HITLER'S CRIME FIGHTER

HITLER'S CRIME FIGHTER

THE EXTRAORDINARY LIFE OF KONRAD MORGEN

DAVID LEE

First published in Great Britain in 2024 by
Biteback Publishing Ltd, London

ISBN 978-1-78590-866-8

10 9 8 7 6 5 4 3 2 1

A CIP catalogue record for this book is available from the British Library.

Set in Trade Gothic and Adobe Caslon Pro

Printed and bound in Great Britain by
CPI Group (UK) Ltd, Croydon CR0 4YY

When you get a cat to catch the mice in your kitchen,
you can't expect it to ignore the rats in the cellar.

Bernie Gunther in Philip Kerr's *March Violets*

CONTENTS

A NOTE ABOUT SS RANKS

The SS (short for *Schutzstaffel*, translated as 'protection squad') had their own system of ranks and titles. In this book, I have used the nearest equivalent British Army rank to give a general idea of the level of responsibility that each member of the SS had. For example, an SS-*Sturmmann* (literally 'storm man') was near the bottom of the organisation, roughly equivalent to a lance corporal. An SS-*Hauptsturmführer* (literally 'head storm leader') was roughly equivalent to a captain. Konrad Morgen finished his SS career as a *Sturmbannführer*, a 'storm unit leader', which was roughly equivalent to a major.

The SS rank for a general started at SS-*Gruppenführer* (literally 'group leader') and had several additional levels, for example SS-*Obergruppenführer* ('upper group leader'). In the British Army, these are equivalent to major generals, lieutenant generals and full generals. Because many of the officers described here moved through the various ranks of general at different times, I have simply described these officers as generals in the narrative in order to keep things straightforward.

INTRODUCTION

MONDAY 25 OCTOBER 1971

Three people are together in a room in Frankfurt, West Germany. John Toland, an American historian, is working on a biography of Adolf Hitler and has come to Frankfurt to meet Konrad Morgen, currently a lawyer. Also in the room is Inge Gehrich, an interpreter.

Toland isn't interested in Morgen because he's a successful Frankfurt lawyer. He has come here today because of the surprising and little-known fact that Konrad Morgen, a former SS investigating judge and Reich police official, carried out the very first successful criminal investigation of a concentration camp commandant and he did it not after, but during, the Second World War.

The tape recording of the conversation is not a good-quality one and it's difficult at times to hear what Konrad Morgen is saying.[1] Sometimes I have to rely on Inge Gehrich's English translation and even then, I am often rewinding the tape and turning the volume up to the maximum in order to make out what is being said. Sometimes a car or truck roars past, and at one stage the telephone rings and a dog barks.

Although the quality of the recording is poor, I pay particular attention because it is the only occasion on tape when Konrad Morgen is being conversational. The recordings of his witness testimony at Nuremberg after the war and then again in the Frankfurt Auschwitz trial in 1964 are very formal. Even his interview for the TV series *The World at War* is much more structured than the conversation I am listening to right now.

It is immediately clear that Morgen has a very good understanding of English; several times he is so keen to get his point across that he speaks directly to Toland in English. Although his English is very good, I think I know why he prefers to speak in German and that's because he's a lawyer who has been in a lot of courtrooms and he wishes to express himself exactly as he wants to on tape, with no possibility of misunderstanding.

Toland asks Morgen about being an SS judge and police investigator. Is it true that SS courts sentenced concentration camp commandants to death for atrocities against inmates? Yes, replies Morgen, who goes on to say that he personally arrested Karl-Otto Koch, the commandant of Buchenwald, and his wife and then went on to investigate Rudolf Höss, the commandant of Auschwitz. Toland says he plans to write a chapter about this and that most people in the West wouldn't believe it.

Morgen tells Toland that the higher-up SS leaders didn't like him and he was dismissed from his job in Kraków. Toland tells Morgen that he's surprised that the Allies didn't honour him for the things he did – after all, he risked his life. Morgen sounds embarrassed and simply mutters *Ja*. Toland adds that it says something about German law that people like Konrad Morgen were able to carry on a legal process. And why not, says Morgen animatedly.

After all, the government may have changed but the judges didn't turn into criminals!

Toland wants to know how many other judges were like Morgen? He tells Morgen, 'You sound like an original to me.' Ninety-nine per cent of judges were like him, says Morgen. Yes, but how many were acting like Morgen, Toland wants to know. Were these other judges also bringing up embarrassing cases? They wanted to, yes, says Morgen. But he had a special investigative talent, he had the right nose to be a detective. Plus, says Morgen, he was interested in international law. You were a bloodhound, says Toland. Morgen is delighted and says yes, yes! He was called a *Blutrichter*, literally a 'blood judge'.

Morgen tells Toland that when he investigated the crimes in Buchenwald, he had been instructed not to investigate political cases. But here he was with a political case. So he investigated on his own initiative, what he calls *auf eigener Faust* – literally with his own fists. And when he told the senior SS officers about what was going on at Buchenwald, they wouldn't take action and kept passing him on to the next person. He went to Arthur Nebe (head of the *Reichskriminalpolizeiamt* or Reich Central Police Detective Office) first, but Nebe said go to Ernst Kaltenbrunner (head of the *Reichssicherheitshauptamt* or the Reich Security Main Office).* Kaltenbrunner said take it straight to Himmler.

At this point in the conversation, Morgen switches to English as Gehrich, the interpreter, hasn't heard of Nebe and he is impatient to carry on with his story. Morgen wrote to Himmler, who didn't cover

* I have translated *Reichskriminalpolizeiamt* as Reich Central Police Detective Office. Other translations use Reich Central Crime Office. The *Kriminalpolizei* (*Kripo*) in a German police department is the equivalent of the CID in the UK.

it up and, he says, he raised hell. Himmler told Morgen to arrest Koch and told him he would also get the authority to clean up the whole place. Koch was indicted, sentenced to death and executed. But Morgen couldn't obtain enough proof to get his wife sentenced and she was still under arrest at the end of the war.

Toland asks Morgen, is it true that lampshades were being made of human skin or is that baloney? Morgen says it was other people who found this out. The Americans threatened to kill him if he didn't testify that Frau Koch had done it but he wouldn't as he had found no evidence. Toland asks if he was treated well by the Americans. Morgen tells him that they threatened to hand him over to the Czechs, Poles or French if he refused to testify. Toland expresses his dismay at this.

Morgen says that after the war lots of people asked him why didn't he go after Hitler? In the same way that a US Army judge couldn't go after President Nixon, or after Kennedy for Vietnam, he couldn't prosecute Hitler. A judge in the army always reports to the army chief of staff.

The conversation turns to concentration camps and Toland asks Morgen what he thinks of the figure of 6 million Jews who were killed during the Holocaust. Morgen answers simply 'yes, it's correct' in a tone which conveys the meaning 'yes, of course it's correct'. Later on, the discussion moves through various senior Nazis to Martin Bormann, head of the Nazi Party Chancellery and Hitler's private secretary. Earlier in the interview, Morgen had mentioned that he had been imprisoned in Oberursel and Nuremberg by the Americans after the war and had talked to many fellow prisoners about Hitler.

Morgen tells Toland that Bormann never left Hitler's side. He always carried a notebook and whatever Hitler said, he wrote down and turned into an order. Toland is interested in this and asks Morgen if he thinks that this was how the order for the extermination of the Jews came about? Was Hitler thinking aloud and then Bormann wrote it down and turned it into an order? Morgen says the extermination of the Jews was always Hitler's intention; it was premeditated and carefully managed. Bormann's role was to facilitate this and make sure that it happened.

Toland asks Morgen where he thinks the order to exterminate the Jews came from. Was it from Hitler? Toland says that many people have told him that Hitler knew nothing about it. Morgen doesn't agree. He says yes, it came from Hitler. What about Himmler's role? Morgen says that Himmler was central to the extermination of the Jews.

Toland tells Morgen how grateful he is that he confirmed the killing of 6 million Jews, as he was on the verge of doubting it but now he's met Morgen and Morgen is the best witness he has come across. It's clear from this that other interviewees from inside the SS and Nazi Party whom Toland has talked to for his book have rejected this figure.

At the end of the interview, Morgen says he would be glad to read Toland's book and Toland promises to send Morgen a copy before it's published in appreciation. When the book is published in 1976, Toland describes Konrad Morgen as 'the man who did the most to hinder the atrocities in the East' and describes his work as 'one man house-cleaning' as well as a 'lonesome attempt to end the Final Solution'.[2]

* * *

The more I read about and listen to Konrad Morgen, the more I am reminded of Bernie Gunther, Philip Kerr's fictional Second World War Berlin detective. Like Gunther, Morgen worked for Nebe in the *Reichskriminalpolizeiamt*, the Central Police Detective Office of the Reich. Like Gunther, Morgen had a career investigating crime during the war and uncovering terrible truths in Nazi Germany, where darkness touched everyone and everything. But while Bernie Gunther was investigating general crimes, Morgen's particular beat was rooting out criminals in the ranks of the SS, including the Gestapo and the police.

Both Gunther and Morgen faced the same problem: how do you stay alive in the Third Reich and perhaps even prosper without selling your soul to the devil? It was a difficult dilemma for any German and a very acute one for Bernie Gunther and Konrad Morgen. But while Kerr could ensure that the fictional Bernie Gunther always lived to return another day, for Konrad Morgen there were no such guarantees. He was on his own. The title of this book, *Hitler's Crime Fighter*, captures the contradiction of an SS investigating judge and police official investigating and prosecuting murder and crime in the Third Reich, which gave itself the legal powers to kill people, especially Jews, and take their money, valuables and property on a massive scale.

While Gunther is a cynical Berlin detective with a large dose of English humour from his creator, Morgen embodied very traditional German values. He had a very strong sense of honour and he was very loyal to his fiancée, Maria, with whom he exchanged constant letters through and after the war, when he was imprisoned by the Americans. He later married her.

Both Gunther and Morgen had a senior Nazi who interfered

in their lives and sent them off in new directions. While Gunther was often called in by Reinhard Heydrich – head of the Reich Security Main Office before Kaltenbrunner – to investigate crimes, Morgen's activities were watched over by *Reichsführer*-SS Heinrich Himmler himself. Morgen's problem was that he worked for arguably the world's most frightening and dangerous employer and he didn't play by their rules.

In the first half of the war, Morgen blotted his copybook by investigating SS officers for corruption without fear or favour. These SS officers used their connections to complain to Himmler, who contemplated sending him to a concentration camp. In the end, he decided instead to reduce him in rank and dispatched him to the Waffen SS Division Wiking (pronounced 'Viking') on the Eastern Front to fight the Soviet Army in winter.

And then in a plot twist worthy of any Bernie Gunther novel, Himmler changed his mind. Having decided that he needed Morgen's skills as a bloodhound after all, he recalled Morgen from the front, restored his previous rank as an officer and sent him to investigate the increasing problem of corruption in concentration camps. Going way beyond his brief, Morgen then charged multiple concentration camp commandants, officers and guards with murder.

His approach depended on a literal interpretation of the law in Nazi Germany. Contrary to popular perception, the law and the legal process were very important in the Third Reich – so much so that there wasn't just one set of laws but two. These were first characterised by Ernst Fraenkel, a German lawyer and political scientist who left Germany in 1938 and wrote a book in 1941 about the twin legal systems in Nazi Germany called *The Dual State* to reflect these two legal systems operating at the same time.

In his book, Fraenkel identifies first what he calls the 'normative state', which he describes as 'an administrative body endowed with elaborate powers for safeguarding the legal order as expressed in statutes, decisions of the courts and activities of the administrative agencies'.[3] In other words, Nazi Germany still had a normal legal system similar to those which could be found in most Western democracies at the time.

But then Fraenkel also identifies what he called the 'prerogative state', which he describes as 'that governmental system which exercises unlimited arbitrariness and violence unchecked by any legal guarantees'.[4] In other words, in Nazi Germany there was a second parallel legal system, which allowed Hitler and other senior Nazis acting with Hitler's authority to decide on courses of action that were deemed as legal and which could not be challenged in the courts. The decisions taken as part of this second legal system had terrible consequences for the millions of people who were killed, especially the Jews. In his interrogation after the war by the Americans, Morgen summed this dual legal system up neatly. He told his interrogator, Fred Rodell:

> Law in the National Socialist state was several things; as previously, it embodied legal norms and included common law but what was new were the orders from the Führer. In the National Socialist state the Führer united all power in his person; he was the head of state, the chief lawgiver and the chief judge.[5]

Alongside these two legal systems in the Third Reich, there was an extensive bureaucracy. This meant that every single killing – whether an execution for murder as part of normal state processes or the killing of someone or groups of people because of an order from Hitler or from another senior officer acting on his behalf – had to be accompanied by the right paperwork. Any killing which was not a result of normative legal processes or not directly ordered by Hitler or someone acting on his behalf was therefore illegal and could be investigated as murder.

For Morgen, this represented the way to bring criminals in the SS to justice, particularly for murders which had been committed with no lawful order authorising them. Officially his job was to investigate corruption in the SS, and Morgen used this as a way to disrupt the work of the SS and as a way to investigate SS officers for murder. In a way, he was copying what the FBI did when it went after Al Capone. The FBI couldn't get evidence for murder, so it prosecuted Capone for tax evasion in order to get him sentenced and imprisoned.

As a prosecution witness in the 1963–5 Frankfurt Auschwitz trials, Morgen set out his approach to the court:

> I saw a way of proceeding. Where the highest legal principle, life itself, is worth nothing and is trampled into the dirt and destroyed, then all other legal principles, whether they be around property, loyalty or something else, must also collapse and lose their value. And therefore – and I had already convinced myself of this – these people, to whom these tasks had been assigned, were set on a path to criminality. And my instructions and the criminal code gave me my duty to prosecute these crimes, namely crimes which were not covered by official orders. And that's exactly what I did.[6]

Morgen was an important witness to events in the concentration camps. But even with his energy and determination, he could not visit all the camps that the Nazis set up. According to the United States Holocaust Memorial Museum there were around 44,000 camps and ghettos, although the exact number will never be known.[7]

Concentration camps were places where people who were seen as enemies of the state were imprisoned. They were also places where targeted killings of individuals and small groups were carried out and they were places where prisoners were forced to work. Concentration camps also had numerous sub-camps – for example, Buchenwald had at least eighty-eight satellite camps, which were run from Buchenwald itself.[8]

There were also a number of dedicated extermination camps or killing centres, whose purpose was to kill people, particularly Jews, who were sent there. These were located in Nazi-occupied Poland and included Auschwitz-Birkenau, Majdanek, Chełmno, Sobibor, Belzec and Treblinka. It is also worth noting that there were three concentration camps at Auschwitz: Auschwitz I, Auschwitz II (Birkenau, the killing centre) and Auschwitz III (Monowitz).

Morgen's wartime career in the SS came to define both his career and his life. After the war he was detained by the Americans for over three years, interrogated extensively and used as a witness in the Nuremberg trials. Even after they were completed and he was released, he was summoned back to various courts to give evidence. By the end of the war, Morgen had conducted 800 investigations into crimes committed by members of the SS, with 200 brought to trial. He personally arrested five concentration camp commanding officers and two were executed after their trials.[9]

He described himself as a *Gerechtigkeitsfanatiker*, a fanatic for justice, and the list of people he went after is a roll call of some of the very worst killers, thieves and sadists in the ranks of the SS.

This is his story.

CHAPTER 1

BEGINNINGS

THURSDAY 6 NOVEMBER 1941

For Walter Krämer and Karl Peix, two concentration camp inmates at Goslar, a sub-camp of Buchenwald, the last day of their lives started like any other. The daily routine was nine hours of work, every day from Monday to Saturday each week. Most of the work carried out by prisoners at Goslar was manual labour at the Luftwaffe base, with some prisoners being sent to work at the mine near the village of Hahndorf.

Most of the prisoners were Poles, Russian political prisoners, Jehovah's Witnesses, so-called career criminals and what were termed 'asocial' prisoners from the Reich.[1] What was unusual about Krämer and Peix was that they had been transferred from the main camp at Buchenwald and they were being used for manual labour at Goslar even though both were skilled in nursing and medicine.

Krämer and Peix were both communists and had served as members of the regional parliament. Krämer had been arrested after the Reichstag fire in 1933, which the Nazis had used to target communists. Following a prison sentence lasting until 1936, he was taken into preventative custody by the Gestapo and sent to Buchenwald, having refused to spy for them.[2] In Buchenwald, Krämer, a locksmith by profession, transformed himself into a nurse and medical practitioner and Peix became his deputy. Together they set about helping their fellow prisoners, and they gained such a positive reputation that even the SS camp personnel came to them for help, preferring to use them rather than their own SS doctors.[3]

One prisoner, Yaakov Silberstein, testified after the war that Krämer had crawled into the Buchenwald 'small camp' at night where Jewish prisoners were held in order to give him medicine for typhus. Krämer also brought another prisoner, seventeen-year-old Artur Radvansky, from the small camp into the 'big camp' where political prisoners were held and operated on him, without anaesthetic, for gangrene due to frostbite. He treated him again for an infection after a flogging. For these acts, Walter Krämer was added to the Yad Vashem list of Righteous Among the Nations, which honours non-Jews who risked their lives to help Jews during the Holocaust.[4]

Alongside their fellow prisoners, Krämer and Peix had also treated camp commandant SS Colonel Karl-Otto Koch for syphilis.[5] They had also treated local SS General Prince Josias of Waldeck for a furunculosis infection after the prince had sought treatment on a visit to Buchenwald as part of his official responsibilities as the head of the SS and police in the local area.[6] This made their transfer to carry out manual labour at Goslar all the more puzzling. Why would the SS at Buchenwald deprive the main camp of two skilled nurses and medics?

General Waldeck had been taking a close interest in Buchenwald concentration camp since he had had SS Colonel Koch arrested on suspicion of corruption the previous year. However, this arrest had not been successful. SS General Oswald Pohl, who ran the SS-*Wirtschafts-Verwaltungshauptamt*, the SS Main Economic and Administrative Office in Berlin where he was in charge of all the concentration camps, and SS General Ernst Kaltenbrunner, head of the Reich Security Main Office, complained to Himmler. Himmler then ordered Koch's release and sent out a general order, which became known as the 'lex Waldeck', saying that a commandant of a concentration camp could only be arrested on the direct orders of Himmler himself.

However, General Waldeck could still make life difficult for Koch and he still visited Buchenwald on a regular basis. On one of his visits, he decided to order the release of the two prisoners, Walter Krämer and Karl Peix. However, unbeknown to Waldeck, instead of releasing the prisoners, Koch ordered them to be transferred to Goslar. The next thing Waldeck heard about the two prisoners was that on 6 November 1941 they had both been shot in the back of the head while trying to escape.

According to the official report, both prisoners had died in exactly the same way. Each had suddenly stopped work and made a run for the perimeter. The guards, including SS Sergeant Johann Blank, had in both cases shouted twice as warnings and then fired at the fleeing prisoners. A telegram was sent immediately from Goslar to Buchenwald and to the SS Court in Kassel. The Buchenwald adjutant, SS Lieutenant Heinz Büngeler, was dispatched to investigate. He drove straight to Goslar, where the bodies were still lying where they had been shot.

Before the bodies were moved, the scene was photographed. A post-mortem was carried out to determine the cause of death and the SS doctor certified that both had been shot from behind at a distance of 30 metres. The officer in charge at Goslar also filed a report stating that the guards were reliable SS soldiers and listing the previous convictions of the prisoners. The conclusion of the investigation by Büngeler was that both men had been shot while trying to escape.[7]

General Waldeck did not believe this report. He knew that one of the prisoners had severely inflamed knees, was overweight and could only walk with a limp. And he knew that Büngeler knew this too, as he had known both men from the camp hospital. Plus, why would prisoners who were going to be released try to escape? He referred the case to the SS Court in Kassel, which summoned the guards, the officer in charge on the day and the adjutant in charge of the investigation to Kassel, where they were interrogated under oath. The guard who shot Krämer and Peix stuck to his story: 'I yelled at the prisoners but they didn't stop. I had to use my rifle,' he told the court.[8] Faced with this testimony, it appeared that there was nothing more that Waldeck could do.

Eighteen months later, in 1943, Konrad Morgen arrived in Buchenwald and broke the case wide open. He had been sent there to investigate corruption but, as part of his wider investigations, the killings of Krämer and Peix caught his attention. He soon gained a reputation among the SS at Buchenwald and prisoner Stefan Heymann remembered how 'Morgen was extraordinarily feared and hated by all SS officers in Buchenwald'.[9] When Morgen looked at the case files for Krämer and Peix, they were so well put together that he said, 'Not even the most conscientious or most thorough judge or criminal investigator could have found the slightest trace of any criminal act in those files.'[10] However, for Morgen, his experience as an SS investigator meant that when he saw reports of prisoners attempting to escape, accompanied by apparently thorough investigations, his suspicions were immediately aroused.

To gather the evidence which would confirm his suspicions that the prisoners had in fact been murdered, Morgen relied on information from other prisoners. But they were initially suspicious of Morgen's investigations. Alfred Miller, a journalist who had been sent to Buchenwald and who helped Morgen with a number of murders inside Buchenwald itself, found it hard to trust Morgen at the start:

> At first I couldn't make up my mind to tell [him] everything and it took me a long time to start trusting [him] ... I was given a document from Prince Waldeck saying that nothing would happen to me and that no one was allowed to harm me. But I said that wasn't enough. Then Prince Waldeck came along in person and said that if I gave a statement which could be verified then he would personally lobby the *Reichsführer*-SS Heinrich Himmler for my release. So I decided to give a statement.

Miller was eventually released on 13 March 1944 after Morgen intervened with the Reich Security Main Office. 'I owe my freedom to Dr Morgen,' he said.[11]

The truth about the killing of Krämer and Peix was entirely as Morgen had expected. Koch and SS Sergeant Blank had drawn up the plan to murder them and put it into effect. The SS guards on duty were sworn to secrecy, especially when it came to any court-authorised investigation, and they were informed that what they were asked to do was a direct order from Himmler himself. They were briefed extensively about what they should say to the investigation, namely, 'Yes, we shot them because I considered it to be the right course of action. I know of no order which protects the lives of the prisoners.'[12]

The first part of the plan was to transfer Krämer and Peix to Goslar well in advance of the date Koch and Blank planned to kill them. On the appointed day, Blank made sure that no other prisoners were around in the area where the prisoners were to be shot. Each prisoner was given instructions to fetch water from a well and, suspecting nothing, picked up a bucket and walked to the well. The guards, including Blank, then fired the fatal shots at a distance of 30 metres, removed the bucket from the murder scene and reported it.

Why had they been killed? In his official report, Morgen speculated that Krämer and Peix had known that Koch was stealing donations that richer prisoners at Buchenwald had been making to the camp hospital.[13] After the war, Morgen pointed to the fact that Koch was suffering from syphilis and he had been treated by Krämer. To ensure that word of this did not get out, he arranged to have the two prisoners killed.[14] Morgen was outraged: 'They behaved just like gangsters, from the camp leadership right down to the lowest man.'[15]

Morgen uncovered many unlawful killings like those of Walter Krämer and Karl Peix at Buchenwald. Their murders were included on the final indictment against Koch. Blank hanged himself when he was arrested.[16] However, their murders were of great interest to another trial, one which took place after the war in 1947 in Dachau, where the Americans put SS General Prince Josias of Waldeck on trial for the crimes committed at Buchenwald, especially those committed at the end of the war. Waldeck was convicted and sentenced to life imprisonment but released due to ill health in 1950 and died in 1967.[17]

At this trial, Morgen appeared as a witness for the defence. But before asking Morgen details about the murders of Krämer and Peix, the defence lawyer, Dr Emil Aheimer, asked Morgen about his past. He was particularly interested in the times when Morgen had incurred the wrath of the Nazi Party and had fallen out with colleagues in cases where he was sitting with other judges.

One of the judges in the trial asked Aheimer what he was trying to prove by asking Konrad Morgen these questions? Was he trying to prove the credibility of his own witness? Aheimer replied:

> No, I want to show the following, the witness, as will be shown, was appointed investigating officer in the complex of questions concerning Koch and what is to be shown here is that the man who was selected for this job was not a man who always did what the SS and the Party always desired him to do. This should serve to demonstrate that the investigation was conducted in a very serious manner indeed.[18]

This was also a theme of other post-war trials where Morgen testified. Before giving his testimony, there were always questions about how he came to be an SS investigating judge. However, the most detailed questions of all were put to him as part of his interrogation by the Americans after he surrendered to them at the end of the war. And these questions started at the very beginning.

EARLY LIFE

Georg Konrad Morgen was born on 8 June 1909 in Frankfurt,

where he also went to school, studied and returned to after the war for the rest of his life. After he left school in 1929, Morgen worked at the S&H Goldschmied bank in Frankfurt for six months as a trainee before leaving to study law. He was always very proud of the fact that his studies had a very international flavour – having been a school exchange student in France in 1926, he studied law at universities in Frankfurt, Rome, Berlin, The Hague and Kiel between 1930 and 1933.[19]

Morgen's interest in international relations led him to join the Pan European Union as a student. This was an organisation which was founded in 1923 and which wanted a politically, economically and militarily united Europe. When Hitler came to power he abolished the German Pan European Union, as he saw it as a dangerous opponent.

Morgen was also a member of the German People's Party, a right-wing liberal party which supported the interests of business and industry. In 1931, he went to hear Hitler speak but came away disappointed – his main impression was that Hitler only talked about himself and had no concrete ideas about how to improve things.[20] But this did not stop him joining the Nazi Party in 1933 as an ordinary member.

The push to join the Nazi Party came from Morgen's mother, Anna. She had been very impressed by the flags, the speeches, the singing and the marching, and she believed that Hitler was responsible for a great turning point, especially in terms of reducing unemployment. Morgen himself knew people who had been unemployed for five, six or seven years. She told him, 'You won't get a job if you want to work for the government. We made so many sacrifices for your studies.' Morgen thought to himself, 'Well, it's just a formality' and joined up.[21] On the other hand, his father, a train driver whom Morgen described as a calm, modest man without any ambition, was, if anything, critical of the Nazis. He just wanted a quiet life as a state railway employee.[22]

In the same year that Konrad Morgen joined the Nazi Party, he also joined the SS. But this was an involuntary membership. In order to take the law exams, students were required to play sport for two terms beforehand and to do this, Morgen had joined an organisation called *Das Reichskuratorium für Jugendertüchtigung* or the Reich Committee for Youth Fitness. Then one day, instructors from the SA and the SS appeared and the training started to become more militaristic, with various uniform items handed out for the students. Eventually, the instructors simply divided the students into two groups. One group were told they now belonged to the SA and Morgen's group were informed that they now belonged to the SS.[23]

The SA – *Sturmabteilung*, translated as 'storm unit' or 'storm troops' – was originally set up after the First World War as a group of men who would provide security at Nazi meetings, which usually meant attacking anyone causing trouble. The SA evolved into an organisation that, alongside putting up posters, beating up opponents and marching up and down, also became a serious military force in its own right.

The SS – *Schutzstaffel* or 'protection squad' – had been set up by Hitler as a unit of personal bodyguards. It then expanded its remit to include protecting other big-name Nazis. In 1929, when Hitler appointed Himmler to head up the SS in the post of *Reichsführer-SS*, the number of SS personnel was given by the in-house SS magazine as exactly 270.[24] Himmler slowly built up the SS with the 'right' sort of people, which included aristocrats like Prince Josias of Waldeck, who had joined the SS in 1930 and become Himmler's adjutant before being promoted to full SS general by the end of the war.[25] Another key appointment was that of Reinhard Heydrich to head up the new SS intelligence service, the *Sicherheitsdienst* (SD), in 1931.

In 1931, Himmler also set up the SS *Rasse- und Siedlungsamt*, the Race and Settlement Office, under Richard Walther Darré, an Argentinian German who had spent some of his school years at King's College School in Wimbledon, London. Darré impressed Himmler with his ideas, which revolved around the need to solve the agricultural problems facing Germany in the early 1930s by improving the 'racial purity' of the German peasantry. His ideas included settlement schemes in the countryside, raising the birthrate and stopping the rural population drift to the towns and cities.

Himmler also introduced new marriage rules for the members of the SS in 1931. The purpose was to ensure that SS men were racially 'pure' and that their future wives were going to continue this racial purity when they had children. To this end, all members of the SS had to apply to the *Reichsführer*-SS via the Race and Settlement Office for permission to marry. This measure did not go down well both inside and outside the SS, and every year the SS expelled men for marrying without permission. This marriage rule would later cause problems for Morgen and his fiancée, Maria Wachter.

One effect of this new rule was that it set the SS apart from other organisations in Nazi Germany, especially from the SA. According to Himmler's biographer, Peter Longerich, the SA saw themselves as tough guys who got drunk from time to time and who tolerated homosexuality, whereas Himmler wanted the SS to be a force of Aryan, disciplined, reserved men who contributed to the 'racial quality' of the German *Volk* by marrying appropriately.[26]

In 1932, the SS was still a small organisation, but in 1933, after Hitler became Chancellor and the Nazis took control of Germany, the floodgates opened and new recruits poured in. One of these was Morgen, who received the SS number 124940.[27] The SS veterans who had been in since before 1933 suspected the new arrivals of joining simply to get ahead and called them 'March violets'.[28] When Morgen joined, the new all-black SS uniform had already been introduced to distinguish it from the brown shirts of the SA. Then in 1934, out went the SA brown shirts – in more ways than one, as Hitler had moved against the SA leadership at the end of June 1934 and had their leaders, including co-founder Ernst Röhm, executed.

In 1933, the first concentration camps, later a key focus of Morgen's investigative talents, had been set up. In the beginning, these were uncoordinated. They were places that the local police, SS and the SA had set up to imprison and mistreat their enemies, whether real or imagined. By the end of 1933, there were over 100 of these camps scattered across Germany, which would eventually grow to over 1,000 by the end of the Second World War.[29] One of these camps was at a place called Dachau in the grounds of an old gunpowder works, which was established on 22 March 1933 and which was initially staffed by Bavarian state police. Their rule over the camp inmates was short and brutal. On the first full day of Dachau's opening alone, the Bavarian police killed four Jewish inmates.

Word of the mistreatment of the prisoners at Dachau soon got out and the Munich prosecutor's office launched an investigation. Although this investigation got nowhere, the pressure on Himmler – who had recently been put in charge of the Bavarian police alongside his duties as *Reichsführer*-SS – was intense and he replaced the Dachau commandant, Hilmar Wäckerle, with Theodor Eicke. Eicke took immediate action to address the situation and he introduced a new model of concentration camp management, which became a template for the other concentration camps once Hitler had given the go-ahead to centralise concentration camps under the control of the SS in 1934.

Eicke's new model involved a much tougher security regime and a uniform set of punishments for the prisoners. Under Eicke's management, Dachau was sealed off from the outside world so no one could find out what was going on there, which meant that the death of prisoners who were shot 'trying to escape' would routinely avoid investigation. He restructured the camp administration and introduced hard work for all prisoners – any work, whether it be useful or pointless. Eicke also introduced a new set of rules for the prisoners, the so-called *Lagerordnung*. This code introduced rules for discipline and punishment, which meant that prisoners could be punished for anything at all that their guards didn't like, with punishments including flogging, solitary confinement and execution.[30]

From the concentration camp prisoner perspective, life under the SS had become worse, more random and more terrifying than when the Bavarian police were in charge. But for Himmler, the dual advantage of this new system was that he could show the world that Dachau had a proper set of rules, while any crimes committed in Dachau by the SS officers could be covered up.[31]

By 1933, while concentration camps were still in their infancy, Konrad Morgen was a member of both the Nazi Party and the SS. For an ambitious young lawyer of that time and place, it seemed like the future was a bright one. But then in 1934, Morgen incurred the wrath of the Nazi Party by refusing to vote on 19 August in the referendum to give Hitler ultimate power in Germany by combining the offices of chancellor and president. On 28 August, he received an icy memo from the head of his local party, who informed him that on looking through the voting records it had been noticed that he did not cast his vote locally and please could he inform them of the place where he did vote?[32]

'I stuck to my old constitutional views, and I could not see it as a good thing that all the power should be in one person's hands and so I didn't take part in the election,' he told his American interrogators after the war:

> As a result, the party started proceedings to expel me but then the SS took over and said, 'This man belongs to us.' I was reprimanded and had to remain as a candidate for SS membership rather than as a full member. I was persecuted for years because of this. In those days whenever you applied for a job the party had to be consulted and they continually made life difficult for me. I couldn't get a job in Frankfurt and I had to leave and go to Stettin where they were short of people.[33]

In 1935, Morgen saw Hitler again. This time it was up close, as work on the autobahn between Frankfurt and Darmstadt had been completed and Hitler came to open it. Students blocked the streets on both sides to prevent the people getting to Hitler's car and Hitler went past Morgen from only a few metres away. In Morgen's eyes, the fact that Hitler was keeping his promises was a positive. People were finding jobs, the autobahns were being built and the whole place looked, well, just generally better. When he was going to university, he passed a factory every day. At first the place looked dreadful but after Hitler had been in power, the whole place was spruced up, flowers were planted and there were benches where the workers could smoke cigarettes on their break.

In his interview with John Toland, Morgen summed up Hitler's success in the early years by quoting the English saying 'nothing succeeds more than success'. Hitler had constantly proved himself to be correct against the opinions of experts. These experts had warned Hitler he wouldn't be able to build autobahns, that he wouldn't succeed in invading France but, of course, Hitler succeeded in these things. Morgen also held the view that right up until the last day of the war, everyone in Germany expected that Hitler would have something in reserve that would have enabled him to win. The fact that he didn't meant, for Morgen, that at least the German people could see that Hitler had failed when he killed himself at the end of the war.[34]

By 1936, Morgen was enthusiastic enough about the Nazi Party that he paid £217 (in 2023 prices) in membership fees to the party.[35] The Nazi Party membership documents contained pages for members to buy stamps from the party and Morgen paid for forty-two individual Reichsmark stamps and sixteen 30-pfennig (penny) stamps. Even having paid this amount for these individual stamps, there were still plenty of pages without stamps in them.[36]

In the same year, his short book *War Propaganda and War Prevention* was published by Leipzig University publisher Robert Noske. In this book, Morgen discussed the role of propaganda in leading to war and how lawyers could contribute to the cause of peace. Along the way, he suggested that the Nazis were actually working towards peace. However, if he was hoping to regain the party's approval by writing this, he was to be disappointed. The official party judgement from the Official Examination Board for the Protection of National Socialist Literature of the National Socialist German Workers' Party was damning:

> The author makes false assumptions and statements for which there is no evidence. The writing contains a number of exaggerations and phrases which have no scientific basis and are therefore worthless and useless. Publication of this book is prohibited![37]

Despite this, the book was published and Morgen later recalled, 'In 1936 I published a book concerning war propaganda and prevention of wars. That book also was considered bad by the Party and was criticised in a derogatory manner. I was told that I hadn't pointed out that the Jews were actually the instigators of the wars.'[38]

The year 1936 was also an important one for the SS because on 17 June, Hitler appointed Himmler as *Reichsführer*-SS *und Chef der Deutschen Polizei* (head of the SS and chief of the German police). In order to centralise control of the police, Himmler created the *Reichskriminalpolizeiamt* with Arthur Nebe, Morgen's future boss, in charge. In November 1938, the Nazis, in the form of the SA and the Hitler Youth, launched attacks on Jews across Germany, Austria and the Sudetenland. These attacks later became known as Kristallnacht or 'night of the crystals', due to the broken glass which littered the streets. Although Morgen did not record his thoughts about Kristallnacht at the time, he later described that he had discovered some of the SS officers at Buchenwald concentration camp had made money from these attacks on the Jews and their property, and this made him angry and all the more determined to take action against them.[39]

THE JULIUS SPECK AFFAIR

While all these changes to the SS would have a huge impact on Morgen's life, for the time being he was not taking an interest in them. After studying, Morgen was occupied in training to be a lawyer in courts in and around Frankfurt prior to his qualification in 1938. This took up so much of his time that he did not get involved in either party or SS affairs. That is until Sunday 6 March 1938. The evening before, Morgen had been round to a friend's apartment where a card game was underway. Morgen's friend Wilhelm Müller was playing with some other acquaintances but when Morgen arrived, one of them, Julius Speck, looked up from his glass of wine and starting baiting Morgen. 'Apparently the number of lawsuits has gone down by 25 per cent. Is that because there are too few lawyers in Germany?'

Morgen had come across Speck before at various courts as Speck was a tax adviser and economist. Having conceded that there were probably too few lawyers in Germany, Morgen asked Speck, 'How are your cases going?' But Speck was having none of it. He was drunk and said, very formally, 'I apologise for my stupid remark; I have often tried to make you understand things and in the future I'll do it in a different way if you don't want to change!' And with this, Speck lifted his arm as if to hit Morgen.

The exchanges carried on for fifteen minutes and eventually Speck told Morgen that if he had as few brain cells as Morgen then he would be apologising. Morgen was outraged and he decided to do something which was very traditionally German and very SS – he challenged Julius Speck to a duel. The very next day, he sent a memo to his SS superior officer, Captain Stroh, setting out the circumstances and asking that the SS act as the go-between for the resolution of this dispute with Speck.

The SS took disputes like this very seriously and they dispatched an SS sergeant and an SS corporal to Speck's house. Perhaps wisely, he didn't come to the door and so instead Captain Stroh wrote to Speck on 11 March asking how he would like to proceed. Would he like to make use of the SS arbitration procedures (in which case Captain Stroh would assign an officer from the SS to assist him) or would he like to settle the dispute voluntarily? And then came the killer sentence: if he didn't reply by 16 March then Captain Stroh would report to his superiors that he, Speck, had refused to resolve the dispute and that this would result in a declaration of dishonour against him by the SS.

Unsurprisingly, this made an impression. Wisely, Speck decided that he would rather avoid being declared dishonourable by the SS and that it would be better if he came to an understanding with Morgen. He eventually apologised to Morgen, albeit grudgingly – Morgen had to draft an apology for him to sign.[40]

After qualifying as a lawyer in 1938, Morgen got his first job with the Reich Ministry of Justice as a judge at the court in Stettin (now the town of Szczecin in modern-day Poland). He knew he had to leave his home town of Frankfurt, as the local Nazi Party was determined to make life difficult for him for refusing to vote in the 1934 referendum.

Morgen did not last long at the court in Stettin. On 25 April 1939, the President of the Regional Courts in Stettin sent him a very formal memo, which ran to seventeen pages, signed only with his surname, Kulenkamp. The memo detailed Morgen's failings in a court case which had taken place on 24 March 1939 in the Juvenile Protection Court.[41]

Morgen was sitting as one of three judges to try a case relating to a schoolteacher who was brought before the court on a charge of grievous bodily harm, having allegedly gone way past what would have been considered reasonable corporal punishment for a schoolteacher to use on a pupil. The consequences of a guilty verdict for the teacher would have been serious, meaning prison and loss of a civil service position. Morgen had been called into this case at very short notice and as a result had not read the case file in advance of the hearing.

As the case hearing progressed, Morgen noticed that the lead judge, Braune, was talking up incriminating evidence and ignoring any evidence that could have helped the teacher. Morgen noted that the teacher was not a member of the Nazi Party. He became suspicious that the Hitler Youth were behind this case, as they were generally opposed to the teaching profession at the time, and that they had Braune in their pocket.

Eventually, it got too much for Morgen and he asked if he could look in the files while the hearing was going on. The vice president of the proceedings became angry at Morgen and barked at him in what Morgen later described as 'Prussian barrack tones' and said, 'You need to give your undivided attention to the hearing!' Morgen saw this as an outrageous rebuke to a fellow judge.[42] After the evidence had been presented, Morgen asked for a break: 'I'm asking as a matter of urgency for a recess so I can raise my concerns about the way this hearing has been conducted.'

Morgen later recalled that no one was listening to their consciences. The other judge was too weak to have an impact in the discussion, so he then stood up and said to the court clerk, 'Write into the record that I refuse to take part in the discussion about the verdict!' Then the lead judge jumped to his feet and told Morgen, 'This will cost you dearly!' The hearing had to be abandoned and Morgen said that the President of the Regional Courts nearly had a heart attack when he heard about it and launched an immediate investigation.

Morgen was fired as a judge and went to work in the German Labour Front, the Nazi organisation that replaced the trade unions after the Nazis banned them. Morgen worked on cases involving wage and holiday disputes. But he had people on his side. Morgen had written to his local bank manager, Friedrich Focken, for advice about the case and how he had conducted himself. Focken wrote back to him on 15 July and told him that, in his view, Morgen had acted entirely correctly throughout and he shouldn't be disheartened. 'Don't lose heart!' he told him. 'You have proved that you are a capable lawyer and a good judge who is aware of his responsibilities and an all-round good guy. You'll soon make your way and if I can help by removing any obstacles, I'll be happy to help as one German man to another!'[43]

KONRAD MORGEN IS CALLED UP

In 1939, two more key developments in the timeline of the SS took place, which were to be decisive in terms of both the Third Reich and Morgen's career. In October 1939, the *SS-und Polizeigerichtsbarkeit* – the SS and Police Judiciary, Morgen's future employer – was set up to investigate and rule on offences committed by members of the SS and the police.

A month before this, in September 1939, Himmler had brought the SS and the police together to create the *Reichssicherheitshauptamt*, the Reich Security Main Office, under Reinhard Heydrich. This office would recruit the desk-based killers who would oversee the Final Solution and the Holocaust. In 1943, Morgen would be transferred into Office V of the *Reichskriminalpolizeiamt* for his investigations into concentration camps.

Other, more ambitious men were ahead of him and were already working in the new Reich Security Main Office. Historian Michael Wildt points to a whole generation of Germans who joined this department and were born between 1900 and 1910 – just like Morgen, who had been born in 1909. These were young men who had not had the experience of fighting in the First World War, and this missed opportunity had become a constant feature of their lives, prompting them to make their own future. According to Wildt, three quarters of the leaders of the Reich Security Main Office were born after 1900 and 60 per cent of them were born between 1900 and 1910.

As adolescents and young men, these leaders experienced Germany after the First World War, a time of violent unrest and poverty. Two thirds of them had degrees, a third had doctorates and they were active in student politics. They used the coming to power of the Nazis to further their careers.[44] Although Morgen was part of this generation, he was focused instead on a career in civil law.

But by the time of both of these developments, something else had happened that was to propel Morgen into a new career in the Third Reich. On 3 September 1939, Britain and France had declared war on Germany. In the same month, Hitler gave Himmler permission to form an armed force of SS men who would fight independently of the Wehrmacht, the German armed forces, as front-line soldiers. This was later called the Waffen SS.

The immediate impact of the outbreak of the Second World War on Morgen was that he was drafted into front-line service with the Waffen SS. He was first sent to a reserve battalion at Breslau (now Wrocław in Poland) and from there he was transferred to battalion HQ at Posen (now Poznań in Poland) where he worked exclusively on legal issues for the battalion, such as maintenance allowances for the families of soldiers.[45]

In 1940, after the German invasion of France, Morgen was demobilised from his battalion. When he reported back to the personnel office in Berlin in October 1940, he asked if he could work as a lawyer. After all, he had only recently taken his final exams and it would be difficult to resume his career, as he had not practised as a lawyer for over a year. The personnel officer was sympathetic. 'The SS judiciary is looking for judges; you'll be posted there,' he told him.[46]

After training at the main SS court in Munich, in January 1941 Morgen was posted to the SS Court at Kraków, which was part of Nazi-occupied Poland in a separate administrative area called the General Government. Hitler had appointed his personal lawyer, Hans Frank, to the post of governor general of the General Government. Frank installed himself in great luxury in the old royal palace in Kraków and proceeded to put in place a reign of terror over both the Poles and the Jews. According to historian Robert S. Wistrich, 'Frank treated the Poles as slaves of the Greater German Reich, to be mercilessly subordinated, exploited and wiped out as a national entity … Frank's policy towards the Jews was even more brutal.'[47]

Konrad Morgen was now an SS investigating judge in the middle of the Nazi reign of terror and he was going to face much sterner tests of his character than a drunken acquaintance at a friend's apartment and a disagreement over a civil court verdict. These incidents had shown that he was passionate about justice and he was very sensitive when his own sense of honour and integrity were challenged. But now his feelings about justice, honour and integrity were to be put to the test in ways he could not have imagined.

CHAPTER 2

INVESTIGATING CRIME IN NAZI-OCCUPIED POLAND

DAY AND MONTH UNKNOWN, 1941

The young Jewish women must have been terrified. They had been put in a group together because of their striking good looks. Then they had been taken into the cellar of the building where they were being held and forced to strip, while Major Oskar Dirlewanger and some of his friends from a Wehrmacht supply unit, whom he had invited along to observe a 'scientific experiment', looked on.[1]

They were each given a high-dose injection of strychnine and died in agony while Dirlewanger and his friends smoked cigarettes and observed their convulsions and deaths. Later, their bodies were moved into the next room, cut up and mixed with horse flesh at a ratio of one part human and nine parts horse flesh, and made into bars of soap.[2]

The reports reaching SS investigating judge Konrad Morgen about the activities of Dirlewanger and his *Sonderkommando* (special unit) were enough to spur him into immediate action. Alongside the report he received from the security police in Lublin about the murder of the unnamed Jewish women in the cellar, there were numerous other reports of abuses by Dirlewanger and his men. Morgen spoke to the local head of the Gestapo, SS Major Johannes Müller, whom Morgen trusted as he had previously been a detective with the Breslau police before being drafted into the Gestapo and SS. Müller said to Morgen, 'If only you could do something to help, I don't know what's to be done, it's just vile.'[3]

One of Dirlewanger's favourite ways of extorting money was to arrest Jews at random in the ghetto in Lublin and accuse them of ritual slaughter. However, they would then be told that they could be released on payment of an amount up to 15,000 zloty. If the prisoners paid up, they would be released; if they didn't or couldn't pay then they would be shot. On another occasion, he and his men surrounded an entire district in Lublin and went on a plundering spree. When they had finished, they sold the stolen items back to the Jews.

Morgen stopped work on his other cases and went to Lublin for two days to investigate personally what was going on. His investigation unearthed some surprising facts. The Dirlewanger Brigade, as it was known, had started out as a group of only fifty or so men who had been sent to Lublin under Dirlewanger in September 1940 and been put under the command of the local SS and police commander for the area, SS General Odilo Globočnik. Together with twenty new recruits and four additional experienced non-commissioned officers, the new unit set to work terrorising the local population.[4]

What was surprising about Dirlewanger and his men was that every single member of the Dirlewanger Brigade had a criminal conviction, including its commanding officer. Dirlewanger, like many other Nazis who rose to positions of power, was a very intelligent man. He gained a doctorate from Frankfurt University for his thesis titled *Zur Kritik des Gedankens einer planmäßigen Leitung der Wirtschaft*, a critique of the concept of planned control of the economy, but his doctoral title was later stripped from him after his conviction and imprisonment for raping a girl under the age of fourteen.[5] He was then convicted again for embezzling a textile factory in Erfurt. However, by 1941 he managed to overturn these convictions and have his doctorate restored.

For all Dirlewanger's failings, it turned out that when Himmler was looking to create a new special unit made up of convicted poachers for special operations in the occupied Eastern territories, Oskar Dirlewanger was exactly the man he needed to head it up. Thanks to Dirlewanger's friend, SS General Gottlob Berger, Himmler's chief of staff for the Waffen SS, Dirlewanger got the job.

For Morgen, Dirlewanger and his unit needed to be stopped and these allegations properly investigated. After returning from Lublin later in 1941, he went straight in to see SS General Friedrich-Wilhelm Krüger, who was the SS and police commander in the General Government, and asked him for an arrest warrant against Dirlewanger and all his officers. Krüger was not happy and he told Morgen, 'There is nothing I can do here. Unfortunately, I am not competent because this unit is subordinate exclusively to the orders of SS General Berger.' Krüger then rang Berlin while Morgen was still in the room. Berger came on the line and Krüger started screaming at him: 'You will see to it that this bunch of criminals will disappear from the General Government within a week or I will act myself and lock them all up!'[6]

Berger did exactly what Krüger asked him to and removed Dirlewanger and his unit from Lublin to Belarus. When he heard, Morgen passed on all his files to the local SS and police authorities in Minsk but nothing happened as a result. Morgen was to come across Dirlewanger again when he was investigating crimes in concentration camps. Dirlewanger had broadened his recruiting efforts and began to recruit convicted criminals in concentration camps who had been sentenced to death or to life imprisonment.

On 2 November 1941, Morgen wrote to his boss at the SS Court headquarters in Munich, SS Major Norbert Pohl, about some of his cases, including Dirlewanger. In his report, Morgen, perhaps mindful of which offences would have the most impact higher up the SS chain of command, restricted himself to detailing the Dirlewanger Brigade's economic crimes and described their tyrannical approach. He wrote that robbery and extortion of the Jewish population were being carried out at night, with the stolen items being sold back to their Jewish owners. Morgen also wrote that Dirlewanger was reported to engage in what he described as 'odd relationships' with Jewish women.[7] Morgen finished his report by asking for something to be done, especially as the local security police in Lublin seemed to have no idea about what to do.

More complaints against Dirlewanger were submitted, including one about a prisoner called Sarah Bergmann, a Jew who was arrested and accused of theft after an anonymous tip-off to the Lublin police. Dirlewanger arranged for her release because he was having an affair with her. Because of the number of complaints, SS General Berger did eventually ask for an investigation, which he intended would clear Dirlewanger's name. As part of this investigation, Dirlewanger told the investigating judge, 'It's true I had Jews (fifty-seven in number) poisoned by the Lublin Doctor, rather than having them shot. I did it to save their clothing (coats etc.) which I subsequently gave to *Hauptsturmführer* Streibel for his forced labourers.'[8]

Finally, Himmler called a halt to the constant requests by the SS courts to investigate Dirlewanger and his unit. Morgen later recalled:

> He went into the concentration camps and recruited volunteers, both criminals and political prisoners. Later I spoke with one of these who told me about the terrible life that they led. Dirlewanger was drunk all day long, lashing out and cursing. A terrible situation. The SS judiciary was always after him. But instead of breaking up this bunch, the *Reichsführer* said one day, 'Enough! The SS judiciary is blocked and Dirlewanger can do whatever he wants.'*[9]

With Himmler's backing, Dirlewanger continued his wartime career. By the end of the war, his unit had grown to division strength and was fully incorporated into the SS. Dirlewanger himself finished the war as a general and is used by Himmler's biographer, Peter Longerich, as an example of how Himmler's 'idiosyncratic approach to discipline produced extraordinary successes precisely in the case of SS leaders whose career histories were seriously flawed. In his hands they became willing instruments of his policies.'[10] Longerich goes on to say that Berger and Himmler urgently

---

* Due to later complaints an SS judge was assigned to the unit in 1944 to improve discipline; however, this had no effect.

needed men such as the Dirlewanger Brigade for the 'fight against "sub-humanity"'.[11]

Given this support from the very top of the SS, nothing was ever likely to happen. The lack of action by senior SS officers and their continued support for Dirlewanger and his unit was to have terrible consequences for the people of Belarus and Poland. In Belarus, a favourite tactic of Dirlewanger was to herd villagers into barns and machine-gun them through the open barn doors. Then the barn doors would be closed and the barns set on fire.[12] During the Warsaw Uprising in 1944, the Dirlewanger Brigade killed and raped its way through the city. In the Wola district, the brigade entered a hospital, shot all the Polish patients and raped all the nurses. Then later that night, they built a makeshift gallows and hanged the doctor and the naked nurses while some of Dirlewanger's unit played flutes and sang songs.[13]

After the war, the Americans were very interested in Konrad Morgen's brush with Oskar Dirlewanger. It was a recurrent theme in their questioning.[14] They wanted to know what Morgen knew about Dirlewanger's subsequent wartime career as well as his current whereabouts – no doubt so they could arrest him and bring him to trial. They also used his evidence in the trial of Gottlob Berger, the SS general who had been friends with Dirlewanger and who had protected him from Morgen's investigation.

Given the scale of Berger's crimes at the top of the Waffen SS, it is perhaps surprising that he was only sentenced to twenty-five years' imprisonment at Nuremberg, which was then reduced on appeal to ten years. After his early release in 1951, he returned to his home town of Gerstetten in Swabia and managed a curtain rail factory. He lived to claim his pension and died in 1975.[15]

There was no peaceful end for Oskar Dirlewanger. He died as he had lived: violently. He was arrested in early June 1945 by the French authorities in Altshausen and imprisoned. Over the course of the next few days, his Polish guards beat him to death.*[16]

THE CASE OF SS CAPTAIN GEORG VON SAUBERZWEIG

Konrad Morgen may have tried in vain to bring Dirlewanger and his officers to justice but he did have a number of notable successes during his posting to the General Government. Having arrived in January 1941, he was immediately struck by the scale of lawlessness in the General Government:

> You have to understand that I had studied law and I had got to know something of the German civil service tradition through my three to four years of legal practice. What I saw there made my hair stand on end, it was as though a swarm of locusts had descended on the country in order to eat it clean ... in every department you would only encounter the most useless officials who wouldn't have been of any use in the Reich. Anyone who didn't want to be a soldier could see an opportunity to feather his nest. One side there was the obvious poverty of the population and on the other there was partying and excess – and corruption. I saw it as my duty to devote my efforts there.[17]

When Morgen arrived in the General Government he was given the rank of SS sergeant, with a promotion to 2nd lieutenant three months later. But the fact that Morgen was a relatively junior SS

* Some sources dispute that he died in Altshausen but first-hand accounts of prisoners who were in jail alongside Dirlewanger set out in detail how he was beaten to death.

officer did not put him off investigating those occupying higher office in the SS. Although relatively junior in rank, Morgen and his fellow SS judge's activities were of great interest to Himmler himself because of his view that the SS had to live up to the higher standards that he imposed, and by the end of the war there were forty SS courts operating at fixed locations across the Reich and a further sixty mobile courts dispensing the SS brand of justice to SS and police personnel.[18]

The laws on taking goods and money for private gain in Nazi Germany were clear. Any kind of theft, embezzlement, bribery or corruption was illegal. In 1943, Himmler set these rules out in plain German to his senior SS officers in a speech in Posen. Under the heading 'The Clearing out of the Jews', he told them:

> I have issued a strict order, which SS-*Obergruppenführer* Pohl has carried out, that this wealth should, as a matter of course, be handed over to the Reich without reserve. We have taken none of it for ourselves. Individual men who have lapsed will be punished in accordance with an order I issued at the beginning which gave this warning: Whoever takes so much as a mark of it is a dead man. A number of SS men – there are not very many of them – have fallen short, and they will die.[19]

There were three big cases which Morgen investigated during his time in the General Government. His first, and probably his biggest success during this time, concerned SS Captain Dr Georg von Sauberzweig, son of a famous First World War general, one-time Berlin city councillor and secretary of a racing club in Munich. Sauberzweig was the commanding officer of a troop-supply warehouse in Kraków, an ideal position for anyone wanting to make a few million Reichsmarks on the side.

Morgen established that Sauberzweig ignored his official responsibilities around procuring and administering supplies for the army and the SS and instead managed to hand over these responsibilities to the Wehrmacht. The Wehrmacht took over the official business of bringing in supplies, which left Sauberzweig and his SS cronies free to make money.

They did this by confiscating, plundering and looting by the truckload and selling it on to buyers whom Morgen described as 'mainly Jews, criminals and pimps'.[20] The system was simple: Sauberzweig pocketed the money he received and spread some of it around his fellow officers and co-conspirators. The best pieces, including carpets and pictures, he kept for himself and sent back to his apartment in Berlin and to his friends. 'It was unimaginable that something like this was happening, that it was even possible,' Morgen later said.[21]

Morgen had started his investigation because of an insult within Sauberzweig's department. One of the SS soldiers accused another of stealing and it escalated from there. Morgen quickly established that Sauberzweig himself was the main perpetrator but this then caused problems for Morgen. Sauberzweig was a friend of SS General Oswald Pohl who headed up the SS Main Economic and Administrative Office in Berlin, which ran the concentration camps. Pohl thought very highly of Sauberzweig and intervened on his behalf.[22]

Morgen then uncovered an old bribery complaint against Sauberzweig, which had been suppressed. This resulted in a complaint against Morgen and the head office of the SS court. The court agreed informally with Morgen that he was doing the right thing, then launched proceedings against him for not following the correct procedure, part of which being that he was of too low a rank to be investigating SS generals.

Along with bribery, routine confiscation and plundering, on one occasion Sauberzweig organised a heavily armed unit of SS soldiers and raided Jewish businesses in the Warsaw Ghetto. He then sold the goods on the black market for 200,000 Reichsmarks, worth over £20,000 at the time and approximately £850,000 at today's prices.[23] But he was always careful to share his loot with his colleagues and superior officers. Those who had taken part received a share of the money, as did the office of SS General Pohl in Berlin.[24]

Sauberzweig's embezzlement was blatant. He told Morgen that he had sent a couple of truckloads of stolen items to Pohl, including one painting of a Polish battle scene. However, Morgen could not make the direct link in his case because Sauberzweig had not personally delivered it to Pohl. 'I made sure I did,' Sauberzweig told Morgen. 'Just make sure you make sure of it [the direct link] too. I told him [Pohl], "You are my superior officer, I will deliver it to you."'[25] The problem for Morgen was that without seeing the pictures on the walls of Pohl's office, he couldn't just accuse him. It would have been seen as a terrible insult.

Morgen's investigations had far-reaching consequences. He arrested Sauberzweig and forty of his men. At the trial, they were found guilty. Sauberzweig was sentenced to death. His appeal went all the way up to Hitler himself, who refused it, and Sauberzweig was put in front of a firing squad and executed. Then Himmler decided that the other verdicts were too lenient, so some of Sauberzweig's officers had their prison sentences overturned and they were shot too. Other officers whose crimes were relatively minor were also punished severely. One officer who had only dealt in a few boxes of stolen items was sent to an SS prison for between three and four years.

The Sauberzweig case was significant for Morgen because it increased his profile. Himmler took a close interest in the work of the SS courts and this was a case which had gone all the way to Hitler on appeal. It was also significant because this was the first time he had tangled with SS General Otto Pohl in Berlin. This poor relationship with Pohl was to continue right to the end of the war and afterwards at Nuremberg as well.

Morgen continued to inadvertently stir things with Pohl. Having investigated Sauberzweig, he turned his attention to SS Captain Paulsen, Pohl's right-hand man and his adjutant in Berlin. Without knowing of his connection to Pohl, Morgen accused Paulsen of being present during the looting and of diverting valuables into his own pocket. At this stage, Morgen was still looking for evidence and had no inkling that the Sauberzweig investigation was anything more than an isolated case. Morgen later said, 'At the time I had no idea about SS General Pohl. I assumed that the head of the SS Administration was an exemplary soldier and I was inclined to trust that he wouldn't surround himself with criminals!'[26]

Morgen used the opportunity of a trip to Berlin to visit Paulsen at his office. Paulsen knew exactly who Morgen was and what he had achieved in Warsaw, and he immediately struck Morgen as being too friendly by half. He invited Morgen to lunch at his expense, an invitation which Morgen declined. Because of the difference in rank, Morgen was treading carefully: he was a sergeant and Paulsen was a captain. Morgen said to Paulsen in a conversational tone, 'It will interest you to know that an accusation has been made against you.'[27]

Paulsen hit the roof, cursing and swearing: 'If you have any doubts about me please search my house!'

Morgen replied, 'Of course I myself have no doubts about you but since you have articulated what you think should happen as an order, I will of course carry it out straight away!' Morgen borrowed another officer and together they went to Paulsen's apartment.

Morgen was immediately struck by how well-furnished Paulsen's apartment was, considering that he was only a captain in the SS. 'You must have inherited a lot of money or made a good match,' Morgen said when he saw it. Paulsen tried to explain it away. It was, he maintained, all honestly obtained through gifts and reimbursement of expenses. Unsurprisingly, Morgen believed none of it and opened a formal case against Paulsen. Technically, Morgen's responsibilities were limited to the General Government in German-occupied Poland but Morgen listed the case as one which arose from the Sauberzweig case, which he had been responsible for.

But at that stage, Pohl made his move and started to make life difficult for Morgen. According to Morgen, Pohl used SS Lieutenant Colonel Kurt Schmidt-Klevenow, who was head of the legal department at the SS Main Economic and Administrative Office under Pohl, to keep an eye on him and obstruct him at every turn. He spread the word round about Morgen: 'Morgen is someone who creates suspicion from nothing, a useless fellow who digs around in the dirt in order to spread it around on to others. His cases are just assumptions on his part which his perverted mind is just making up.'[28]

Schmidt-Klevenow then proceeded to send complaints about Morgen and the Sauberzweig case to Himmler and to the head of the SS and police courts at the time, SS General Paul Scharfe. Morgen was forced to drop some of his proceedings against suspected criminals in the SS and the police due to lack of evidence. 'First this guy says a great big Hello and then he's too cowardly to admit he was wrong and he just says "it was due to lack of evidence" leaving suspicion hanging over innocent men,' said Schmidt-Klevenow.[29] As a result of this campaign, Morgen missed out on promotion opportunities and was given extra work so that he had to work evenings and weekends. Paulsen himself told Morgen that if he ever got the chance, he would shoot him like he would a mad dog.

But Morgen was undaunted by these threats. It was a feature of his wartime investigative career that he carried on working on cases even when powerful forces within the SS were working against him. He continued his case against Paulsen but in the end, because he had completed his case against Sauberzweig, the only course of action open to him was to send his case against Paulsen to the main SS court in Munich.

THE CASE OF SS COLONEL HERMANN FEGELEIN

Morgen's case against Sauberzweig had caused him to come up against vested interests inside the SS. And now a second case presented itself for him to investigate and to make even more enemies.* This one had started on the day Morgen arrested Sauberzweig.

* Most of the detail in this section comes from Morgen's own recollections in his post-war interrogation by the Americans. This means there may be historical issues with his narrative, as there are no other sources available that could corroborate his account.

When Morgen took him into custody, he turned to his wife and said, 'Call Colonel Fegelein immediately and tell him that I've been arrested!'[30]

This immediately aroused Morgen's suspicions and he opened an investigation into SS Colonel Hermann Fegelein. Together with SS Major Albert Fassbender, whom Morgen described as the adopted son of a Berlin chocolate manufacturer, Fegelein had come to Warsaw in 1940 with instructions from Himmler to set up an SS cavalry regiment.[31] Fegelein, who had previously been in charge of the SS riding school, was described by the historian Hugh Trevor-Roper as an 'illiterate jockey' and 'ignorant horse fancier'.[32] He was a favourite of Himmler and his SS cavalry units killed thousands of innocent people in the war in the East.[33]

Morgen had already come across the SS cavalry during his investigation into Sauberzweig because they had been requisitioning an unusually large number of items. Morgen's suspicions led him to another surprising fact: that Fegelein and Fassbender had taken over a fur company called Nathan and Apfelbaum in Warsaw, which also had branches in New York and London.

When Morgen started investigating, the company was wound up and the assets, rumoured to be in the region of 14–16 million Reichsmarks (roughly £1.43 million to £1.63 million at the time and £59.5 million to £68 million at 2023 prices) were sold off for a mere 50,000 Reichsmarks (roughly £5,100 at the time and £213,000 in 2023 prices).[34] Morgen was left asking himself about the missing millions.

He then found out that they had confiscated a further forty fur companies in Warsaw. But Fassbender then made a mistake. He confiscated a shipping company and with it, forty boxes of tea.

These turned out to belong to a German company in Danzig (now Gdańsk) who were not pleased about the loss of their tea and started legal proceedings against the General Government in occupied Poland. Fassbender promptly denied having anything to do with it.

Fassbender had become infatuated with Jaroslawa Mirowska, who had been a saleswoman in the firm and later the mistress of one of the owners of the business, Apfelbaum, who had fled Poland at the start of the war. Mirowska helped Fassbender and Fegelein to strip the company of its assets. They even managed to present her to Himmler, who was utterly charmed by her. According to Morgen, she was treated as 'the first lady of the SS'. Morgen, however, was suspicious of her and thought that she might be a spy.

With everything going so well, Fassbender and Mirowska decided to get married and have children together. There was only one problem with this plan: they were both already married to different people. Fassbender's wife Countess Stollberg refused to grant a divorce and Mirowska's husband was a Polish army staff officer. The next thing Morgen heard was that Mirowska's husband had gone in front of a court martial for illegal possession of a weapon and been found guilty and shot.

Morgen investigated further and established that this was a case of premeditated murder. While her husband was out, and prior to his own arrest, Sauberzweig had placed a pistol in the oven of the house where the Mirowskas were living. Then, when the husband was back at home again, the Gestapo suddenly appeared and carried out a search of the house. Of course, they found the pistol and arrested the husband. Conveniently, possession of a weapon by a Polish national was an offence that the Gestapo had responsibility for, so they could arrest offenders and try them. They took the husband into custody where, despite the regulations prohibiting visitors, Jaroslawa got in to see him and got him to sign a power of attorney over his bank accounts. Less than an hour later, her husband was taken out and shot.

On his own initiative, Morgen decided to search Fassbender's apartment. He had a discussion about the case with the head of the Gestapo in Warsaw who advised him, 'This is not my area of responsibility, it is a matter for the SS. As a judge you know what you have to do. If you ask me for help, I will find an officer to assist.'[35] Because Morgen was still only an SS sergeant, he took him up on his offer and went to Fassbender's flat to carry out a search.

Once there, he met Mirowska, who lost no time in ringing her husband's regiment which promptly dispatched three officers to the apartment, 'What are you doing here?' one of them asked. 'I am not answerable to you,' replied Morgen.

'Well, do you mind if we stay around during your operation?'

'No,' replied Morgen. There was a lot of coming and going as they kept an eye on Morgen's search. He and his Gestapo colleague quickly turned up piles of secret documents lying around in the apartment, which contravened the SS regulations around confidentiality.

While all this was going on, the regiment had radioed through to both Fegelein and Fassbender. Both were at the front with their units. Fegelein was the commanding officer of a cavalry unit in East Prussia and Fassbender was the commanding officer of a reconnaissance unit at the head of the advance into the Soviet Union. Once the news of Morgen's search reached them, they lost no time in abandoning their men and travelling back to deal with Morgen's investigation. Fassbender got on to a motorbike and in only five hours made it back to Warsaw. Fegelein, thinking more strategically, got into an aeroplane and headed straight to Berlin to talk to Himmler himself.

Morgen travelled back to Kraków and reported his investigation to SS General Friedrich-Wilhelm Krüger, who was in overall charge of the SS and police. Krüger, according to Morgen, was pleased and said, 'Bring it on!' On his way out of Krüger's office, Morgen met Fassbender on the stairs. Then Morgen was summoned back in by Krüger, who told him, 'Fassbender came to see me and has complained about you, how you forced your way into his apartment, ransacked the place, insulted his wife etc. He was exaggerating, of course.'

'What did you say to him?' Morgen wanted to know.

'I said to Fassbender, "Is your conscience clear? Of course it is. So now you've got nothing at all to worry about. Just report what has happened and Morgen's actions will come to light and God have mercy on him!"' With that, Krüger had dismissed Fassbender, who went straight to Munich and the headquarters of the SS judiciary to complain about Morgen.

Fegelein had more luck with Himmler. On the same day he went to see him, a telex arrived in Kraków in Himmler's name. Morgen was informed that what he had done was improper, and he was therefore reprimanded and ordered to stop investigating because Himmler was reserving the case for himself. Morgen therefore sent the case through to his superior officers at the main SS judiciary headquarters in Munich, who were having none of it. They said to Himmler that they were going to continue investigating but this time a more senior officer to Morgen would take the case on. SS Colonel Martin Tondock was assigned to take over from Morgen.

Himmler tried to have the case stopped but the SS judiciary pointed out to him that only Hitler, as head of state, had the power to stop criminal investigations. Himmler eventually had the relevant authority transferred to him from Hitler and stopped the investigation.

Meanwhile, Jaroslawa Mirowska's life was becoming more interesting. Her case was taken over by the Reich Security Main Office and she was arrested, but she was then installed in a six-bedroom apartment in Berlin on the condition that she did not go back to the General Government. Four weeks later, she was gone. One year later, the Polish resistance was raided and Mirowska, the 'first lady of the SS', was arrested as a spy and one of the main agents in the underground. Himmler, however, instructed the Gestapo to let her go.[36]

Himmler's protection of Fegelein was perhaps surprising given his own views on the need for SS officers to behave appropriately. For example, Himmler himself always insisted on paying for the cigars he smoked in the SS mess room in Berlin.[37] But he was involved in a power struggle with Hans Frank, the governor general, and could not afford to lose Fegelein.[38] Later, Fegelein would repay Himmler for his actions in saving him. He went on to become an SS general and gained entry into Hitler's inner circle by marrying Gretl Braun, the sister of Eva Braun, Hitler's mistress. Because he was Himmler's friend, Fegelein was then a key link between Himmler and Hitler's inner circle. But ultimately, Fegelein's principal interest was always in himself and this was to lead to his downfall.

Because of Fegelein's marriage to Gretl, he was part of the group of loyal Nazis in the bunker with Hitler as the end approached.

But with Hitler's fate sealed, Fegelein had no plans to share it with him and he went missing from the bunker. He was later arrested in civilian clothes and brought back to the bunker, where he was put in front of a court martial and shot for desertion and complicity in Himmler's treason in reaching out to the Allies.[39]

THE CASE OF SS LIEUTENANT COLONEL ERICH LEKEBUSCH

Konrad Morgen's third big case in the General Government involved SS Lieutenant Colonel Erich Lekebusch, who commanded an SS training camp at Dębica in the area of the General Government. A former employee reported financial irregularities in the camp and the initial investigating officer, SS 2nd Lieutenant Katlak, asked Morgen for his help. However, Lekebusch had contacted Governor General Hans Frank straight away, who stopped the investigation and sent Lekebusch a memo saying that there were no investigations against him. Lekebusch then had this memo copied and distributed around the SS housing complex in Zehlendorf in Berlin.[40]

But this apparent setback did not put Morgen off and, with Katlak, he carried on investigating at Dębica without informing the official channels. Together they calculated that Lekebusch had embezzled 1.25 million Reichsmarks, equivalent to approximately £127,500 or over £5.3 million in today's prices.[41]

He had formed a limited partnership with three businessmen, two brothers called Präger and another called Dannenberg. They supplied the Polish employees and workers at the Dębica SS training camp with clothing and consumer goods at vastly inflated prices. Lekebusch placed his shares in the enterprise in the names of his father-in-law and a friend. The initial purchases were made with money advanced by Hans Frank from the Reich Treasury. In order to assist with cash flow, Lekebusch also traded food, tobacco and medicine on the black market in Kraków. When he was arrested, 80 per cent of these goods were still in his possession.[42]

According to Lekebusch's own statement, he continually bribed a couple of hundred SS officers in Berlin with fur coats, food, fridges and radios. At one stage, he had around 1,000 items stored in Berlin for this purpose. He even supplied Morgen's colleague Katlak with food and he gave Frank two fur coats, for which no payment was received.

However, Morgen was to be deprived of his day in an SS court with Lekebusch. He committed suicide shortly after his arrest. This meant that there wasn't enough evidence to convict the three local businessmen and they escaped with their reputations intact. Morgen did arrest five SS officers from the training camp administration and three of these were given prison sentences of between seven and ten years. Charges against the remaining two were dismissed for lack of evidence.[43]

* * *

Morgen had been very busy since he had arrived in the General Government. He had brought corrupt SS officials to trial and made enemies in all the big cases he had investigated. And he had had enough of the criminality that he saw all around. On 27 March 1942, he wrote to the SS judiciary in Munich asking for a transfer: 'The corruption in the General Government is so great and property crimes and offences of a revolting nature so numerous that I am deeply convinced that any judge, in time, must find himself somewhat dulled and the danger therefore exists that his natural sense of justice will be damaged.'[44]

What Morgen wanted was a transfer to a quieter backwater of the Reich like Norway, but the reply that he got was not one he expected. In May, Morgen went to Dresden for the Pentecost break, a public holiday in Germany. However, the same day he left he was called back to the office in Kraków, where there was a letter waiting for him from the head of the SS judiciary: 'The *Reichsführer* has ordered that you be relieved of your duties with immediate effect, you are to stop work and you are to report to the headquarters of the SS judiciary immediately.'[45] Morgen went straight to Munich, where he was informed that he had now been demoted from his newly acquired SS officer's rank of lieutenant down to an ordinary soldier. His officer's shoulder rank insignia were removed.

It is unlikely that Morgen would have had an easier life in Norway and, given his record in the General Government, he would undoubtedly have made just as many enemies there, if not more. The SS judiciary normally only had jurisdiction over members of the SS and the police but the SS court in Oslo was given jurisdiction over ordinary Norwegians who were deemed to have worked against Nazi rule, and it gained a reputation among the general population for the severity of the punishments that it handed down, including frequent use of the death penalty. The head of the SS court in Norway, SS Lieutenant Colonel Hans Paul Latza, was charged with war crimes after the war, although he was eventually acquitted by the Norwegian Supreme Court.[46]

What had happened? Konrad Morgen's powerful enemies had moved against him. Although Morgen was an investigating judge, he also sat as a conventional judge in trials of SS officers and men. And now, one of these cases had been dug out to use against him. This concerned a charge against a police officer of having sexual relations with a Polish woman. Himmler had decreed that these offences should be punished very severely but Morgen dismissed the charge as trivial.[47] In the normal course of events, this would not have been noticed, as acquittal decisions were seldom checked, but for Morgen's enemies it was an ideal opportunity to show that he wasn't up to the job. According to Morgen, Oswald Pohl persuaded SS General Wilhelm Koppe that he had nothing better to do than to fly down to Munich in person to show the SS judiciary the case.[48]

While he was in Munich, Morgen ran into the SS judge who had been appointed as his replacement, SS Major Sachs. Sachs told him that Himmler had drawn up an order that would have sent Morgen to a concentration camp for two or three years but the SS judiciary had complained, saying, 'That's not how it works, what about judicial independence? This isn't about Konrad Morgen but about the general principle of justice. A verdict can be appealed but a judge shouldn't be punished for it.'[49] Himmler backed down but decided that Morgen should be demoted, transferred out from the SS judiciary and sent to the front as an ordinary soldier.

Senior SS officers were no doubt relieved that the troublesome Konrad Morgen was being sent to the Eastern Front to fight the Soviet Army as an ordinary soldier. They were undoubtedly thinking to themselves, 'Wouldn't it be great if he were to be killed in combat?'

As for Morgen himself, he was off to war and, given the nature of the heavy fighting in the East with no quarter given or taken by the Waffen SS, his life would be on the line and he knew he would be lucky to come back alive.

CHAPTER 3

AT WAR WITH THE WAFFEN SS

MONDAY 31 MARCH 1958

Fans of James Bond had been looking forward to this day with eager anticipation.[1] The sixth book in the series featuring the famous British secret agent was due to be published. When they opened it, fans found it lived up to all their expectations. One reason was that it was in this book, *Dr No*, that Ian Fleming introduced readers to the trademark handgun for James Bond, the Walther PPK, 'a real stopping gun'.[2] Apart from its firepower, the Walther had another advantage for the secret agent – at just over an inch wide, it could be easily concealed in a holster or a waistband.

Using the Walther PPK was simply a matter of moving the safety lever and pulling the trigger. Sounds simple? Could you kill an enemy agent? Ian Fleming couldn't.

Towards the end of the Second World War, Fleming was in Toronto with naval intelligence where he had got himself on to a Special Operations Executive course for a couple of days. He distinguished himself so much that he was considered to have real potential as an agent.[3] For the final exercise, Fleming was given a loaded revolver and told to make his way to a certain hotel where he was to shoot dead an enemy agent. This 'agent' was in fact an expert unarmed combat instructor from the Special Operations Executive called William Fairbairn, who was ready to disarm Fleming when he entered his room. However, Fleming never made it; at the last minute he turned around and left. 'I couldn't kill a man that way,' he was later reported as saying.[4]

The creator of James Bond was not alone in discovering that he could not kill the enemy. In 1947, US General S. L. A. 'Slam' Marshall surprised the military world with his book *Men Against Fire*. Marshall was a combat historian who had travelled with the US Army and interviewed soldiers after battle. In the book, he made the startling suggestion that in the Second World War, 'On an average not more than 15 per cent of the men had actually fired at the enemy … the best showing that could be made by the most spirited and aggressive companies was that one in four had made at least some use of his fire-power.'[5]

Although Marshall's methods were later heavily criticised, there does appear to be some truth in his assertion. During the Sicily campaign in 1943, Lieutenant-Colonel Lionel Wigram of the British School of Infantry had found that only a quarter of the men in a typical British platoon could be relied on to try to engage the enemy in battle.[6]

Whatever the truth of Marshall's research, the US and British armies did review the way they trained their soldiers after the war, so that they became much more effective. The problem lay in the traditional training which US and European armies gave to their soldiers. Endless drill, marching up and down, was supposed to teach soldiers how to respond unthinkingly to orders. Shooting their weapons on the range was supposed to teach them how to kill. Finally, fieldcraft, the art of movement under fire, was supposed to equip them with the skills they needed to move around the battlefield. The problem with this was that it didn't produce very many effective soldiers – i.e. soldiers who killed the enemy.

But there was one military formation in the Second World War that had worked out how to train their soldiers to kill the enemy and that was the Waffen SS. They still trained their soldiers the traditional way but they had worked out the three additional elements which were necessary to turn ordinary Germans into killers. These elements have been identified and characterised by former US lieutenant colonel and psychologist Dave Grossman as desensitisation, conditioning and denial.[7]

Desensitisation in modern armies is all about getting soldiers used to the idea of violence and killing, for example through bawling out by non-commissioned officers and bullying. Conditioning, arguably the most important of these three factors, is all about training to kill enemy soldiers. Instead of aiming at stationary targets on a firing range, soldiers practice battle drills over and over again. These drills involve firing at pop-up targets in realistic battle scenarios, which fall over when hit. According to Grossman, this is based on operant conditioning. The stimulus is the target appearing, the response is that the soldier fires his weapon and the reward is to see the target fall. If this is done enough times in training, then it becomes automatic on the battlefield. The last element, denial, is about removing the humanity from the enemy soldier. For modern soldiers, denial means talking about enemy soldiers as targets instead of as human beings. For the Waffen SS, denial fitted right in with the Nazi ideology of seeing other races as *Untermenschen* or sub-humans.[8]

When Konrad Morgen arrived in Stralsund to begin his Waffen SS training with the regiment 'Der Führer', none of this was on his mind. He was writing love letters to his fiancée Maria Wachter and reassuring his parents that he would be fine. Having written to them on 28 April 1942 telling them that they would be pleased to hear of his promotion to lieutenant, his subsequent letters from Stralsund were written to keep their spirits up in the face of this setback.[9]

Although Morgen had already received military training at the start of the war, now he was treated as if he had just joined the Waffen SS. But with one important difference – he was assigned to a punishment company and there he was put through what he called 'all the amusements of Prussian training'.[10]

Recruits in the 'Der Führer' regiment went through a standard military training routine. New arrivals were issued with steel helmets, tunic, trousers, jackboots, coat, three shirts, black tie and underwear. The SS trouser belt clasp was engraved with the SS motto *Meine Ehre heißt Treue* (for me, honour means loyalty). The long johns were designed to be worn in both winter and summer. These items were stored in wooden lockers, which were kept unlocked as SS men did not steal from one another. They were shown how to make their beds the SS way and then every morning during inspection, the non-commissioned officer of the day would measure the folds with a ruler and any beds which did not conform exactly to the SS standard would be upended so the recruit had to start again from the beginning.

All soldiers were trained on the Karabiner 98 kurz, the German Army rifle, as well as the Luger Po8 handgun before being assigned a main weapon that they would specialise in: the heavy machine gun SMG 34 or the 8 cm mortar. The battle drills were around the operation of the SMG 34 or mortar, so that each member of the team knew instinctively what to do whenever they were in action. The mortar was operated by a four-man team and the SMG 34 heavy machine gun was maintained and operated by a five-man team of riflemen, each with his own task. Two operated the machine and two more supplied the ammunition and dug the position, with a fifth to liaise with the battlefield commanders.

Alongside heavy weapons practice, there was endless marching and practice on the range as well as against pop-up cardboard soldiers. The day often started with press-ups at 8 a.m., with anyone not giving their all during the marching and singing of SS songs being forced to run carrying a heavy machine gun tripod until they fell over with exhaustion.[11] Punishments by the training staff were out of all proportion to the mistakes made by the soldiers. One soldier from Morgen's future unit, Waffen SS Division Wiking, reported how he dropped a cartridge on the ground and was ordered to do fifty knee bends with his rifle held out at arm's length. After twenty he could do no more and as a punishment for weeping with exhaustion, he was ordered to clean out all the toilets for a week.[12] Morgen used one word to describe his Waffen SS training: 'horrible'.[13]

The other key element of Waffen SS training, which modern armies use to condition their trainee soldiers and which the Waffen SS pioneered during the Second World War, was training under live-fire conditions. SS soldiers carried out their battle drills while being exposed both to live small arms and artillery fire. The artillery was positioned as close as possible for realistic training, and shells would be fired in the direction of the soldiers from as little as 100 metres away.[14] This aspect of training was also used by elite British units like the newly formed commandos. All of this training, including the key elements of denial, desensitisation and conditioning, was designed to produce combat-ready Waffen SS soldiers who would be supremely effective in battle and who would kill enemy soldiers without hesitation.

At Christmas 1942, Konrad Morgen was dispatched to his new unit, SS Division Wiking. In common with other Waffen SS divisions, this was a mobile, heavily armoured SS division with tanks, armoured personnel carriers and weapons including mortars as well as heavy and light machine guns. To reflect this change, the division had been officially renamed SS Panzergrenadier-Division Wiking on 9 November 1942. The order for Morgen's departure to the front came from Waffen SS headquarters and was only for him. No one else from Stralsund was dispatched with him. His departure was so quick that he was not given a winter coat and so travelled in winter to the Soviet Union to join up with his division in his ordinary summer uniform.[15]

The reason as to why someone might want Morgen at the front and exposed to maximum danger soon became clear when he arrived at his new division. SS General Felix Steiner, who commanded the division, had received new orders just before Christmas to proceed to Stalingrad to relieve the German Army there. For whoever wanted Morgen out of the way, this was an ideal opportunity to expose him to maximum danger. Steiner, while being one of Himmler's more effective Waffen SS generals, would get himself into trouble with Himmler in July 1943 because of critical attitudes within the division towards Himmler. Although Morgen had endured a horrible training with the Waffen SS, it is likely that his new division would have been more agreeable for him because there was more opportunity to express his own opinions. Having visited the division, Himmler wrote to Steiner in August 1943 and told him off for the way his officers spoke to and about Himmler: 'Even in the messes of the Wiking Division it should be unheard of for SS leaders to discuss the actions of the *Reichsführer* in a tone of criticism that goes beyond the proper limits of mess discussions.'[16]

Morgen's new unit was the 2nd SS Panzer Grenadier regiment Germania. Across the SS Wiking Division, his new comrades were Waffen SS recruits from other European countries who were deemed suitable for the Waffen SS by virtue of race. They included Scandinavians, Dutch and Belgian soldiers. At Christmas 1942, soldiers from the Wiking Division arrived at the small village of Zimovniki, the farthest point in the division's push towards Stalingrad, about 180 miles from the city itself. Morgen arrived as units of the Wiking Division were defending the village against attacks from the Soviet Army.[17]

The Waffen SS was dug in along the main road through the village. The Soviet Army attacked Wiking positions in a snowstorm and used their T34 tanks to knock out the Luftwaffe Stukas that were parked on the airstrip. The SS Wiking Tiger tanks were parked up with no crews available to drive them. Together with their infantry, the Soviet T34 tanks moved into the village as darkness fell and the fighting went house to house. Soviet artillery then opened up, pounding the village, and before long all the houses were on fire and the Waffen SS were falling back. The wounded were abandoned in the haste to retreat and the Soviets were only halted when the big German 88 mm guns opened up and starting destroying the Soviet T34 tanks.

The fighting went on all through Christmas and it was only on New Year's Eve that the village of Zimovniki was abandoned by the Waffen SS.[18] This was now the start of the division's withdrawal all the way back across the steppes to Rostov. Along with other Panzer Grenadier regiments Nordland and Westland, Morgen's unit, Germania, had the most dangerous task of all, which was to cover the fighting retreat during the depths of winter, and these Panzer Grenadier regiments were often reduced to company strength because of the intensity of the fighting.

On 24 and 25 January 1943, the Germania was exposed to the full force of a Soviet Army attack at the village of Yegorlykskaya. At one point, a motorcycle patrol ran into a Soviet Army emplacement in in the middle of a snowstorm. Having captured the gun, the SS soldiers were astonished to discover that it was being towed by camels because of the problems caused by freezing conditions to motorised vehicles on both sides. At the beginning of February, Morgen's unit was defending the Rostov bridgehead, one of the last to cross the River Don at Rostov. The Panzer Grenadiers were split into small groups fighting individual battles and contact was lost with many groups as they were swallowed up by the snow and the Soviet Army.

In early February, Morgen was in action again, this time as part of the counter-attack at the Donets River where the SS Wiking Division was ordered to stop the Soviet Army's advance. It was bitterly cold and while the Panzer Grenadiers' mortars continued to work, the machine-gun crews constantly had to move into abandoned houses to try and warm them up enough to function. As they moved forward, their lorries would seize up from the cold and they had to be abandoned and blown up with the men crammed on to the lorries that were working. Once they reached the Donets, they dug in for a war of attrition against the Soviets on the other side of the river.[19]

By May 1943 there were only seventeen men left in Morgen's company and in the five months since he had joined the division at Christmas 1942, they had lost 570 men. It was a vicious war on both sides. Later, Morgen recalled the brutality of the Soviet troops against the Waffen SS, with SS soldiers being killed by being hung on meat hooks.[20]

But for Morgen, his time on the front line was at an end, having survived the winter war in the East. At the end of May 1943, Himmler pulled him out of the front line and restored his rank so that he was now an officer again. Himmler wanted Morgen back for his investigative abilities. His instructions were that Morgen was to report to the *Reichssicherheitshauptamt*, the Reich Security Main Office, in order to take charge of investigations into corruption in Buchenwald concentration camps. This was a real vote of confidence in his abilities by Himmler, who was increasingly concerned about the losses to the central Reich treasury because of theft, embezzlement and corruption. Morgen himself pointed to an article he had written for a magazine about investigating corruption during his time on the front line as being a factor in Himmler's decision to bring him back.[21]

The historian Michael Wildt describes the modus operandi of the Reich Security Main Office (RSHA) in one German word: *Entgrenzung* or dissolution of boundaries:

> The RSHA proved to be a new type of political institution, one extremely capable of adapting to circumstances, one able to increase or decrease in size, to implement new divisions and sections or dissolve old ones, to shift and re-establish its focus, to initiate cooperation among its different offices, and, despite all the bureaucratic procedures, to pursue the project of a racist reordering of Europe.[22]

On 23 June 1943, Morgen reported to Office V of the Reich Security Main Office, the *Reichskriminalpolizeiamt* or the Central Police Detective Office of the Reich. Office V was home to the only female head of section in the RSHA, Friederike Wieking. Her section was responsible for identifying and monitoring children and young people who were thought to be at risk of criminal behaviour. She was also responsible for the youth concentration camps at Moringen and Uckermark where conditions were inhumane and the young prisoners were subject to serious abuse.

But Morgen had other things on his mind. On 27 June he sent a memo to the *Rasse- und Siedlungshauptamt der SS*, the SS Race and Settlement Office, asking for the papers he would need to submit in order to marry.[23] Whatever hopes he may have had of a quick marriage were destined to be unsuccessful; the wheels of SS bureaucracy moved very slowly, especially with forms to complete and references to obtain.

Morgen's new boss was SS General Arthur Nebe, who was unusual in the Reich Security Main Office because he was older than other RSHA senior officers and had fought in the First World War. Nebe had a long police career before the Second World War. When he was in the Berlin CID, he used to send any Jews who asked for the office to office 429 on the fourth floor, which was the toilet. According to another CID detective, Bernd Wehner, who assisted Morgen at Buchenwald, Nebe said he did this 'to get their flat fleet moving'.[24]

Nebe combined a career as Nazi crime-fighting senior detective with leading *Einsatzgruppe B*, which killed more than 45,000 people in the Soviet Union in 1941. The RSHA organised these mobile killing units, which moved into areas invaded by the German Army so they could identify and eliminate potential enemies of German occupation. Nebe would later be involved in the plot to kill Hitler in 1944. Despite not being suspected of involvement, he went on the run, which caused Himmler and the heads of the RSHA and the Gestapo to wonder where he was.[25] Eventually, he was betrayed and executed in early 1945.

Morgen's appointment as a police official in Office V made the SS judiciary nervous and its head, SS General Franz Breithaupt, wrote to Himmler with his concerns. The problem for Breithaupt was one of authority: to whom would Morgen report? If Morgen were to remain an SS investigating judge employed by only the SS judiciary then the chain of command was clear – Morgen would report to him as head of the SS judiciary and Himmler as *Reichsführer*-SS. But now he was both an SS investigating judge and police official, a senior police detective in all but name, and this was going to muddy the waters. Breithaupt pointed out to Himmler that Morgen would now have two more bosses, SS General Ernst Kaltenbrunner, head of the Reich Security Main Office, and Nebe. This, said Breithaupt, was untenable.

Instead, Breithaupt asked Himmler if existing liaison arrangements with the Reich Security Main Office could be used instead via SS judge Lieutenant Colonel Kurt Mittelstädt, who was the appointed point of contact between the SS judiciary and the Reich Security Main Office.[26] Breithaupt's request turned out to be perfectly valid because these multiple lines of responsibilities would cause Morgen problems at Buchenwald when his investigations uncovered illegal killings. But for now, his request fell on deaf ears. Konrad Morgen was to be an SS investigating judge and police official.

It had been a year since Morgen had been stripped of his rank and sent to join the Waffen SS. He was back from war with the award of an Infantry Assault Badge in bronze, awarded on 20 April 1943 for fighting on the front line.[27] Now, battle hardened and with a war record that no one in the SS could argue with, he was back and about to take on the biggest case of his SS judicial career.

CHAPTER 4

THE INVESTIGATION AT BUCHENWALD CONCENTRATION CAMP, PART ONE: CORRUPTION

MONDAY 16 APRIL 1945

The town of Weimar is on the move. One thousand smartly dressed people are walking along a road through the woods in the sunshine. One of them covers her face with her coat as the camera captures their trek from a US Army jeep. Otherwise they walk along talking and looking into the camera. The woods are named for the type of trees which were planted here and which give the forest its name: *Buchen* or beech trees. It is six miles from Weimar to their destination, a concentration camp named after the woods where it is located, called Buchenwald.

When they arrive, American soldiers and military police meet them and take them round the camp. The previous day, US General George S. Patton had inspected the camp and ordered that 1,000 citizens of Weimar should visit and see the full horror of what the Nazis were doing in their name. The sweetness of the countryside is replaced by the smell of the bodies, which are still lying on the ground piled up. The camera captures the Weimar citizens holding cloths over their noses and mouths. Some faint and one elderly lady is supported by a camp inmate in his striped uniform.

The American soldiers show them body parts, shrunken heads and tattooed pieces of skin. The soldiers wave the visitors closer so they can see properly and the visitors respond by holding on to themselves and to each other. The film is silent but a *Guardian* special correspondent accompanying them on the visit wrote that most of the women and some of the men were in tears as they moved around the camp.[1] There were 48,000 inmates in Buchenwald when the people from Weimar visited, and despite the help from the Americans they were dying at a rate of forty every day.[2] As the *Guardian* reporter went inside one hut with the German visitors, one of the inmates died and was taken away.[3]

But the emotion shown by the Germans on the film was not the whole story. The Americans were angry that the Germans weren't taking their visit as seriously as they should. On the way out of the camp one group started laughing, which enraged one of the officers. He ordered his men to turn the Germans around and they were forced to go back through the camp for another tour.[4] Others protested that they knew nothing about what had happened there, and after the visit, three of the town's leading dignitaries wrote to General Patton arguing that they hadn't known about Buchenwald. In addition, the Lutheran superintendent of the Weimar diocese instructed all churches to read out a statement saying that they had not been aware of what was happening at Buchenwald and that they did not share the responsibility for the atrocities there.[5]

The letter to Patton referred to Weimar as the 'old culture town', a clue to the defensiveness of the residents when confronted with the reality of Buchenwald.[6] Weimar is a town of traditional German buildings and cobbled streets; it has four palaces and was the birthplace of the twentieth-century Bauhaus architectural movement. But in their reference to Weimar as the 'old culture town', the townspeople were thinking more about Weimar's importance to European history and culture. Johann Sebastian Bach, Franz Liszt and Richard Strauss lived, performed and composed music in Weimar. More importantly for German culture and German national identity, Weimar was home to Johann Wolfgang von Goethe and Friedrich Schiller, two of Germany's most famous and important writers, who both lived in Weimar in the latter half of the eighteenth century and who became the most famous writing duo in German history. Their output was prodigious and can best be summed up by Goethe himself, who said that Schiller 'preached the gospel of freedom; I didn't want to diminish the rights of nature'.[7]

The third important figure in German history who lived in Weimar during the same period was German philosopher Johann Gottfried Herder. Herder and Goethe had met at the University of Strasbourg in 1770 and Herder encouraged Goethe to read widely, including Shakespeare whom Goethe credits with inspiring his own literary awakening. Goethe later wrote, 'When I had finished the first [Shakespeare] play I stood there like someone who is born blind and on whom a miraculous hand bestows sight in a moment.'[8] It is not just Goethe who loved Shakespeare – throughout German history, Shakespeare has been almost as much, perhaps even more, of a national figure than in Britain. The world's oldest Shakespeare society was founded not in England but in Weimar, and it is still going strong today.[9]

Although Herder is less well known today than other German philosophers of the eighteenth century, such as Immanuel Kant and Friedrich Schlegel, he is important because he was the first advocate of a Germany where people who shared the common German language should consider themselves as *Ein Volk* united by *Ein Volksgeist* – one people united in spirit. Herder was a philosopher working in an age when rulers were absolute, and despite the French revolution of 1789, the German-speaking peoples across the border were not in a position where they were able to challenge the established order. As a result, Herder's writings were of a general nature: he encouraged German-speaking people in philosophical abstracts rather than in revolutionary provocation. But this did not prevent him castigating his fellow German speakers who had chosen to speak French instead of their own language and he told them to stop speaking French and speak German.

During Goethe and Herder's lifetimes, the country we know today as Germany was still split into numerous small duchies, kingdoms, principalities and city states, which loosely formed part of the Holy Roman Empire. Over time, these small independent states consolidated and by 1871, twenty-five of these came together to form the first united Germany. These twenty-five states then formed the new *Länder*, or federal states, which then, as now, had a great deal of freedom to make their own laws.

In Goethe's time, the ruling duke lived in what is today called the *Stadtschloss*, or the town palace, in order to distinguish it from three other palaces in Weimar. This palace was where Johann Sebastian Bach carried out his duties as court organist from 1708 to 1714 and then as concertmaster from 1714 to 1717. In the following century, the pianist and composer Franz Liszt was the director of the court orchestra. Bach composed most of his organ music in Weimar and his children were baptised at the church of Saint Peter and Saint Paul.

Weimar, the centre of so much of Germany's cultural heritage, had a very small Jewish population. By the 1920s, it was a very hostile place for German Jews and Hitler visited the town on a regular basis during the time of the Weimar Republic, when it was the place where the national constitutional assembly sat. In 1933, there were just forty-three Jewish families in the town, one quarter of the national average.[10] By 1940, the remaining members of these families were confined to three houses in the town until April 1942, when they were sent to Majdanek extermination camp along with other Jews who were brought to Weimar and housed in the Gestapo prison pending onward transportation.[11]

The Jewish community in Germany had been big fans of Goethe, and Jewish authors researched and wrote most of the biographies of him. According to Professors Klaus L. Berghahn and Jost Hermand, the Jews who left Nazi Germany:

> clung to their belief in the humanitarian promises of Goethe's works. They could not understand the paradox that Germany, the country of so many great philosophers, poets, composers and scholars, would also be inscribed in the annals of history as the land in which the Holocaust took place. A few survivors returned to Germany after 1945 but the country had lost Goethe's most devoted audience, the German Jews.[12]

Goethe loved the countryside around Weimar and he often walked and rode in the woods on the Ettersberg Mountain. The SS chose this same location for the site of Buchenwald concentration camp 105 years after his death. The first prisoners built the camp using the local clay to make bricks for the huts and camp buildings. The proximity of the camp to Weimar and the links between the two meant that the people of the town must have known what was going on at Buchenwald when they wrote to Patton denying they knew anything about it. According to historian Michael H. Kater, 'The Weimar citizens, in particular the museum director, mayor and divines, all were lying, and if they did not see what was going on at Buchenwald, they did not want to see.'[13]

One Weimar citizen who certainly knew what was happening at Buchenwald was businessman Thilo Bornschein, whose relationship with the Buchenwald commandant was to prompt the SS and police investigation conducted by Morgen. He was a member of the town council and a local Nazi Party official, so he was a man of considerable influence and power in Weimar and the surrounding area. One of the senior detectives in the local police, Emil Holtschmidt, became concerned at the relationship between another Nazi Party official working in the police's fraud department and Bornschein. He started to investigate the arrangements by which Bornschein supplied Buchenwald with food. One of the detectives brought in with Morgen said later that Holtschmidt either fell out with this official or he was simply an honest and courageous police detective. Whatever his motives, his investigations were initially secret.[14]

What Holtschmidt discovered was startling. As well as from holding the contract to supply food to Buchenwald, Bornschein had been drafted into the SS as a private by the camp commandant, SS Colonel Karl-Otto Koch, and assigned to the Buchenwald camp headquarters, where he became the main buyer for Buchenwald. The suspicion was that he could, in this position, order supplies from himself at prices that he set and the goods which he bought could be sold on the black market with the profits being shared all around.[15]

Once Holtschmidt started taking statements from witnesses, it wasn't long before word of his investigation reached Bornschein and he confronted the detective. 'I demand to know what is going on,' he said to Holtschmidt. 'What are you going to do with these witnesses who have given statements against me?'[16] The answer was straightforward. Holtschmidt searched his house and obtained an arrest warrant against Bornschein, who was put in jail while further investigations were carried out. The jailing of a prominent local businessman caused a real stir among the population of Weimar but after six months he was released because of lack of evidence.[17]

There was another problem. Koch had put Bornschein beyond the reach of the local Weimar police by drafting him into the SS. Only the SS could investigate and prosecute one of their own and Holtschmidt was a police officer, not an SS officer. The case went to the responsible SS court at Kassel where one of the local judges, SS Lieutenant Colonel Werner Paulmann, soon realised that the Buchenwald investigation was likely to be long and complex. Doubtful that either he or the local police in Weimar had the expertise to investigate properly, Paulmann sent a request into the *Reichskriminalpolizeiamt* for an expert to lead the investigation. Morgen, newly returned from the Eastern Front, was assigned to the SS and police court in Kassel to lead a team of detectives on the Buchenwald case.[18]

THE CASE OF SS COLONEL KARL-OTTO KOCH

By the time Morgen arrived in Buchenwald at the end of June 1943, Koch was no longer there. He had been transferred to Majdanek concentration camp in Lublin in Nazi-occupied Poland in September 1941, where he only lasted twelve months. In August 1942, eighty-six Soviet prisoners of war escaped from Majdanek and Himmler suspended Koch. At the start of Morgen's investigation, Koch had been working in the Reich Security Main Office with the postal service before being posted to Eger in German-occupied Hungary to take charge of SS security for the postal service there.[19]

Koch's transfer from Buchenwald came after the earlier investigation into his behaviour, as outlined in Chapter 1. Koch had been arrested on 17 December 1941 but, as outlined in Chapter 1, this inquiry went nowhere. Himmler had ordered Koch's release a day later and then sent out a general order known as the 'lex Waldeck' saying that a commandant of a concentration camp could only be arrested on the direct order of Himmler himself. Further enquiries by SS investigating judges Lieutenant Colonel Vogt and SS Major Schaper revealed only mistakes but no financial irregularities.[20] It was only because of the suspicions surrounding Thilo Bornschein that the investigations into Koch were started up again under the leadership of Morgen.

SS General Oswald Pohl, who had complained to Himmler about Koch's arrest in 1941, had written to Koch after the episode and said to him, 'My dear Kamerad Koch. If anytime in the future any unemployed lawyer stretches out his vicious hanging hands after your innocent body, then I shall place myself in his way with all the strength of my personality and woe betide him!'[21] Koch had then taken copies of this letter and distributed it widely. Not only that but SS General Richard Glücks, inspector general of the concentration camps, had visited Buchenwald and called the SS and the inmates together to harangue them. He told them that all statements and suspicions against Koch were malicious slander and that he personally would see to it that anyone who uttered a word against Koch would be punished.[22]

Historian Tom Segev, who wrote a study of concentration camp commandants in the 1970s based on documentary evidence and interviews with surviving family members of the commandants, writes about Koch, 'The worst of them all was Karl-Otto Koch. His life and death mix cruelty with passion and corruption, including undercover investigations, threats, forgeries, anonymous letters, liquidation of witnesses and a secret trial, all against the background of the intrigues at the top of the SS.'[23]

Given what Morgen would later discover about Buchenwald, it is surprising that his first impressions of the place were good. Having moved into the camp for six weeks with his fiancée Maria, who helped him with typing during the investigation, he told his American interrogators after the war:

> My first impression was positive, the prisoners' accommodation was good and they were well fed. I myself ate the food on a number of occasions. The working conditions were good; so much had been done for the prisoners to make their lives easier that I was amazed. At the time, the impression I had was that the concentration camps were a big step forward when compared to other justice institutions. People are outside, almost in freedom,

they have a positive work ethic and they have much more freedom. In addition the commandant, Senior Colonel Pister, made an excellent impression on me.[24]

Morgen's first impressions were undoubtedly carefully curated by SS Senior Colonel Hermann Pister, Koch's replacement, and the SS staff for his visit. After all, the visit of an SS judge must have caused considerable tension among the camp staff. Alfred Miller, one of the prisoners at Buchenwald, observed the effect of Morgen's investigations on the SS personnel at Buchenwald, later recalling, 'Faced with Dr Morgen the SS were shaking. Dr Morgen was seen as the devil himself. I even saw commandant Pister make the sign of the cross in his presence.'[25]

The concentration camp inmates saw things very differently to Morgen's first impressions. One prisoner, Franz Eichhorn, the camp barber, recalled, 'Under Koch a regime of true arbitrariness prevailed, whereas Pister attempted to organise the Nazi terror more correctly and bureaucratically. He was of course brutal and ruthless, but always within the framework of his orders – to which he adhered in a painstakingly exact manner.'[26] This obsession with the rules led Pister into a long correspondence about the rules concerning free travel for staff on furlough; they could travel for free when they left Buchenwald but the rules about the return journey were unclear and Pister wanted to know exactly what he should do.[27] Of course, Pister had seen the way Morgen was going after any member of the SS who stepped outside the rules, which might have accounted for some of his paranoia.

For prisoners arriving at Buchenwald, the routine was very different to that enjoyed by the SS. After a rail journey often lasting days in crowded conditions, they were either marched the six miles from Weimar, with their arms in the air while being hit with canes by the SS and threatened with rifles and pistols, or they were crammed into lorries. On arrival, they would face a reception committee of SS sergeants who would kick them, hit them and pour cold water on them. They had to stand for hours with their arms crossed behind their heads and knees bent to increase the pain before being forced to strip – at which point their valuables and possessions would disappear – then shower and parade naked outside even in winter before being given their uniforms, which caused many inmates to die of pneumonia.[28]

The Buchenwald Report – written in the camp by American intelligence officers with the help of the inmates themselves just after liberation – records, 'The life of the camp inmates stood in sharp contrast to the life of the SS. Crowded quarters, cold, hunger, slave labour and constant fear governed their existence.'[29] Koch's Buchenwald was a place where what Morgen called 'brutal arbitrariness' reigned.[30] He documented how Koch forced inmates to stand for hours in all weathers on the parade ground. Many fell to the ground through exhaustion or sickness, where they were beaten, kicked and had dogs set on them by the SS guards. Koch made the prisoners take their gloves off in severe frosts, which resulted inevitably in many cases of frostbite. When members of the SS pointed out that other concentration camps managed without these measures, Koch despised them for being weak. Morgen's assessment of Koch was that he wanted the reputation of being the most notorious concentration camp commandant.

The most feared place in Buchenwald was the quarry because this was where the SS, especially in the form of SS Sergeant Johann

Blank, were brutal in their treatment of the prisoners. Individuals were selected to run while carrying heavy stones and they were beaten with clubs as they ran, especially on their heads. Witnesses, including both prisoners and SS guards, told Morgen and his team that anyone who bled after their beating was placed in front of a red-hot oven so that the skin became raw and inflamed. SS guards would pour water into prisoners' mouths with a funnel and then they would stamp on the prisoners' stomachs with their boots. The prisoners were then forced to run through the sentry lines so they could be shot.

Morgen also discovered how Koch treated his staff, the SS officers and soldiers who ran Buchenwald. Koch would not talk to his officers if something had gone wrong. Instead, he would write a formal letter and send it or, better still, physically give it to the officer concerned. In the officers' mess there was an open book on one of the tables, where Koch would write observations and thoughts, no matter how trivial, so that his officers could see what he was thinking. He also interfered in their private lives. Two hours before the daughter of his deputy at Buchenwald, SS Major Alfred Rödel, was due to marry and have the wedding reception in the officers' mess at Buchenwald, Koch withdrew his permission on the grounds that the groom and brides' ranks were not equal.[31] Rödel himself was an especially brutal and sadistic SS officer. Just before midnight on New Year's Eve 1939, he forced several thousand prisoners to line up for inspection, selected five men at random and had them whipped in time to the camp orchestra through the night.[32]

Koch's method of running Buchenwald was to divide and rule by playing each group in the camp against each other. He played the prisoners against the Kapos – prisoners who were in charge of other prisoners – the Kapos against the prisoners and prisoners against the SS. He had a mailbox in the camp where prisoners could report individual members of the SS to him. On one occasion, one of the two Kapos in the quarry, who had a reputation for brutality, was beating a prisoner when one of the SS guards intervened and instructed him to stop. The Kapo ignored the guard and the guard said to the Kapo, 'If you hit this man once more, I shall shoot you.'

'I shall report you to commandant Koch,' was the reply from the Kapo. As a result, the guard was relieved of his duties and the guard who was sent in later shot the prisoner. The two Kapos were later killed by the inmates of Buchenwald.[33]

It is interesting that Morgen's American interrogator, Deputy Director of the Evidence Division Benno Selcke, did not challenge his description of Buchenwald when he described his initial impression of the camp in such positive terms. However, Morgen had previously given a more realistic assessment of concentration camps in a sworn affidavit dated 13 July 1946. In this affidavit, Morgen set out how the lives of prisoners were supposed to be protected and then listed a series of negatives in the concentration camps: the arbitrariness of decision making; the fact that prisoners were hardly ever released because they were needed to work; the use of some prisoners as Kapos who had power over other prisoners; the fact that concentration camp staff were not suitable for the job they were doing; the secrecy of concentration camp operations, which was achieved by isolating the camps from the outside world; the censorship of mail; the lack of change among camp personnel, which meant that secrecy was preserved; and the atrocities that took place in the concentration camps. He mentioned mass killings, especially in the gas chambers; the execution of individuals; medical experiments on prisoners; mistreatment and torture of prisoners in order to obtain statements; the harsh treatment of prisoners; the sacrifice of prisoners through work; and the death marches that took place at the end of the war.[34]

* * *

Morgen's investigation in 1943 centred on the activities of Thilo Bornschein. A number of former camp staff under SS Colonel Koch had kept their houses in Weimar, and Morgen searched these houses and found valuable furnishings and gold whose worth was far in excess of what they could have purchased from their SS salaries. Morgen promptly sent arrest warrants out for the return of these officers so that they could come under the jurisdiction of his investigation at Buchenwald. These included SS officers Köhler who was working in Majdanek extermination camp and Hartmann who was in the Balkans.*

Morgen also undertook an investigation into SS Sergeant Gotthold Michael, who theoretically ran the stores which housed prisoners' property. But the reality was that he was busy making money both for himself and for Koch. Morgen quickly established that Michael had an unusually close relationship with Koch – the prisoners of Buchenwald would describe him as either Koch's nephew or brother-in-law.[35] Michael would act as Koch's informant in the camp and he had greater access to the commandant than other SS personnel. In his official report, Morgen sets out that just like other camp SS officers, Michael's personal wealth shot up after the arrival

* Morgen states in his September 1946 interrogation that Köhler was in the South of France but in the interrogation that took place on 11 October 1946, his location is given as Lublin (Majdanek).

of the Jews following Kristallnacht in 1938.[36] He acquired an expensive car from a Jew who was emigrating, although Morgen was unable to prove that this was a crime because even the head of the Gestapo in Weimar was allowing his officers to buy cars cheaply from Jews who were leaving Germany.

Morgen arrested Michael on 7 August 1943. In his report, Morgen describes the fact that Michael was isolated from Koch's other money-making crimes as the key factor in charging him separately to the main indictment against Koch and others for crimes committed at Buchenwald. During his interrogations, Michael confessed everything to Morgen. He was used by Koch to buy textiles, shoes and books with the prisoners' money, which Michael was the custodian of, and would obtain discounts and bribes from the various firms he was dealing with. He stole items from the store himself and on one occasion he told the prisoners he would be travelling to Holland so if anyone wanted anything, they should give him the money upfront. He duly travelled by first-class train and stayed away for nearly two weeks, so long that the prisoners assumed that he wouldn't be coming back. When he did return, his prices for cigarettes, cigars, chocolate and condensed milk were extortionate.[37]

Morgen charged Michael with bribery, embezzlement, theft, favouritism and forgery – this last because as soon as Michael heard about Morgen's investigation into Koch, he promptly conspired with a prisoner called Meiners to falsify the records, creating fictitious receipts and forged signatures to cover the money that passed between them. The purpose of these was to ensure that the transactions could be balanced back to the bank records and cash holdings, whereas the reality was that both Michael and Meiners were stealing from the camp canteen.

The investigation into Michael led to a falling out between Morgen and his boss, SS Lieutenant Colonel Werner Paulmann. In early 1944, Morgen wrote to the chief of the SS judiciary head office, SS General Franz Breithaupt, to inform him of their differences. Paulmann had some criticisms of Morgen's enquiries and Morgen felt that these were getting in the way of his investigation. He also sent a copy to SS Senior Colonel and judge Horst Bender, who was on Himmler's staff.[38] Fortunately, Morgen and Paulmann settled their differences quickly in a mediation session with SS General Prince Josias of Waldeck and before their dispute was escalated to Himmler.[39] Himmler took a close interest in every aspect of the lives of his SS officers and was in the habit of devising unusual mediation arrangements where two officers could not reconcile their differences. On one occasion, he made two senior SS colonels live together for six weeks in one room so they could iron out their differences.[40]

At this early stage of Morgen's investigation, there were several leads to Koch. But because of the previous ban on any investigations of Koch, and because in his new job Morgen had been told not to investigate political cases, Morgen had to carry out his enquiries on his own initiative. In his interrogation session with Benno Selcke, Morgen used the phrase *auf eigener Faust* – literally with his own fists – to describe the fact he was now out on a limb in choosing to investigate. He told Selcke that he decided to do this because of two factors. Firstly, the fact that enquiries into Koch had been expressly forbidden, and secondly, because of the events of Kristallnacht. Morgen was enraged at the stories he had heard about the way in which staff at Buchenwald had lined their pockets off the back of Kristallnacht.[41] Morgen told Selcke that he investigated

Koch '*Weil ich nun einmal Gerechtigkeitsfanatiker bin*' – because I'm a fanatic for justice.[42]

The other factor in Morgen's decision might well have been his experiences on the Eastern Front. Morgen was not only back in an SS officer's uniform, he also had his Infantry Assault Badge and front-line experiences with the Waffen SS, which must have given him an added sense of confidence. After all, if he could survive five months fighting the Soviet Army in winter and spring with the Waffen SS, then surely he could take on an SS colonel and his backers at the top of the SS.

The first prisoners at Buchenwald had arrived in 1937 to start building work, but it was the arrival of a large number of Jews at Buchenwald after Kristallnacht in 1938 which presented the SS officers in the camp with their first real opportunity to enrich themselves and their bank accounts. When Morgen investigated, he found out that the Jews who were sent to Buchenwald had been arrested with very little notice and that they had used the little time they had before being taken away by the SS and the Gestapo to pick up their money and their most valuable possessions. The Gestapo then separated the Jews from some of their possessions and brought these items separately to Buchenwald.

The separation of the Jews from their valuables started immediately on arrival. The concentration camp regulations required the Jews to hand over their possessions in front of witnesses and for these possessions to be stored in containers, with each possession being logged into a register. These regulations were ignored at Buchenwald. Instead, the Jews were forced to walk past large tables and throw their valuables into boxes. No entries were made into any registers. The items which the Gestapo brought to the camp had not been catalogued or listed either – these were simply added to the general store of valuables. Any Jews who were subsequently released, because they had been given permission to emigrate for example, had to sign a form on leaving Buchenwald which stated, 'I herewith declare that I did not hand in any money, any valuables and any effects in the concentration camp Buchenwald and that such were not taken from me: therefore I make no claims on the concentration camp Buchenwald.'[43] Unsurprisingly, Jews who were released signed this form without complaint.

Morgen also established that a number of Jews managed to keep their valuables, especially their money, for use inside the camp. From the beginning, Buchenwald had been afflicted by a power struggle between political prisoners (mainly communists) and the ordinary criminals.[44] And now these criminal prisoners set about stealing money from the Jewish prisoners. They spread rumours that the SS was going to shoot any Jew found with money or valuables, so some Jews threw theirs away. Others used their money as toilet paper and the criminal inmates devised schemes to retrieve this money from the latrines and clean it. Jews were attacked by gangs and robbed. Individual Jews were tripped up and robbed by their 'helpers'. The criminals then used this money to bribe SS guards and to obtain cigarettes, food and alcohol.[45]

Historian Tom Segev studied concentration camp commandants, looking for common factors. He notes, 'They were all soldiers – soldiers by choice. Political soldiers in the service of evil.'[46] Segev goes on to state that because of the different ways they came to concentration camps, each commandant's story had to be studied individually. For SS Colonel Karl-Otto Koch, his road to Buchenwald started in 1931 when he joined the Nazi Party and the SS after an unremarkable and ordinary career in administrative jobs in businesses and factories, interrupted only by service on the front line in the First World War and being held as a prisoner of war by the British. After the war, he managed a comb and hair ornament factory in Erbach but in the later 1920s, he spent a long time without a job. In 1928, he was caught cashing forged postal orders.[47] In 1932, Koch was expelled from the Nazi Party but when he appealed this was reduced to a warning. In 1935, he was investigated for embezzlement but this was later dropped because of lack of evidence.

Segev cautions against reading anything into the mediocre jobs which were held by Koch and other concentration camp commandants: 'Their mediocrity is misleading; they were not Germans like all the Germans, they were not Nazis like all the Nazis. It is not the banality of evil that characterises them, but rather inner identification with evil.'[48] After joining the SS in 1931, Koch worked in a number of administrative jobs before being transferred into the early concentration camp system, where he was deployed in setting up units of SS to run the camps. After spells running the smaller concentration camps at Esterwegen and Columbia-Haus in Berlin, Koch was appointed to Buchenwald from 1 August 1937.[49]

Morgen's investigation had initially focused on the businessman Thilo Bornschein. But after a thorough investigation, Morgen did not pursue the Bornschein case himself because it turned out that he had not abused his position in Buchenwald in respect of the prisoners.[50] However, Bornschein was convicted by an SS court for the crimes identified by Emil Holtschmidt and sentenced to nine years in prison.[51]

Instead of Bornschein, it was one of the prisoners, Meiners, who turned out to be of much more interest to Morgen's investigation.

He had eighteen convictions for theft and fraud and had become close to Koch, so much so that Koch had put him in charge of the Buchenwald canteen. In order to help Meiners with his responsibilities, Koch allowed him to come and go from the camp as he pleased in ordinary civilian clothing and without having the regulation camp haircut.[52] As a reward for this trust which Koch placed in him, Meiners proceeded to inflate the prices of the food to the prisoners in order to make money. For example, a vegetable salad which cost 60 pfennigs to buy was sold to prisoners for 2.60 Reichsmarks.[53] These extortionate prices meant that Meiners was able to pass on large amounts of money to Koch.

Having decided to investigate Koch, Morgen took two steps which had the potential to land him in serious trouble with the SS. He had been instructed not to pursue political cases but now Morgen was about to do just that. He contacted the head of the Postal Monitoring Service without any authority and arranged for letters to and from Koch and his wife Ilse to be sent to him so he could read them.[54] He had already looked at the bank accounts of the SS personnel whose houses he had searched but now he went to the banks in Weimar without any official papers, relying only on his SS uniform, and asked to see Koch's bank accounts. He got them.[55]

When Morgen looked at the bank accounts, he was immediately suspicious. Koch had 45,000 Reichsmarks in his bank accounts plus another 9,000 Reichsmarks in a safe at one bank, totalling 54,000 Reichsmarks – worth £34,500 at the time or £207,535 in 2023 prices.[*56] Morgen was nothing if not thorough. He even obtained the divorce proceedings between Koch and his first wife in 1931 and

* In his *World at War* interview, Morgen uses a figure of about 105,000 Reichsmarks. This is the final figure for all Koch's assets (which actually worked out at 103,500 Reichsmarks).

noted that Koch told the court that he was poverty stricken and he had to rely on his family for support. From this, Morgen knew that Koch had not come into the SS with much money and theoretically, his bank account should therefore only show the money which Koch had managed to save from his salary as an SS officer. Given that Koch had a family and had expensive tastes, all these savings seemed to Morgen to be unlikely, to say the least.

THE ARREST OF SS COLONEL KARL-OTTO KOCH

Having gathered new evidence against Koch, Morgen went to see local SS and police leader, SS General Prince Josias of Waldeck, who had previously been told off by Himmler for investigating and having Koch arrested. He laid out all his evidence and Waldeck gave Morgen his full support.[57] With the backing of Waldeck, Morgen submitted everything he had to *Reichsführer* Heinrich Himmler. During his initial investigations, Morgen had also established that there were grounds for suspicion against Koch during his time at Majdanek extermination camp. He had found out that Koch was behaving the same way in terms of theft, embezzlement and corruption there, having noted from the start that the SS guards were pocketing items of value which fell from prisoners' pockets as they arrived in Majdanek or were taken for execution.[58] For Morgen, this represented an opportunity to ask to extend his investigation.

Instead of heading to Munich, where the SS judiciary was based, with his initial findings, Morgen decided instead to travel first to Berlin. His superiors in Berlin were not keen on a new investigation, so Morgen headed to the SS judiciary in Munich instead, where they were much more supportive. They told Morgen that a light needed to be shone on to Koch and that it wouldn't be right if nothing were done. However, Morgen was told that because of the previous order from Himmler, he would now have to go to Berlin and approach Himmler directly. Morgen travelled straight back to Berlin where he met with Himmler's liaison officer with the SS judiciary and judge Horst Bender who was on Himmler's staff and to whom Himmler had delegated some of his own powers and functions as chief judge of the SS and the police.[59]

When Morgen spoke to Bender, he presented him with the results of his investigations so far into Koch and Buchenwald concentration camp. He told Bender, 'It appears that extensive crimes have been committed in concentration camps; for example there is the case of Lublin [Majdanek]. Please order me to conduct more wide-ranging investigations.'[60] Bender told Morgen that he had arrived just at the right time, as Himmler had just signed an order suspending the investigation into Koch. In addition, Himmler was going to reduce Koch in rank from SS colonel to SS major and post him to a road-building unit in the East in order to wean him off his money-making behaviour. Morgen told Bender that Himmler's proposed measures for Koch did not match up to the seriousness of Koch's crimes and that Bender should tell Himmler that the investigation should be carried out properly so Koch could face the most severe punishment.[61]

Morgen got his way. As a result of his initial investigations, Himmler refrained from taking action against Koch and he gave Morgen new orders on 8 August 1943 to investigate Koch properly. In addition, Morgen now had the authority to investigate all concentration camps. Not only that but Himmler threw his weight behind Morgen's investigations and instructed other departments and the Reich Security Main Office to support him. This meant that Pohl could not obstruct him. In the space of three months, Morgen had gone from an ordinary front-line Waffen SS soldier to an SS judge and police official in charge of wide-ranging investigations into concentration camps.

Morgen returned to Buchenwald and wasted no time in continuing his investigation into Koch, this time with Himmler's full support. The first action he took was an extensive search of the premises on 9 August, the day after Himmler issued his order. Morgen then decided to arrest Koch and sent orders for him to return to Buchenwald from Eger where he was stationed. Morgen anticipated that Koch would probably not respond to an order from him so instead he wrote to Koch's boss, SS General Gottlob Berger, whom Morgen had previously encountered in German-occupied Poland when he had tried to have Oskar Dirlewanger and his officers arrested and Berger had transferred Dirlewanger and his unit away to the East. Morgen wrote, 'In the name of the *Reichsführer* I am writing to inform you that Koch is to be arrested. To this end please would you give him orders to report to Buchenwald immediately.'

Koch did not appear. By this stage, Morgen had his own office in Buchenwald and he got on the phone to the office in Berlin and asked what was happening, 'Where is Koch?' he asked.

'Yes, he's here,' was the reply.

'Did you not order him to come to Buchenwald?' asked Morgen. It seemed that Koch had gone to Berlin to talk to his friends to find out what was going on. 'Listen,' he told the office in Berlin. 'Your responsibility is to me. You will find Koch and take him to the train station. There's an afternoon train which will get him to Buchenwald at 11 p.m.' Morgen then sent several cars to the station for 11 p.m., when Koch was supposed to arrive along with a non-commissioned officer. However, Morgen received a telephone call: 'Koch was not on the train!'

Morgen was just thinking to himself that Koch had done a runner when the phone rang again. 'Koch's car has been spotted driving at top speed towards Buchenwald. One of our cars is in pursuit!' Fifteen minutes later, the pursuit driver appeared at Buchenwald and reported to Morgen, 'I was following Koch's car. On the way to Buchenwald he must have turned off into the forest. I couldn't find him; he must have gone!'

Morgen's boss SS Lieutenant Colonel Werner Paulmann was in Buchenwald for the arrest and he said to Morgen, 'There is a possibility that he has driven straight to his house in Buchenwald.' By now it was midnight, so Morgen and Paulmann went straight to the villa that Koch still maintained and where his wife was living. It was pitch dark and there was no noise. There was no sign of the car. Morgen rang the bell. Still nothing, just silence. Morgen kicked the door with the heel of his boot. By this time a storm was brewing and they could see flashes of lightning. But still nothing from the house – until suddenly, there was the sound of someone slurping. Paulmann said to Morgen, 'Get your gun out, the shooting's about to start!' And then Koch appeared in a dressing gown, very calm, and asked, 'What do you want?'

'We have to question you; it would be best if you got dressed,' replied Paulmann.

'Yes,' replied Koch. 'I've just arrived home and I wanted to freshen up.'

Koch had driven straight to see his wife to find out what was happening in Buchenwald. Morgen had been monitoring their telephone calls and letters and he knew that Koch's wife had noticed what had been going on.

Paulmann and Morgen questioned Koch through the night. Morgen later described Koch during that interrogation as 'the smartest fox I have ever seen and ice cold! He lacked any human feelings. We had the impression that he was very calculating, he answered very carefully and had an excuse for everything. I didn't believe a lot of what he said.'[62] Paulmann and Morgen arrested SS Colonel Koch and after a search of the house they arrested his wife, Ilse Koch, as well.

Morgen was now able to carry out a detailed assessment of Koch's net worth and compare it to his income as a colonel in the SS. Alongside the 54,000 Reichsmarks already identified in bank accounts and cash, Morgen now identified an additional 49,500 Reichsmarks from insurance premiums, furniture, jewellery and a car, giving a total of 103,500 Reichsmarks, worth at the time about £10,500 and £398,000 at 2023 prices.[63] Morgen then sent in a team to trawl through Koch's income and expenditure, and they identified a significant gap between what he was earning and what he was spending, both on living expenses, including a maid which the Kochs employed, and in building up cash and other assets. Koch had used an architect to renovate and enlarge his official house at Buchenwald which cost between 50,000 and 60,000 Reichsmarks (between £192,000 and £230,000 at today's prices).[64]

Throughout all of this, Koch continued to provide explanations. He enjoyed gambling and was often at the races, where he backed the winning horses. He conducted a number of affairs and often visited Norway where his brother was stationed. Morgen's final, very detailed analysis showed that of Koch's total assets of 103,500 Reichsmarks, he could not account for how he obtained 78,000 Reichsmarks.

However, when it came to embezzlement, Koch did cooperate with Morgen's inquiry and confessed to running off-the-books accounts, from which loans were made to SS staff for various enterprises and from which Koch helped himself.

These secret accounts received money from a number of different sources. These included the theft of money and valuables from Jews who were imprisoned at Buchenwald after Kristallnacht in 1938 and the inflated sale of goods. Alongside the activities of the prisoner Meiners, who ran the canteen, there were sales of clothes, blankets and food as well as 'voluntary' contributions which prisoners were forced to make to support life at the camp, such as buying books to help poorer prisoners or the camp orchestra. Other sources of income included arbitrary fines, which were levied on the prisoners for no reason at all. For example, on two occasions when an animal ran into the barbed-wire electrified fence, the prisoners were fined for having killed the animals.

Money and valuables were confiscated from prisoners and wealthy inmates offered money for their release. Koch himself admitted to Morgen that on one occasion a Jewish prisoner offered 1 million Reichsmarks (about £3.8 million in 2023 prices).[65] When prisoners left the camp, they always had to leave their possessions behind. If they died or were executed at the camp, gold was extracted from their teeth and melted down.

There was an officers' mess at Buchenwald, which ensured that, in contrast to the prisoners, the SS officers dined in style with real coffee, liqueurs and the best wines. Meals were also served from the mess to the SS officers' homes. Morgen was surprised to learn there were no cooking utensils in the homes of the SS officers, as they and their wives lived from the mess. Koch and the camp staff even ensured that the meat from the pigs, fed on the waste from the kitchens at Buchenwald, made its way to the officers' mess. There was a watch repair shop, which restored confiscated watches so they could be sold. There was a woodworking workshop, which made items for the SS, and there was a falconry and zoo, which charged admission fees. There was a photographic section, which charged prisoners to have their photographs taken for their official registration card, and there was livestock and a nursery, which provided food and flowers to the staff.

Money from all of these activities flowed into Koch's off-the-books accounts. But since so much was cash and there were so many missing records which were never completed, the investigators could not trace all the transactions. Koch himself was evasive when questioned and he blamed others for his own lack of supervision of his staff. In one of his final interrogations, he did admit to misappropriating 20,000 Reichsmarks, which he spent on a grand piano and other living expenses as well as giving some of it away. Koch blamed lack of official supervision for his actions.[66]

Not only was Morgen's investigation hampered by lack of records, it was also hindered by a lack of witnesses. Morgen's priority in his initial investigation had been the arrival of Jewish prisoners in 1938 after Kristallnacht and the way in which the Jews were robbed of their money and valuables. When Morgen looked further, he realised that most of the prisoners who might have known more about this and who could have been witnesses had died. Nearly all the Kapos from 1938 had died. Morgen was also struck by the fact that other prisoners, who were not connected in any way to the arrival of the Jews after Kristallnacht and who knew nothing, lived for years at Buchenwald in apparent good health and were still there during Morgen's investigation.

Until now, Morgen was proceeding in accordance with his authority from Himmler, which was to root out corruption, embezzlement and theft. These crimes deprived the Reich of the financial resources it needed to fight the war and run the Greater German Reich. But murder, i.e. premeditated killings not allowed under the conventional legal system (the normative state) and killings which were not covered by a legal order direct from Hitler or someone he had delegated his powers to (the prerogative state), was a different matter. Morgen had no authority to investigate these and had been instructed to stay away from political cases. He had already successfully overcome the ban on investigating Koch and gained permission to investigate him for corruption. Now he was contemplating going out on a limb and looking into murder as well. He didn't hesitate.

Morgen's next step was to look at the files concerning the prisoners who had died and who could have been important witnesses for his corruption inquiry. He noted that the prisoners had died at different times with lengthy intervals, and in each case a different cause of death was recorded. But the one common factor he did notice was that most had been admitted to the camp hospital or had been arrested and put in the cells – or bunker, as it was known in the camp – shortly before their deaths. Morgen's suspicions were aroused. He had a murder investigation on his hands.[67]

CHAPTER 5

THE INVESTIGATION AT BUCHENWALD CONCENTRATION CAMP, PART TWO: MURDER

SUNDAY 12 SEPTEMBER 1943

SS Sergeant Rudolph Köhler was dying and there was nothing anyone could do about it. He was semi-conscious, sweating, vomiting and his skin had gone blue from cyanosis.[1] A doctor in Buchenwald had been called and now he was in the military hospital in Weimar where the doctors were trying to save his life. But they weren't having much success.

Konrad Morgen was standing in the office of SS judge Lieutenant Colonel Werner Paulmann in Kassel when the call came through from Buchenwald. Paulmann picked the phone up, listened and went pale. 'What are you saying? What has happened?' he demanded. He listened and turned to Morgen: 'The concentration camp is saying that Köhler has attempted suicide but was stopped in time.' Morgen was powerless to act; the detective he had left behind in Buchenwald had gone on holiday for the weekend and there was no one there he could ring. While he was talking this through with Paulmann, the phone rang again. The first call had been a mistake. Actually, Köhler was seriously ill in hospital in Weimar with the symptoms of poisoning and his death could be expected at any minute. Morgen and Paulmann looked at each other with the same thought: he had been deliberately poisoned.

Rudolph Köhler was key to Morgen's inquiry into the murders at Buchenwald. It had only been a few days since Morgen had interrogated him again after bringing him back from Majdanek extermination camp at the start of the investigation. At first, he had denied everything, but then he had broken down and confessed the name of the murderer. It was a crucial piece of the puzzle. Morgen now knew the identity of the key person who was murdering the prisoners at Buchenwald and how. And now his witness was dying.

Morgen had left strict instructions with Pister, the Buchenwald commandant, that no one was to see Köhler in his cell. With Köhler's confession in the bag, Morgen had left Buchenwald and gone straight to Kassel to see Paulmann to ask for an arrest warrant. Paulmann had just said to Morgen, 'Yes, I agree, he must be arrested,' when the phone had rung from Buchenwald for the first time with news of Köhler.

Morgen and Paulmann then went to see SS General Prince Josias of Waldeck, the local SS and police chief, who signed the arrest warrant. However, when Morgen called Buchenwald, he was told that his suspect had left the camp the previous day. Morgen rang the Gestapo in Weimar and gave them instructions to arrest him, and then he called the universities at Jena and Leipzig to ask them to send a pharmacologist and an internal medicine specialist doctor to try and save Köhler's life.

Morgen then hurried back to Weimar to try and speak to Köhler before it was too late. He went straight to the hospital, where he spoke first to the doctors and nurses but they had little more to report to him. He then went into see Köhler, who was still conscious but looked like he was very close to death, a shadow of the man Morgen had interrogated not long before. Morgen had to bend over to hear his whispers. 'What's up with you?' asked Morgen.

'I don't know,' Köhler whispered.

'Did you try and take your own life?' asked Morgen.

'No, that's very far from my mind.'

'Have you eaten something which you cannot tolerate?' Morgen needed to run through all the possibilities.

'I don't know,' came the reply.

'Was anyone else with you?' After more questions, Morgen established that Köhler could not remember anything at all from midday on Friday until 8 p.m. on Saturday. He did remember being secured on to a stretcher and saying, 'What nonsense is this? Why are you tying me up?' He then remembered vomiting and being very weak, drinking a glass of water and collapsing again. Morgen stayed with him for an hour but was unable to find out what had happened.[2]

* * *

Konrad Morgen's suspicions had been aroused when he discovered that witnesses to the crimes being committed in Buchenwald had been admitted to the hospital or arrested and confined in the cells or, as the inmates called it, the bunker. He had put one of his best investigating officers, a detective called Cohen, on the case to find out what was happening. Meanwhile, Morgen continued his investigations into corruption at Buchenwald. As he got to know the SS there better, he started putting names to faces. He had been impressed by one of the camp doctors, SS Captain Dr Waldemar Hoven, who was very friendly towards him and invited him to come and visit him in his office. One day, Morgen, who was overworked and on edge, decided to go and see him for some medical advice.

Hoven was very friendly and welcoming and very keen to help Morgen. He got hold of a large supply of glucose for him, typically used to treat hypoglycaemia, which instantly aroused Morgen's suspicions. How was it possible to obtain such large supplies when there was a shortage of glucose because of the war? Did Hoven want something from him, Morgen asked himself. But Hoven seemed genuine. Either he wanted to get on well with Morgen or he was simply a capable and helpful doctor. Morgen went away and thought about this. He started to see more and more the close relationships at work within the camp headquarters. Being a suspicious judge and detective, Morgen wondered if they were all in cahoots with each other.

Morgen was keen to look around more at Buchenwald and understand how the whole place worked, so Hoven invited him to see the hospital and the operating theatre. Everything looked perfectly in order. But when they went into the kitchen, Hoven gave Morgen a glass of milk and some bread and then he placed a pound of butter next to it. This was very unusual in wartime conditions and Morgen had the distinct impression that this was a bribe, deciding to keep his distance from Hoven. But Hoven redoubled his efforts to keep Morgen sweet.

One evening, Hoven visited Morgen unexpectedly. Without any prompting from Morgen, he told him that he killed people with phenol. Morgen was speechless. He couldn't believe what he had just heard, so he said nothing and waited for Hoven to continue. Hoven told him that prisoners had no idea what was happening to them when he injected them with phenol; it was painless and quick. Meanwhile, Morgen was asking himself: why are you telling me this? Me of all people! Criminals aren't so stupid that they betray themselves to a judge. Morgen pondered Hoven's motives in telling him. Was he telling Morgen something that was blatantly untrue, in the hope he might investigate and find there was nothing in it? Or was Hoven telling him because he believed that these killings were lawful, so he was safe anyway? Since Morgen was already suspicious of Hoven, he was inclined to think that his intentions were hostile, and since concentration camps could be dangerous places for judges, Morgen was on his guard. His next step was to make enquiries among the prisoners at Buchenwald. But these didn't get very far as the people he did talk to were, naturally, very circumspect and the people who could shed some light on these deaths were all dead themselves.

A couple of days after this extraordinary conversation with Hoven, General Waldeck came to Buchenwald to meet Morgen and to receive a progress report. As they were walking around, Morgen told him of his suspicions that prisoners who were witnesses to the crimes being committed at Buchenwald were being murdered and asked him if he knew anything about it. Waldeck had no idea that this was happening. At that moment, Hoven was walking past, so Morgen called him over and Waldeck asked him if it was true that concentration camp inmates were being killed by injection. Hoven replied that he knew nothing about it. Morgen looked closely at him. He wasn't even blushing as he spoke, even though he had willingly and enthusiastically told Morgen all about murdering prisoners by injection only a few days before.

Morgen was now even more suspicious of Hoven. But there was a problem. Detective Cohen, who had spent two weeks interviewing prisoners and staff and looking through the records for the hospital and the bunker, reported back to Morgen. Not only could he find nothing wrong, he couldn't see any point in continuing to look. He even went so far as describing Morgen's suspicions as a 'fairy tale'.

Eventually, Morgen found the clue he needed. He discovered that some potential witnesses to the corruption at Buchenwald were in the records of the camp hospital on the same day as they were in the records of the bunker. In one particular case, he found that a prisoner was recorded as being discharged from the prison at midday – on the same day as being recorded in the camp hospital as having died in the morning. Clearly, entries were being falsified.

Morgen won over two of the long-term prisoners in the bunker who had been aware of what was happening – Dr Roman Hädelmayr and Alfred Miller. With their help, he established that what was happening was that the prisoners he was interested in were being taken to a cell in the bunker and murdered there. Then reports of illnesses and death certificates were prepared and put into the files, so that anyone looking into these deaths would think that the prisoners had suffered serious illnesses and died. For this reason, these deaths were not reported to the local SS and police court in Kassel.

THE CASE OF SS SERGEANT MARTIN SOMMER

Morgen had already arrested SS Sergeant Martin Sommer, one of the non-commissioned officers who worked in the bunker and who was murdering the prisoners there. Sommer was a notoriously brutal

SS non-commissioned officer, and Morgen said of him, 'Sommer regarded his job of torturer and executioner with great pride and vicious enjoyment.' One of the prisoners, Dr Roman Hädelmayr, who became a witness and gave evidence against Sommer said, 'If there should be a hell after death as a punishment, it cannot be worse that the cell-block under Sommer.'[3]

Sommer was always on hand with his whip and told Morgen that he delivered up to 2,000 lashes per day to the prisoners in the bunker, in order to obtain confessions from them. In his official report, Morgen suggests that doing this day in, day out over the years turned him into an *Unmensch* – an inhuman being – and that outside a concentration camp environment, he would probably not have behaved in such an inhuman manner. One of the prisoners he tortured was Protestant pastor Paul Schneider, who was given twenty-five lashes and put into the bunker for refusing to obey the rules and take his hat off when he passed the flag. He remained there for eighteen months, and every time Sommer opened his cell door he would hit him with his whip. After continuous mistreatment at the hands of Sommer, he died on 18 July 1939. But it wasn't just Protestant priests who Sommer targeted. At the end of May 1940, he hung Roman Catholic priest Otto Neururer upside down and naked until he died thirty-four hours later because he had baptised another prisoner. Neururer was beatified in 1996 by Pope John Paul II.

Sommer was greatly feared among the prisoners because of his habit of hanging them from their hands so their feet couldn't touch the ground and their shoulders dislocated. Sommer and another officer, SS Captain Hermann Hackmann, would whip them while they were hanging there for hours at a time.[4] Pastor Paul Schneider received this treatment often because of his habit of calling out Bible verses to his fellow prisoners and of calling out the SS as murderers.[5] In 1938, after the increase in Jewish prisoners at Buchenwald, Sommer personally beat a number of them to death. After Koch left Buchenwald, Sommer tried to get a transfer to join him in Majdanek extermination camp but was forced to remain in Buchenwald. The arrival of Pister had meant that the killing stopped but the torture continued.[6]

Having arrested Koch, his wife Ilse Koch and Martin Sommer, and having obtained a confession from Köhler, Morgen went straight to Kassel to see Paulmann, where they agreed to arrest Dr Hoven. But although Morgen's instructions to camp commandant Pister had been to make sure that no one got in to see Köhler in his cell, it later emerged that Hoven had somehow gained entry on several occasions to see Köhler and on one occasion had spent several hours with him. Morgen alerted the Gestapo and they arrested Hoven and put him in a cell in the Gestapo prison in Weimar. With Hoven denying everything, Morgen carried out an immediate search of his house and office. He later recalled that while he found lots of letters from different women and various potions designed to improve sexual performance, he found nothing which would help the investigation.

Meanwhile, the specialist internal medicine doctor who Morgen had requested arrived at the hospital in Weimar. But he was too late. Köhler had died by the time he'd got there.

Weimar coroner Dr Friedrich Timm arrived two hours after Köhler had died. He decided that a post-mortem should be carried out immediately and he assembled a group of six doctors, including the pharmacologist who Morgen had requested. The doctors noted that there was no damage to any of Köhler's organs but the coroner decided that the cause of death was poisoning. The only problem was that they didn't know which poison had killed Köhler. The verdict of the post-mortem was poisoning, possibly by an unknown poison from South America or by a combination of poisons.

Hoven was questioned again and denied everything. His assistant at Buchenwald started to agitate on behalf of his boss and sent out complaints that Morgen had broken into the infirmary and confiscated various items. He also complained that Morgen's investigation was undermining his own authority with the prisoners. Hoven's wife also complained to the local Weimar dignitaries. With Morgen firmly caught in the crossfire, Arthur Nebe called Morgen to Berlin to report.

Morgen drove to Berlin where he found Nebe and all his staff officers gathered together. One of them, the head of the murder squad, Bernd Wehner, later said, 'Morgen's visits always brought thousands of news items to the Reichskriminalpolizeiamt!'[7] Nebe suggested to Morgen that since this was now a political case, it might be better if the Berlin office took over as they had access to specialist murder detectives. Morgen didn't agree to this but he told them he would find it useful if some of their detectives came to work on the investigation. Nebe then allocated Wehner to go to Buchenwald and work with Morgen. Wehner was a very experienced Berlin detective. After Buchenwald, he led the investigation into the attempt on Hitler's life in July 1944 and later led the hunt for his boss, Nebe, who had been a part of the plot. He became head of the CID in Düsseldorf after the war.[8]

* * *

What was clear in the autumn of 1943 was that Morgen had uncovered a den of lethal and brutal iniquity at Buchenwald. With Koch and Hoven under arrest and active investigations underway against others, it was evident that the law and the rules concerning concentration camp administration and control were being systematically broken at Buchenwald. The law in Nazi Germany was clear: only *Reichsführer* Heinrich Himmler could determine the life or death of a concentration camp inmate and he had delegated that power to the Reich Security Main Office. What this meant in practice was that a prisoner at Buchenwald could only be killed legally if there was an order from either to do so.

Once the prisoner had been killed, a report had to be made immediately to both the *Reichsführer* and the Reich Security Main Office and relatives had to be informed. If an inmate died in unnatural circumstances, then the coroner and the Buchenwald doctor had to meet and decide if an investigation needed to take place. If not, then only once this had taken place could the body be released for cremation.[9] Any member of the SS who had killed without a legal order was now going to be investigated and prosecuted by Morgen and his team.

The problems identified by Morgen weren't just confined to Buchenwald. Koch had been transferred to Majdanek extermination camp in Nazi-occupied Poland and had taken key staff with him from Buchenwald. Morgen already had the authority from Himmler to investigate other concentration camps, and now the Reich Security Main Office and the SS judiciary decided that Morgen needed more support.

A new SS court was set up to oversee Morgen's investigations, to be based in Kassel and headed up by Paulmann, with General

Waldeck as another judge and others drafted in as well. This new court was described as *zur besonderen Verwendung* – 'for a special purpose'. Morgen was the chief investigator and, in addition to Wehner, more staff were transferred in from the Reich Security Main Office and the Central Police Detective Office of the Reich.

It didn't take Wehner long to identify the difference between detective work in the Berlin murder squad and Morgen's murder investigations. 'You've got a unique set of circumstances,' Wehner told Morgen. 'With us, we have one corpse and then we have to look for the perpetrator. Here you have a hundred corpses and you know who the perpetrator is. And even though it's totally obvious, it's still really difficult to get a result!'[10] But Wehner's first task at Buchenwald was to investigate the death of Rudolph Köhler, which more resembled the detective work that he was used to. He had a body and two suspects – Hoven and Koch – but as yet no concrete proof that they murdered him. His instructions from his superiors in Berlin were clear. 'This case must be solved immediately,' his boss told him.

Wehner's first enquiries were with SS Major Dr Erwin Ding-Schuler, one of the Buchenwald doctors and head of an institute in Weimar for the study of typhus and virology, a partnership between the Wehrmacht and the local health authority. He was surprised to learn that Ding-Schuler had authorisation from Himmler to experiment with the poisons that might have killed Köhler and which Hoven could have had access to. These experiments were performed on prisoners who were sentenced to death. Ding-Schuler told Wehner that he could arrange an experiment with the poisons that might have killed Köhler. He would inject camp inmates and the prisoners could be observed to see if they had the same symptoms as Köhler as they were dying. Wehner told Ding-Schuler that under no circumstances would he agree to anything like this.*[11]

Weimar coroner Dr Friedrich Timm suggested that the drug Pervitin might have been used to murder Köhler, together with a soporific. Pervitin, a methamphetamine, was used extensively by the Nazis during the Second World War to keep its forces awake and alert. In order to test this, SS General Heinrich Müller, head of the Gestapo, authorised an experiment on five Soviet prisoners at Buchenwald who had been sentenced to death. According to Morgen, who was present at the experiment, they all volunteered. The idea was to see if any of the prisoners showed any symptoms similar to those of Köhler and if not, to rule this suggestion out. None did and all were reported healthy after the experiment.[12]

Wehner's investigation into Köhler's death would turn out to be anything but quick. It became such a complex inquiry that he still hadn't reported by the time Morgen wrote up the results of the main investigation at Buchenwald.

While Wehner was investigating Köhler's death, Morgen was busy interviewing his four main suspects in his investigation into corruption and murder at Buchenwald: Karl-Otto Koch, his wife Ilse Koch, Martin Sommer and Dr Waldemar Hoven. On the day

---

* After the war, one inmate, Dr Eugon Kogon, wrote a book called *Der SS-Staat: Das System der deutschen Konzentrationslager*. In the book, he describes an experiment taking place, similar to the one suggested by Ding-Schuler. Kogon claimed that both Morgen and Wehner were present at this experiment. Wehner strongly denied this and Kogon corrected his book. When Morgen was going through the de-Nazification process after the war, the court wanted to find out if this accusation was true and took statements from Kogon and Morgen. Morgen denied it absolutely and Kogon backtracked, saying it was a story that Ding-Schuler had told him and he hadn't wanted to incriminate anyone. In his affidavit to the Nuremberg Doctors' trial (USA v. Karl Brandt et al.), Morgen states that the experiment Kogon might have been alluding to was the one with Pervitin, which was designed to exclude the possibility of the drug being used in the murder of Köhler and which Morgen did attend. See Chapter 9 for more information.

that Wehner had arrived in Buchenwald, another witness came forward to assist Morgen with his investigation. One of the prisoners who worked with Hoven in the hospital and who had just been given his release came forward and told Morgen how Hoven would inject the prisoners and cover their deaths up.[13]

THE CONFESSION OF SS COLONEL KARL-OTTO KOCH

Morgen had the evidence from the records of the hospital and from the cell block, he had witness statements and now he presented all his evidence to Koch, who confessed. Over the course of several interrogation sessions, Morgen came to understand the full extent of the killings ordered by Koch. These murders weren't just confined to individuals either. In 1939, when there had been an unsuccessful attempt on Hitler's life in Munich, Koch had decided that he would have eighteen to twenty Jews shot as a measure of atonement and he agreed with his officers that these would be recorded as a mass escape. Unfortunately for Koch, some of his officers changed their minds and would not agree to this cover so other officers had to change their stories and say that they had killed lots more Jews than they had previously stated. As part of his investigation, Morgen talked to officers from SS General Theodor Eicke's office. He had set up the system of concentration camps but he had not issued an order allowing Koch to shoot Jewish prisoners without permission.

At the trial of Hermann Pister after the war, the question of what precisely constituted a legal order to execute a prisoner was raised. The order was always written and it always had the approval of SS General Heinrich Müller, head of Office IV at the Reich Security Main Office.[14] While Morgen was at Buchenwald, he witnessed an execution carried out with the right paperwork under Pister, Koch's successor. Morgen was unhappy about what happened: 'I objected to the fact that the convicts had to undress prior to the hanging and that they were hanged in the presence of all of them, one after another. I described my feelings about this to commandant Pister.'[15]

What became clear from Morgen's investigations was that Buchenwald under Koch was a place where prisoners were murdered for no other reason than Koch wanted them dead. Koch would trawl the lists of newly arrived prisoners in order to decide whether they deserved to be alive. He was particularly interested in criminals and anyone whose behaviour he considered immoral, and he would mark these prisoners' records with a special letter, typically a 'K' or an 'L' so he could review their records again. Koch would then make lists of prisoners he wanted to be murdered and give this list to Sommer. After a while, Koch stopped the lists. Instead he would just telephone Sommer, tell him the names and say to him, 'You know what needs to be done with this prisoner.' The prisoners concerned would then be taken to the bunker by Sommer who would murder them within a number of days. He would then report back to Koch, 'Sir, your order has been carried out.' Morgen estimated that 100 prisoners were murdered in this way.

At first, the doctors would murder these prisoners but then Sommer took over and murdered them himself. The death of the prisoners would be entered as a 'release' in the bunker records and at the same time, in order to make the whole process look legal, the death would be recorded in the hospital records with a fictional account of an illness. Sometimes a post-mortem was carried out and the records were made to fit the story. Mistakes had been made with this cover-up in one particular case, which then in turn alerted Morgen to what was going on.

As well as the prisoners whom Koch considered to be unworthy of life, he also murdered any inmate who could have known anything about his financial crimes. All the Kapos who had been in post during the arrival of Jewish prisoners following Kristallnacht were murdered. Morgen also found one case where Koch had a prisoner murdered because he noticed that he had been in three concentration camps where Koch had worked. 'This fellow won't follow me around anymore,' he said.[16]

Koch had an excuse for all these deaths. He told Morgen that they had been authorised by Theodor Eicke, former inspector of concentration camps, and Reinhard Heydrich, former head of the Reich Security Main Office. Which, as Morgen noted cynically, was handy as both were dead by the time of his investigation.

One area where Eicke had been keen to clamp down on killings in concentration camps generally was when prisoners were shot 'while trying to escape'. This wasn't because Eicke cared about the prisoners being killed; it was simply because such shootings were supposed to be investigated by the local authorities and word occasionally reached the outside world about what was happening inside the camps – Eicke had isolated the concentration camps from the outside precisely in order to hide what was going on there. But this didn't stop Koch.

In order to make a cast-iron case for the prosecution, Morgen and Wehner focused their investigation on two prisoners for whom Koch could have no 'legal' justification for murdering: Walter Krämer and Karl Peix.

The events surrounding their murders are outlined in Chapter 1, but the starting point had been an investigation that Koch had launched against the camp hospital under the camp provost,

Marshal Hubert LeClaire. He was another SS officer whom the prisoners feared and he worked closely with Sommer to terrorise and abuse the inmates. Koch's aim in launching this investigation was to demonstrate his authority over some of his officers and to start the sequence of events that would lead to the murder of Krämer and Peix.

LeClaire arrested Hoven, Krämer and Peix from the hospital as well as SS Lieutenant Dumböck from the garden nursery and all the prisoners who worked with him. Koch accused Hoven of allowing communist meetings in the hospital where Krämer, a communist, was working and Dumböck of being the head of the Jehovah's Witnesses in the camp. After a short spell in the cells, all were released. Krämer and Peix were sent to the sub-camp at Goslar, where Koch arranged for their murder.

THE CASE OF ILSE KOCH AND MORALS IN THE SS

Why would Koch arrest Hoven who, after all, had been carrying out Koch's orders in murdering prisoners? One reason may have been the tangled love lives of the Kochs. Karl-Otto Koch had had a number of affairs and Morgen's official report details the liaisons between Ilse Koch and two SS officers at Buchenwald, Hoven and SS Major Hermann Florstedt, one of the deputy commandants at Buchenwald. Both officers were vying for the attention of Ilse. Hoven had told her that her husband was having an affair with a dancer in Weimar, while Florstedt was busy warning her that eventually his greed and corruption would come out. Each had different motivations, with Florstedt's being that he wanted her husband out of the way so he could become commandant at Buchenwald instead. Hoven simply wanted an affair.

Ilse was torn between loyalty to her husband and the need to rethink her own situation. In the end, she decided she would write to Himmler personally and put herself under his protection. This horrified both Florstedt and Hoven and they persuaded Ilse to seek the advice of SS General Paul Hennicke, the Weimar chief of police, instead. He didn't know about what was happening at Buchenwald and his visit resolved nothing. Hoven then suggested to Ilse that she should talk to her husband about their marriage in order to resolve their differences and she should offer to move in with Florstedt to test the strength of his feelings for her. He refused, the Kochs were reconciled and Hoven became her lover, which had been his plan all along.

Morgen also investigated Ilse for her crimes in Buchenwald – not just her knowledge and support of her husband's financial offences but also her behaviour in the camp. In his report he described her as 'the most hated person in the whole camp' and set out how she would dress provocatively, then note the names of any prisoners who looked at her so they could be beaten later by her husband with twenty-five blows of his club. She also had her own private riding hall constructed, which was built in the style of a riding school with mirrors all around the interior. She would ride here several times each week while the SS camp orchestra played. She wanted the hall built quickly and during its construction, up to thirty prisoners lost their lives.[17]

Why would Morgen include details of the Kochs' affairs in his official report? One reason might well have been because of *Reichsführer* Himmler himself and his strict views on behaviour within the SS. Alongside the SS virtues of loyalty, obedience and comradeship, Himmler prized 'decency', which for the SS meant behaving in a chivalric way towards the 'right' enemies. Himmler maintained that anyone the SS killed should be eliminated 'decently'. Of course, while the SS claimed to behave decently, this was far from the reality. Peter Longerich, Himmler's biographer, examines this: 'Decent treatment could be expedient, but there was always the danger of treating enemies too well and thus doing damage to one's own cause – and that was morally reprehensible. Accordingly, it was decent not to treat one's enemies decently.'[18]

Himmler also extended his ideas about decency into the private lives of his SS officers. He did not hesitate to interfere when his officers' relationships with their wives were not as harmonious as he would have liked. In cases like the Kochs, where a criminal investigation brought to light the fact that the SS officer concerned was having an affair, Himmler's instructions were not to inform the wife so that the marriage could continue. If any divorce proceedings on the grounds of adultery went through the SS courts, then Himmler himself made the final decision on the couple and he was particularly sensitive to any children in the family. One of Himmler's concerns about children of SS officers was that there were not enough of them. He allowed one SS officer whose wife was ill to move in with another woman, on the condition that they had children. He lectured single SS officers on the need to marry and have children and even wrote to one SS officer – and his father – to urge prompt action on finding a wife. He instructed the SS to ensure that SS wives should be given the opportunity to holiday near the places where their husbands were posted so that they had maximum opportunity to produce the minimum number (four) of SS children.[19]

The issue of SS couples bearing children was also on Morgen's mind. He had already set in motion the process of applying to the SS Race and Settlement Office for permission to marry. But this was proving to be complicated. He had been in a relationship at the start of the war, but because he was drafted into the SS he had ended it. Then Morgen had met another woman, Maria Wachter, whom he had fallen in love with. While Morgen in many ways was an ideal candidate for the SS in terms of party membership and his avoidance of politics, in the eyes of the SS, Maria Wachter was not an ideal SS officer's wife.

The first problem was that, unlike Morgen, she had been politically active and had been put in front of a court in 1934 on charges of treason but had been acquitted because of lack of evidence. After this, she had been banned from joining the Nazi Party. After having met and fallen in love with Morgen, Maria suggested she try to join the Nazi Party in order to facilitate the granting of a marriage licence by the SS. But Morgen was against this. He may have joined the party himself to advance his career, as many lawyers did, but he did not want his fiancée joining as well.[20]

The second problem for Morgen and Maria was the issue that Himmler was obsessed with: children. With their application to get married in the slow lane of SS bureaucracy, Konrad and Maria decided that they would do the one thing which would help their application and would have a child. In their initial discussion with a doctor, he advised that they were not well suited because of the age difference – Maria was four-and-a-half years older than Morgen. Despite this setback, they had grown closer together, writing love letters to each other constantly, and they hoped to prove their suitability in the eyes of the SS by having a baby. In 1943, Maria became pregnant but in early 1944, tragedy struck. She was injured in an air raid on the town of Prien am Chiemsee in Bavaria where she was living. She lost the baby and with it their best chance of obtaining permission to get married.[21]

While all this was going on in his private life, Morgen was still driving his investigation forward at Buchenwald. His enquiries had uncovered adultery but in the Kochs' case, Ilse already knew about her husband's affairs so there was no need to keep the details from her. It is likely that by including these details in his official report, Morgen was also strengthening his case against the Kochs, Hoven and eventually against Florstedt as well.

In addition to the murders of Krämer and Peix at Goslar, Morgen also investigated Koch for a murder committed at Majdanek extermination camp as part of the Buchenwald enquiries. When Koch had left Buchenwald, he took with him a number of prisoners who were useful and whose services he wanted to retain. One of these was a German prisoner called Wendel, who was accused by Koch of having stolen from him. One day, Wendel escaped from the camp together with a Polish woman but surprisingly, he then returned to Majdanek. Before Koch was summoned back to Buchenwald to be arrested by Morgen, he had given instructions to SS Captain Hackmann that Wendel was to be killed at the earliest available opportunity. Hackmann passed the instruction to one of the doctors, who refused to comply with the order because Wendel was German. Wendel was eventually killed by one of the non-commissioned officers, SS Sergeant Endres.

THE CONFESSION OF SS SERGEANT MARTIN SOMMER

As Morgen's investigation continued, he was looking for more cases like those of Krämer, Peix and Wendel. After initial evasion, lies

Konrad Morgen in SS uniform. In 1941, Morgen was appointed as an investigating judge in the SS judiciary, where the SS soon learned to fear him and his investigative zeal. After 1943, he was additionally appointed as a police official.

Morgen with his wife Maria in 1959. The SS never gave them permission to marry and it was only after the war, in 1948, that they were able to tie the knot. (Note: the official caption in the archive reads, 'Konrad Morgen with unknown person 1959.')

Oskar Dirlewanger and his unit were notorious for their cruelty and corruption. They were an early target for Morgen. This picture shows Dirlewanger (*left*) and his officers. Dirlewanger was detained after the war and killed by his captors. Source: *Antifaschisten in SS-Uniform* by Hans-Peter Klausch. Edition Temmen, 1993

In 1942, Morgen crossed swords with senior SS officers and as a result he was sent to the Eastern Front as an ordinary soldier with the Waffen SS in the Wiking Division. He would have served in a machine gun or mortar section in a unit like this one. The Waffen SS were early adopters of camouflage uniforms and this picture shows Panzergrenadiers of the Waffen SS in action.
Source: National Museum of Denmark, photo by Kriegsberichter Melters

In 1943, Morgen was reinstated as an SS judge and sent to investigate corruption at Buchenwald concentration camp, where he soon uncovered illegal murder too. Here, SS and police officials are pictured speaking among themselves during a roll call of Polish prisoners at Buchenwald. SS Colonel Karl-Otto Koch, camp commandant, is second from the left. Source: United States Holocaust Memorial Museum, courtesy of Robert A. Schmuhl

As a result of his investigations, Morgen arrested Karl-Otto Koch for murder and corruption. Koch is shown here in a photograph taken by his wife Ilse.

Source: Personal photographs of Ilse Koch, US National Archives 153-IK-2

As well as arresting Koch, Morgen also arrested his wife Ilse. This picture shows the couple in their new home together prior to their arrests. Source: Personal photographs of Ilse Koch, US National Archives 153-IK-1-48

After the war, Ilse was put on trial by the Americans and sentenced to life imprisonment. Morgen testified at her trial but refused to cooperate with the Americans when they wanted him to testify that she had made lampshades out of human skin. This picture shows her in US custody. Source: US National Archives via Buchenwald and Mittelbau-Dora Memorials Foundation

Morgen charged Dr Waldemar Hoven, chief doctor at Buchenwald, with murder, but he ultimately escaped justice from the SS. After the war, Hoven was arrested, sentenced to death and hanged at Nuremberg. Here, he testifies in his own defence at the trial. Source: Photographs relating to the minor Nuremberg trials, US National Archives 238-OMT-I-D-128

Morgen carried out extensive investigations at Auschwitz, including one into its former commandant Rudolf Höss, who was eventually executed by the Polish government. Here, three SS officers socialise on the grounds of the SS retreat of Solahütte, outside Auschwitz, in 1944. From left to right, they are: Richard Baer (commandant of Auschwitz), Dr Josef Mengele (doctor at Auschwitz) and Höss.
Source: United States Holocaust Memorial Museum, courtesy of an anonymous donor

At Auschwitz, Morgen charged Maximilian Grabner, head of the Gestapo there, with murder. However, Grabner escaped justice and was sent to Poland after his trial, where he was hanged in 1948.
© Archive of the Auschwitz-Birkenau State Museum in Oświęcim

Morgen's investigations were continually hampered by SS General Oswald Pohl, head administrator of the concentration camps. Here, Pohl pays an official visit to Auschwitz, accompanied by its commandant Richard Baer, who had previously served as his adjutant.
Source: United States Holocaust Memorial Museum, courtesy of an anonymous donor

After the war, Morgen reported to the US authorities and was detained until 1948, during which time he gave evidence in various trials and was extensively interrogated. This picture shows him in American custody.

Source: Photographs relating to the minor Nuremberg trials, US National Archives 238-OMT-III-W-11

During his time in American custody, Morgen gave evidence on behalf of both the prosecution and the defence at a number of trials. Here, he is testifying in defence of the SS at the International Military Tribunal, 8 July 1946.

Source: US National Archives 111-SC-251755

ABOVE Morgen was called as a defence witness for Oswald Pohl, though his testimony did Pohl no favours. Here, Pohl is being sentenced to death at Nuremberg for his role in running the concentration camps and destroying the Warsaw Ghetto.

Source: Photographs relating to the minor Nuremberg trials, US National Archives 238-OMT-IV-D-86

LEFT Pohl used SS Lieutenant Colonel Kurt Schmidt-Klevenow, who was head of the legal department at the SS Main Economic and Administrative Office under Pohl, to keep an eye on Morgen and obstruct him at every turn. Morgen's and Schmidt-Klevenow's mutual animosity spilled over into the Nuremberg trials, where they both gave evidence. Here, Schmidt-Klevenow (with raised hand) takes the stand at the trials.

Source: Photographs relating to the minor Nuremberg trials, US National Archives 238-OMT-IV-W-9

and prevarication, SS Sergeant Martin Sommer made a full confession. But he wouldn't accept that he had done anything wrong. He told Morgen that he had to abuse the prisoners due to his position and that all the murders he was accused of carrying out were in line with lawful orders. He told Morgen that Koch had justified his instructions by telling him about special orders from the *Reichsführer* allowing Koch to make decisions about executing prisoners. But the way in which Sommer went about murdering prisoners contradicted his statements. Sommer's job under Koch had two elements: firstly, murdering prisoners whom Koch identified to him, and secondly, torturing prisoners either to force a confession from them or to make their lives so miserable and unhealthy that they died anyway.

Sommer murdered prisoners at night in the bunker. He instructed prisoners to come into his office and lie on the bed and he informed them that he was going to inoculate them for their own health. He then injected the prisoner with phenol and when the prisoner was dead, he would roll the corpse in a blanket and store it under the bed. When phenol wasn't available, Sommer would strangle or suffocate the prisoner instead. Under the floor in his office, Sommer had chiselled a hole which was 40 centimetres deep. He kept everything in a box in this hole. Morgen's official report points out that any official and legal execution order against a prisoner would not have needed such a cloak-and-dagger approach.

Sommer was able to get away with murder and mistreatment for a long time because of the secrecy under which the bunker operated. The windows were protected against the outside world by steel shutters. To gain entrance, the visitor had to ring a bell and an SS duty guard would appear. He would inspect the visitor through a spy hole in the door and only when he was satisfied would he open the door and allow the person through. In order to further protect the secrecy of his actions, Sommer operated alone and at night, typically between 12.00 a.m. and 4.00 a.m. He would also sometimes bring prisoners to the orderly room, which was the room farthest from the cells themselves. The door of the orderly room was very thick and Sommer would murder prisoners in there and take their bodies to the crematorium while it was still dark.

In the end, Morgen charged Sommer with three murders. The first was a Jewish prisoner who was only identified by his last name, Goldstein, in the official documentation. He tried to commit suicide by slashing his wrists and was lying in the wash house in the Jewish section of the camp, shouting for someone to come and help him. Sommer hurried across but instead of trying to save him, he put his hands around his neck and promptly strangled him.

A similar incident happened with another prisoner whose name is only given as Schiltmeyer. He tried to escape from Buchenwald after Pister arrived to take over from Koch. His plan was simple; he snatched a rifle from a guard and ran. He was immediately grabbed by the other SS guards who beat him brutally. Pister ordered him to be locked in a cell in the bunker and threatened to hang him.

After Pister had started as commandant of Buchenwald, he had searched the guard house and had confiscated Sommer's syringes. This upset Sommer, who then looked for ways to get back at Pister. His main method of murder, using phenol injections, was now denied to him and so he looked for other ways to murder prisoners in his power in the bunker. Schiltmeyer presented an ideal opportunity and now Sommer seized it with both hands.

After Schiltmeyer was locked in a cell, both Sommer and Hoven visited him and proceeded to murder him. According to their story, Schiltmeyer had wanted to commit suicide so both Sommer and Hoven decided to help him. Sommer tore up a wet towel and showed Schiltmeyer how to hang himself. When the towel broke at Schiltmeyer's first attempt, Sommer fetched a rope and he and Hoven then hanged Schiltmeyer. Sommer put the rope around his neck and Hoven lifted his legs while Sommer pulled on the rope. When Schiltmeyer was unconscious, they dropped him to finish him off.

Sommer was delighted at the fact that he had murdered Schiltmeyer and he went around bragging about his success in outwitting the new commandant. He referred to Pister as a *blödes Schwein*, a stupid pig, and *Nieselpriem*, misery guts. This behaviour represented another opportunity for Morgen and he charged Sommer with grave military insubordination along with his other crimes.

In his official report, Morgen set out the legal argument for Schiltmeyer's death to be treated as murder instead of assisted suicide. Sommer went far beyond helping someone commit suicide because he participated directly in the act of killing. The official report also set out in detail the legal position in the Third Reich for the murders of Goldstein and Schiltmeyer. Morgen was relying on the normative legal system – in other words, the system that was similar to systems in place in other European countries at the time. In fact, sections of Morgen's official report would be familiar in courtrooms today when considering similar issues. He goes on to say in his official report, 'The law does not permit anybody to kill others without being authorised by the state, regardless of the reasons he may have. Special motives are given consideration by the law in providing milder punishment for them.'[22] It is also worth noting that Morgen is using the murders of Goldstein and Schiltmeyer as representative cases for all the prisoners who Sommer murdered – these two murders were just the ones he had the best evidence for.

Morgen also accused Sommer of the attempted murder of another prisoner, one whose name is given only as Titz. Titz was a trusted prisoner and Koch employed him in his own house where he did the housework and looked after the Koch children, whom he often took out for walks. In return for this, Koch gave him a special food allowance. However, Titz and another prisoner were caught drinking by Koch's wife Ilse and he was put in the cell block under Sommer. He made it through this experience and eventually went back to work in the Kochs' house, where once again he got drunk, smashed some furniture and was caught dressed in Ilse's underwear.

However, this wasn't the only reason Sommer and Hoven wanted to murder Titz. He had also given evidence in the corruption investigation against Koch. Pister's solution was to send Titz to another concentration camp, but before that could happen, Sommer and Hoven came up with a plan. Hoven called Titz into the hospital for a check-up and recommended that Titz be kept at Buchenwald. Prisoners Roman Hädelmayr and Alfred Miller gave statements to Morgen saying that they then overheard Hoven and Sommer talking about poisoning Titz's food. Hädelmayr warned Titz but to no avail. He ate some goulash and immediately felt sick, dizzy and was unable to see. When Morgen questioned Sommer about it, he only admitted to giving Titz castor oil. Hoven claimed that he liked Titz and wanted to spare him the transfer to another camp. After this incident, Titz was immediately transferred out of Buchenwald.

THE CASE OF SS CAPTAIN DR WALDEMAR HOVEN

Of all the SS officers whom Morgen investigated, Waldemar Hoven probably had the most colourful backstory. In the early 1920s, Hoven emigrated to the US where he found a well-paid job as an extra in Hollywood films thanks to his relationship with a woman he was having an affair with. He then worked with Baron Adolph de Meyer, the fashion correspondent for *Harper's Bazaar* in Paris. Hoven returned to Germany, studied as a doctor and became a medical assistant at Buchenwald, using the inmates to write key parts of his dissertation to become a fully qualified doctor. Clearly, Hoven wasn't a very good doctor, which meant he needed some other way to stay in the good books with the SS hierarchy at the camp.

Morgen had been very impressed with Waldemar Hoven when he first met him, and Hoven's general friendliness and willingness to help played a part in making sure that Hoven's relationships with the other SS officers were very good. Hoven also recognised his own weaknesses as a doctor and so he looked for talented prisoners among the inmates who had been imprisoned at Buchenwald because of their political affiliations and could help fill the gap – among them, Walter Krämer and Karl Peix. This was pointed out to Morgen by SS Lieutenant Karl Dumböck who ran the garden nursery at Buchenwald. Dumböck suspected Hoven of murdering two of his prisoners who had openly renounced their communist party affiliations and who were ordered into the hospital, under what Dumböck considered false pretences, where they died.

One prisoner, Jan Robert from Amsterdam, was used by Hoven to provide massages to the higher-ranking SS officers in the camp, in order for Hoven to stay in their good books. Robert later recalled that he gave the adjutant, SS Captain Hans-Theodor Schmidt, a massage every day for two years and this was a deeply unpleasant experience because Schmidt was invariably drunk. He also used Robert to obtain eggs, butter and milk from the hospital. When the commandant – Robert didn't say if it was Koch or his successor, Pister – saw this, he wanted to know what was happening, which Robert duly told him. Hoven then informed Robert not to leave the hospital as Schmidt had ordered him to murder Robert.

Robert survived and also gave massages to Morgen, who was living in Buchenwald while conducting his investigations. Robert recalled:

> I had another experience with Konrad Morgen, who had come to Buchenwald as the investigating judge in the case of the previous commandant, Koch. Although he was not sick he took a steam bath and got a massage every morning. The electrical heating box was broken and one morning, despite my warnings, he played around with the hinges on the box and burned himself horribly. The box snapped shut and the ten heat lamps burned his skin. He accused me of intentionally abusing an SS officer. That would have meant an unconditional death sentence. Since Morgen was very unpopular with all the SS officers, who were afraid of him, nothing happened to me.[23]

This account by Robert illustrates the contradictions that Morgen embodied. On the one hand, he had gone beyond his brief at Buchenwald and was investigating the murders and mistreatment of inmates in pursuit of justice. Yet at the same time he was using his status as an SS officer to enjoy the facilities which Buchenwald offered, courtesy of those inmates. His use of the hospital facilities for a steam bath and massage stands in direct contrast to the suffering endured by the inmates all around him. As an SS officer investigating the SS itself, Morgen was well aware of the power which he wielded and in this case he appears to have used his power to threaten a prisoner. This tension between Morgen's self-appointed role as a 'fanatic for justice' and his status as an SS officer was a feature of his SS career and is explored further in Chapter 10.

Hoven organised the hospital so that skilled prisoners did as much work as possible and this meant that he had plenty of time on his hands to dabble in other areas. Morgen noted in his official report that Hoven appeared on the fringes of everything that was going on at Buchenwald. Although Morgen suspected Hoven of being involved in the various financial frauds, thefts, embezzlement and other scams that were going on at Buchenwald under Koch, Morgen was unable to obtain sufficient evidence with which to charge him.

However, Morgen did have enough to charge him jointly, together with Martin Sommer, with murdering Schiltmeyer and the attempted murder of Titz. Morgen also charged Hoven with the murders of three other prisoners and the manslaughter of another, named only as Collinet in the official report.

Another murder which Hoven was charged with was that of a Russian prisoner called Prince Gregor Kuschnir-Kuschnarev. He had been imprisoned at Buchenwald during the period when Nazi Germany was pursuing good relations with Soviet Russia, for no other reason than he had been an adviser to the Tsar in pre-revolutionary Russia. Because of his Imperial Russian links, Kuschnir-Kuschnarev hated communists and for this reason, Koch used him as an informant against the communists in the camp. However, this meant he was a threat to Hoven, who relied on communist prisoners to run the hospital for him. Hoven got it into his head that Kuschnir-Kuschnarev had played a part in the murders of two of his key helpers, Walter Krämer and Karl Peix.

Koch was well aware of the threat which Hoven posed and he took measures to protect Kuschnir-Kuschnarev. He lived in the garden nursery rather than in the general prisoner blocks. One of the camp doctors, Karl Köbrich, looked after Kuschnir-Kuschnarev personally and Koch ordered that under no circumstances was he allowed to go to the hospital. But none of this stopped Hoven. He had Kuschnir-Kuschnarev brought to the hospital, where within a week he was dead.

When Morgen questioned Hoven, he claimed that he had been ordered to kill Kuschnir-Kuschnarev by one of the senior SS officers because he knew too much about the killings of the Russian commissars. These were Russian political prisoners who were brought to Buchenwald and shot in the stables by the SS in an operation called 'Kommando 99', after the first two numbers of the internal telephone number of the stables.[24] Florstedt, in an attempt to stir things up for Koch, whose job he wanted, told Morgen he had overheard Koch saying, 'That bird has to be done away with.' But Morgen refused to believe Florstedt. Koch had no motive for murdering Kuschnir-Kuschnarev and in fact needed him as an informant, whereas Hoven did have a motive for murder. Hoven told

Koch that Kuschnir-Kuschnarev died of typhus and that was what he wrote on his death certificate.

Morgen's final charge of murder against Hoven was in respect of two prisoners whose names are simply given as Freudemann and May. These prisoners were sent from Buchenwald to a work party at the airfield at Quedlinburg, which was next to a chicken farm, under SS Sergeant Blank. The farmer soon noticed that chickens were going missing and he complained to the local police that the prisoners were responsible. The local police found that Freudemann was travelling around on a motorcycle, having an affair with a local woman who worked at the airfield and often spending the night with her. It later emerged that Blank was allowing his work party all sorts of liberties: they would steal chickens, go hunting and have parties and even orgies. Now Freudemann and May presented a danger to Blank, as their testimony could cause him all sorts of problems. He therefore conspired with Hoven to murder both prisoners.

The method chosen by Hoven was to bring Freudemann and May in for participation in a medical experiment. On their return to Buchenwald, he admitted them to Block 46, which was used as an isolation block for these experiments. One control group of prisoners would be given a live virus, then an injection, and their symptoms would then be observed and recorded. The other group was given the live virus with no injection and their symptoms would also be observed and recorded. These experiments at Buchenwald were under the management of Ding-Schuler. But because he was away from Buchenwald, Hoven acted as his deputy and seized his opportunity to murder Freudemann and May. This is not to say that

Ding-Schuler himself was any better – his experiments on prisoners at Buchenwald included one where he deliberately burned five prisoners with ignited phosphorous in order to test various creams and ointments for burns. The prisoners suffered extensive burns, excruciating pain and permanent injury as a result.[25]

The first attempt to murder Freudemann did not work because the virus used to infect him failed. But now there was a problem for Hoven: because of the police enquiries into Blank, the SS headquarters at Buchenwald started to put together an official complaint against him because he did not control the prisoners at Quedlinburg properly. As soon as Pister found out about this, he ordered that Freudemann was not to take part in any more medical experiments. He was too late. Hoven told him that Freudemann was very ill and not expected to survive – though witnesses later informed Morgen that actually Freudemann was in the best of health when Hoven wrote this letter.

Hoven, having lied to Pister, transferred Freudemann and May to the camp hospital and interrogated Freudemann about the woman he had had an affair with at Quedlinburg. Freudemann was evasive in his answers and Hoven decided to encourage him to cooperate, so he asked one of the Kapos to beat and whip Freudemann. This clearly had no effect either, since a short time later Hoven murdered Freudemann and May by injecting them both with phenol.

Hoven had powerful friends in Berlin. Morgen was asked to go and talk to SS General Ernst-Robert Grawitz, the chief Reich physician, who told him that Hoven's killings at Buchenwald were covered by orders, either those from Hitler or those from him as Hoven's ultimate boss. Morgen told him that he hadn't arrested

Hoven for carrying out those orders that were covered by the law but because Hoven was operating outside the law when he murdered the people that Morgen had arrested him for.

The use of prisoners for medical experiments in concentration camps was notorious. In one of his interrogations after the war, the interrogator, Selcke, asked Morgen about his attitude towards them. In his reply, Morgen said, 'It's nothing out of the ordinary, science has been doing this for centuries.' Selcke then asked him, 'On living test subjects?'

'Yes, of course. After all, how does one try out a new drug or a new vaccine if not on living people? Of course, one tries it on all kinds of animals first, but ultimately it has to be tested on people too,' replied Morgen. He then went on to qualify his answer: 'One must clearly understand here that one must distinguish between what was done on a scientific basis and what was ordered and what individuals did on their own initiative. When one hears about what Rascher did this is where things become mixed up.'[26] The Rascher Morgen refers to here is Sigmund Rascher, a notorious SS doctor who carried out freezing and high-altitude experiments on prisoners, killing many in the process. In the end, he was executed on the direct orders of Himmler because he and his wife had kidnapped babies when he had told Himmler he and his wife had conceived them naturally.[27]

Although Morgen references the Rascher case, his analysis of the use of prisoners in medical experiments in concentration camps does not address the fact that these were carried out against their will. He did, however, interfere in the process of selecting prisoners for medical experiments at Buchenwald because he was concerned that these experiments were being used to murder prisoners. Morgen tried to persuade the SS to restrict these experiments so that only prisoners who had been lawfully sentenced to death could be used but he was unsuccessful.[28] In the end, in early 1944, an order was issued putting Nebe in charge of selecting prisoners for experiments and this removed the role of the Buchenwald doctors from the process. A local officer from the Reich Central Police Detective Office supervised the process, which meant that political prisoners could no longer be used and removed the risk of them being murdered in this way.

The evidence against both Blank and Hoven was strong but in the end, only Hoven was charged with the murders of Freudemann and May. When Morgen sent Wehner to arrest Blank for the murders of Freudemann, May, Krämer and Peix, Blank hanged himself.

Meanwhile, Wehner continued with his investigation into SS Sergeant Köhler's death. This would continue even after Morgen completed his official report into Koch, Ilse Koch, Sommer and Hoven at Buchenwald on 11 April 1944. They would have to wait until September 1944 for their trial.

Morgen had been critical of Wehner, who was not making headway with the case and had told Morgen that he needed lots more time and more detectives in order to complete his enquiries. Wehner had not been able to prove murder in the Köhler case; instead he concluded that it was an accident. Morgen did not agree and wanted him to keep looking in order to strengthen the case against Koch, but the result stood.[29] Hackmann was also detained while further investigations took place into his corruption and his part in the murder of Wendel at Majdanek. In the end, despite

Morgen's best efforts, no one was ever prosecuted for Köhler's murder.

Alongside his investigation at Buchenwald from mid-1943 and into 1944, Morgen had also started investigations at other camps, particularly camps in Nazi-occupied Poland. And what he found at these camps was to be a severe test for his conscience.

CHAPTER 6

THE INVESTIGATION AT MAJDANEK CONCENTRATION CAMP

WEDNESDAY 3 NOVEMBER 1943

Roll call at Majdanek, a concentration camp on the outskirts of the city of Lublin in Nazi-occupied Poland. For Pola Braun, this day had started like any other. The barrack leader had woken her and her fellow prisoners at 5 a.m., the signal to start a well-practised routine. First, dress quickly, make her bunk, go to the toilet, drink a cup of coffee and clean around the barracks. Then outside, whatever the weather, for roll call, which always started promptly at 6 a.m. Outside the windows, some of the prisoners noticed a truck had been parked near the camp gates and that the watchtowers had more guards in than was normally the case.[1]

For Pola, who was also known as Paulina Braunówna, there were few other signs to suggest that today was going to be any different to previous days. Pola was a composer, musician and poet, who wrote in both Polish and Yiddish. Before the war, she had worked in the editorial offices of a satirical magazine called *Szpilki* while performing cabaret in the evenings and weekends and writing poetry. As a Jew, she had been forced into the Warsaw Ghetto in 1940 where she continued her artistic endeavours. She sang about life in the ghetto, about her Jewish identity, about deportation, and her audiences listened and took heart. In May 1943, after the Warsaw Ghetto Uprising, she had been sent to Majdanek where she continued to encourage her fellow prisoners by composing, singing and playing on the piano, which was in the barracks where they were held.[2]

By 6 a.m., Pola and her fellow prisoners had to be standing in the roll call square facing their own barrack block. Then came the familiar commands: *Stillgestanden*, *Mützen ab*, *Augen links!* Attention, caps off, eyes left! Anyone who didn't obey the commands immediately was beaten by one of the SS guards. Pola's line of women prisoners then waited for the next command: *Arbeitskommando formieren!* Form up into work parties!

It never came. Instead, they were sent back inside for the morning. They could hear dance music blaring from the loudspeakers which were mounted on the truck they had seen earlier. More music was coming from a second truck that was parked outside the camp next to the ditches, which had been dug over the course of the previous three days. But the music wasn't loud enough to conceal the other sounds which the SS hadn't wanted them to hear. Gunfire.

At midday, the SS came for Pola and her fellow prisoners. They were told to fall in outside in groups of five. Knowing what was to come, a number of the female prisoners hid themselves among the bunks but there was no escape. The SS guards went through the barracks, dragging out anyone who was hiding. Anyone who was sick was loaded onto trucks. Because the sick were only wearing underwear, one of the prisoners, Stefania Perzanowska, threw blankets over them until one of the SS guards – Elsa Ehrich, who was supervising the loading – noticed. She pulled them off, lashed Perzanowska with a whip and told her not to waste hospital property.

Pola and her fellow prisoners were marched out of the camp. The SS ordered them to undress, and once they were naked they were forced to walk through two lines of SS to one of the execution ditches. These were carved into the earth in 100-metre-long zigzags; each was 6–7 metres wide and 1.5–2 metres deep. In his official report on the massacre, Morgen noted that the men were being executed in one ditch, the women in another and any children were being shot with their mothers.[3]

When Pola and her group of five prisoners reached the ditch where they were to be shot, they were right next to the music from the loudspeakers on the truck. Foxtrots, dance tunes: the musical selection was designed to disorientate and confuse the prisoners.[4] Alongside each ditch there were three SS who were doing the shooting and there were three others behind them whose job was only to fill and provide fresh magazines. Pola was instructed to walk forward, climb on top of the dead naked body already there and lie on her front. Once she lay down, one of the SS leaned down and shot her in the neck. Then the next prisoner and the next one. The SS had started the slaughter at 6 a.m. and by 5 p.m. they were finished.

The next day, Thursday 4 November, the Majdanek sub-camp at Poniatowa was liquidated. Around 15,000 people were killed over the course of a single day. Ludwika Fiszer, one of the very few survivors, later related how she arrived naked at the execution pits with her daughter:

> We lay down quickly to avoid looking at the bodies. My daughter asked me to cover her little eyes because she was afraid, so I put my left hand around her head, and with my right hand I held her right hand, and so we lay, faces down. In a moment shots were fired in our direction; I felt my left hand burn and [the bullet] go further through the head of my ten-year-old daughter, who didn't even twitch … Several minutes later, an SS-man brings a woman and a child; I hear her begging to be allowed to kiss her child, but the murderer refuses; she lays down on my right, resting her head on mine. A shot is fired and her blood spurts on my head, splashing on my nape and hair, from the back I must have looked dead.[5]

When the SS left the execution pits, Ludwika stayed still and derived some warmth from the bodies which surrounded her:

> The wind shook the bodies as if saying *Kaddish* for us. The Ukrainians came a few times. I heard them spit aloud on us, saying, 'Job twoja żydów' [fuck the Jews] and leave … My first glance was at my daughter: she always had an oval face, but now her face was round and deathly pale. I touched her hair and back with my lips and her hand slipped out from mine.[6]

Ludwika Fiszer made it to Warsaw and later on to America where she remarried (her husband had also been shot at Poniatowa).

In total, the SS shot over 40,000 people over 3 and 4 November 1943, from Majdanek and the sub-camps at Poniatowa and Trawniki. Alongside Pola and Ludwika's ten-year-old daughter, other victims included famous Jewish figures from the Warsaw cultural and scientific community, actors, poets, historians and theologians.

The SS had a name for this mass shooting. They called it *Aktion Erntefest* – Action Harvest Festival.

* * *

Shortly after the massacre, Morgen arrived in Lublin. He had travelled there to meet with his investigative team, headed by Inspector Dennerlein, which had started work at Majdanek while he was still working on the Buchenwald case. Morgen and his team had already had some success: the camp commandant SS Major Hermann Florstedt had been arrested in October and transferred to Buchenwald before Morgen arrived for this visit. But by shooting all the prisoners in Majdanek and its sub-camps, the SS had also shot all the witnesses Morgen and his team wanted to interview as part of their ongoing investigation into corruption and murder at Majdanek.

Morgen consulted with his boss, SS Lieutenant Colonel Werner Paulmann, who agreed that they should investigate what had happened. Morgen talked to witnesses and provided an official narrative report of the events, describing the way the Jewish prisoners had been forced to climb into execution ditches before being shot as 'the old and trusted method'. Morgen's use of the phrase 'old and trusted method' comes across as very callous in this context. He may have been repeating standard SS terminology but he was never asked about it after the war, so we do not know why he used it.

The local SS commander, SS Major George Wippern, told Morgen that the order to shoot these Jewish prisoners had come direct from *Reichsführer* Heinrich Himmler after a report by SS General Ernst Kaltenbrunner, Chief of the Reich Security Main

Office, who was concerned about action by the Jews against the SS after uprisings had taken place at extermination camps Sobibor and Treblinka. However, despite clear evidence to the contrary, both Morgen and his boss Paulmann thought that the primary motivation for shooting these prisoners was that they were potential witnesses to crimes committed by the SS.[7]

During Morgen's investigation, the SS proceeded with burning the bodies of the Jewish prisoners who had been shot on 3 and 4 November. SS Sergeant Erich Mußfeldt was given the job by the new commandant at Majdanek, SS Lieutenant Colonel Martin Weiß, together with a group of Jewish prisoners who had temporarily been spared execution so they could carry out the work. Their job was to remove any valuables, including gold teeth, from the corpses and to pile the bodies up in the centre of the execution ditches. Once they were ready, Mußfeldt poured methanol over the bodies and lit the fires.[8] The smoke and ash covered Majdanek, causing breathing difficulties among the prisoners and SS. Once the burning of the bodies was complete, the ashes were transported to an SS factory near the camp and turned into fertiliser for the soil. It took from November until Christmas 1943 for the burning of the bodies to be complete and once the work was done, the Jewish prisoners who had been carrying it out were sent to Auschwitz to the gas chambers.

When he was interrogated on 12 October 1945 by the Allies, despite the fact he was the chief of the Reich Security Main Office, Kaltenbrunner denied all knowledge of this massacre. He claimed he hadn't seen Morgen's report, he had no idea what 'the old and trusted method' might refer to and he had no idea who Konrad Morgen was. No one believed him. He was found guilty of war crimes and crimes against humanity and executed on 16 October 1946.

Before Morgen arrived in Lublin, he had already arrested SS Major Hermann Florstedt. Florstedt had taken over command of the camp from SS Colonel Karl-Otto Koch, who had been relieved of his post because of the escape of eighty-six Soviet prisoners of war. Florstedt's approach to running a camp was to continue with Koch's habits of helping himself to as much money and property as he could and ensuring that prisoners lived in a continual state of arbitrary terror. In fact, Florstedt's reign of terror at Majdanek was if anything worse than Koch's at Buchenwald because Majdanek had started operating as an extermination camp and Florstedt made full use of his power as commandant to personally oversee the selection of the prisoners for the gas chambers.

Florstedt was in the habit of pronouncing arbitrary death sentences for prisoners. One Jewish prisoner did not return from work for lunch and so a search was ordered. The prisoner was found asleep, brought back to the compound and Florstedt ordered that he be hanged on the spot. He would also send Jewish prisoners straight to the gas chambers on arrival instead of first registering them. Over the spring and summer of 1943, Florstedt made Jewish prisoners arriving at the camp on the larger transports spend their first night in the open air. The next day, together with Mußfeldt and SS Lieutenant Anton Thumann, he would personally oversee the selection of the prisoners, sending any old or weak prisoners and children to be gassed immediately and allowing the younger healthy ones to live. For prisoners arriving on the smaller transports, Florstedt preferred more brutal ways of slaughtering them. They would be assembled in a line outside the shed next to the crematorium. The SS then summoned them into the shed one by one, where they were beaten to death with metal bars.[9]

One reason why Florstedt took a personal interest in the arrival of Jewish transports was to continue the practice which he had taken part in at Buchenwald: robbing them of money, jewellery, gold and other valuables. Morgen had started investigating Florstedt along with Koch as the trail at Buchenwald led to Lublin and the Majdanek extermination camp.

OPERATION REINHARD

One day, Morgen was in his office in Buchenwald when he received a report from the security police in Lublin about a Jewish wedding where over 1,000 guests and SS had come together for a wedding celebration. According to the report that he received, 'gluttonous' amounts of food and alcohol were consumed.[10]

Morgen immediately suspected a corruption case and left Buchenwald for Lublin to investigate. At first, he could not find the camp where this wedding was supposed to have taken place but after asking around, he arrived at one of the camps in the area surrounding Lublin and met the commanding officer, SS Major Christian Wirth. In his testimony to the Nuremberg trials, Morgen described this man as *Kriminalkommisar Wirth*, which reflects his pre-war police rank of detective inspector before he was taken off police duties and put in charge of the Nazi euthanasia programmes. By the time Morgen met Wirth in 1943, he had been in charge of the extermination camps at Chelmno, Sobibor, Belzec and Treblinka in Nazi-occupied Poland as part of *Einsatz Reinhard* or Operation Reinhard, the plan implemented by the Nazis to systematically slaughter Jews in the General Government and a key part of the Final Solution and the Holocaust.

Wirth was a notorious figure. After a distinguished career in the Imperial German Army during the First World War, he had become a builder before joining the police. He had been part of the first experiments in Nazi Germany that used gassing to eliminate people diagnosed as 'incurably insane' at the end of 1939. As an extermination camp commandant, Wirth was known for brutality and efficiency. He claimed it was he who devised the system of *Sonderkommandos*, units composed of Jewish camp inmates, who were selected for their physical strength and who were forced to dispose of the bodies of Jews in the extermination camps before they too were eliminated. His management style was simple: he preferred his own company and relied on his Ukrainian servant to bring him reports from the camp each day.[11] But the SS in the camps he ran were terrified of him. SS Captain Franz Stangl, who served under him in the extermination camps, described him as 'a gross and florid man' and recalled his first day in Treblinka when Wirth took over the camp:[12]

> I remember Wirth standing there, next to these pits full of black blue corpses. It had nothing to do with humanity – it couldn't have, it was a mass of rotting flesh. Wirth said, 'What shall we do with this garbage?' I think unconsciously that started me thinking of them as cargo.[13]

When Morgen asked Wirth about the reports of the Jewish wedding, to Morgen's surprise, Wirth told him the reports were true.

Wirth said his orders were from Adolf Hitler himself and that they were to eliminate the Jews in Nazi-occupied Poland. The way in which Wirth accomplished this, he told Morgen, was through deception. He built pretend towns in the General Government area so that when the Jews arrived, they would think that they were simply being resettled. After their arrival, they were told that they must shower to prevent the spread of infection and so after having removed all their clothes they were shown into the shower rooms, which were then locked and the gas pumped in.

Wirth told Morgen that the wedding had been organised as a part of this programme of deceiving the Jews. Morgen later recalled:

> At first Wirth's description seemed completely fantastic to me, but in Lublin I saw one of his camps. It was a camp which collected the property or part of the property of his victims. From the piles of things – there were an enormous number of watches piled up – I had to realize that something frightful was going on here.[14]

He also learned about the orders to destroy the evidence of the extermination camps and massacre all remaining prisoners in Majdanek and its sub-camps. Although Morgen suggested in his Nuremberg testimony that this was as a result of his investigation into corruption, the timings were coincidental. The decision had already been made to remove all traces of the camps.

Alongside Wirth, Morgen also took the opportunity to investigate SS General Odilo Globočnik, the local SS and police commander in Lublin. He was in charge of the programme of building and running the four extermination camps – Belzec, Majdanek,

Sobibor and Treblinka – where around 1.7 million Jews lost their lives.

Alongside the slaughter of Jews, Globočnik had also been tasked with collecting their property and valuables. In his final report on Operation Reinhard, he told Himmler the operation had yielded 180 million Reichsmarks, about £18.3 million at wartime prices and with a value today of about £691 million – this despite Globočnik, Wirth and other officers helping themselves to money and valuables for their own use.[15] After the conclusion of Operation Reinhard and after Morgen's first visit, Globočnik, Wirth and their officers were posted to Trieste, where they set up concentration camps as well as fighting partisans in Yugoslavia. And once there, Globočnik asked Morgen for his help. He wanted Morgen to investigate and arrest Wirth and to keep him informed of his enquiries.

Morgen suspected Globočnik's motives. After all, it would have taken any heat off him from Himmler and others in the Reich Security Main Office if one of his subordinates was being investigated for crimes which he, Globočnik, had also committed.

Morgen flew to Trieste in early 1944 to meet Globočnik and spent an evening with him. Globočnik could be charming and friendly when he wanted to and he turned all of this on to Morgen. But Morgen was giving nothing away – he had already decided to investigate Globočnik himself and when he returned to Berlin, he visited Globočnik's ex-wife who was working in the propaganda ministry. Unfortunately, she knew nothing about Globočnik's wealth and his enquiries petered out.[16] Morgen did, however, continue his investigation into Wirth while he was in Yugoslavia, until Wirth was eventually killed by Yugoslav partisans in May 1944.

Something that Wirth had said to Morgen in Lublin had started

Morgen thinking. Wirth had called Rudolf Höss, commandant at Auschwitz, his 'untalented disciple'. Morgen had already sent an investigation team into the complex of camps at Auschwitz and now he decided to get involved personally. And an opportunity presented itself straight away.

CHAPTER 7

THE INVESTIGATION AT AUSCHWITZ

SUNDAY 1 AUGUST 1943

Three Reich Security Main Office transport trains arrive at Auschwitz from Bendin (Będzin) in Nazi-occupied Poland. Each train carries about 2,000 Jews from the ghetto and they arrive at staged intervals in order to give the SS time to process each group. The numbers are approximate for a reason: after the selection process, those who have been chosen to live are given numbers and registered and those who have been chosen to die are taken straight to the gas chambers. About 4,600 are sent to the gas chambers and 1,271 are chosen to live. Later the same day, two more Reich Security Main Office transport trains arrive at Auschwitz, this time carrying Jews from the ghetto at Sosnowitz (Sosnowiec). Of the 4,000 arrivals, more than 3,000 people are sent to the gas chambers.

All week, the trains from Bendin and Sosnowitz continue to arrive, along with transports from Belgium, France and Berlin. On Wednesday 4 August, the resistance movement in Auschwitz smuggles a message out to Kraków to report the arrival of the transports from Bendin and Sosnowitz. They count 20,000 Jews arriving, with

90 per cent being sent straight to the gas chambers. The transports continue to arrive even after this message is sent. Throughout the week, the chief of police in Sosnowitz makes claims for provisions to feed the police officers who are carrying out the deportations of the Jews to Auschwitz.

On Thursday 5 August, the patients and nursing staff from the hospital at Sosnowitz arrive at Auschwitz, numbering about 1,000. Following the selection process, only twenty-four women are judged to be fit enough to be saved. The remainder are sent to the gas chambers. On Friday 6 August, SS Captain Hans Aumeier, in charge of protective custody at Auschwitz, announces to the SS that they can have the weekend off from Saturday lunchtime in recognition of their hard work in processing the arrivals from the Bendin and Sosnowitz ghettos. On Saturday 7 August, the chief of police in Sosnowitz reports the deportation of approximately 30,000 Jews from the ghettos at Bendin, Sosnowitz and Dąbrowa Górnicza. He also makes a claim for further provisions to feed his police officers, who have yet to fully finish deporting the Jews to Auschwitz.[1]

Time off for the SS would also have meant no work for the Jews of the *Sonderkommando*. Once the SS had carried out the process of selection, the work of these units began. These were Jewish prisoners who were picked out on arrival at Auschwitz and sent to live apart with other members of the unit. It was their job to deal with the dead. Their work started at the place where the Jews who had been selected for death had to undress, a process which usually lasted for no more than twenty minutes and which the *Sonderkommando* had to make sure went as quickly and smoothly as possible, usually by calling out *Schnell, Schnell!* (Quickly, quickly!) and *Bitte, ziehen Sie sich doch aus!* (Please take off your clothes!) If necessary, they would physically prod the prisoners.[2] Any hesitation or compassion on the part of a *Sonderkommando* could result in them being forced into the gas chambers as well. Once the Jews were in the gas chambers and the doors locked, the SS poured in the Zyklon B gas pellets. The next job of the *Sonderkommando* was to go in and clear out the bodies of the Jews they had just seen alive.

Because the gas rose from the floor, the strongest climbed over the weakest in order to preserve their access to cleaner air. But this did not save them and the Jews of the *Sonderkommando* had to untangle the bodies and look at their faces, which were contorted in pain. Once the bodies were removed from the gas chamber, the *Sonderkommando* had to clean the floor so that the next group to be gassed would have no idea what was about to happen. Meanwhile, the clothes and valuables which had been left behind in the undressing room were collected and taken to the warehouses, which were nicknamed Kanada I and Kanada II.

Another group of *Sonderkommando* were responsible for removing gold teeth, hair and any jewellery from the bodies. They forced open the mouths of the corpses and used dentists' pliers to remove gold teeth. Leon Cohen, one of the *Sonderkommando*, who carried out this job in 1944, said that he was given only ten minutes to extract the teeth from sixty to seventy-five corpses.[3] The time pressure was so that the *Sonderkommando* could quickly load the bodies into the furnaces and the production line of death was kept moving ready for the next transport to arrive and for the process to start all over again. Sometimes, Cohen would keep gold from a tooth in order to barter with an SS guard for extra food or alcohol.

In 1944, the gold extracted from the teeth of the bodies was melted down into ingots, which measured 2 cm wide by 5 or 6 cm long. But this hadn't always been the case at Auschwitz. Up to and including 1943, dental gold had been tossed into boxes without having been melted down and one of the *Sonderkommando*, Ya'akov Gabai, witnessed high-ranking SS officers come and help themselves every week.[4] These boxes were then transferred to the dental unit for processing and onward distribution. In 1943, an order came through to the dental unit from Berlin in response to the amounts of gold going missing: dental gold now had to be registered and each piece of gold from a tooth had to be accompanied by a paper form showing the prisoner's name, the prisoner's number, the number of teeth extracted and the amount of gold which had been recovered.

This was clearly completely unrealistic. For a start, anyone who was selected for the gas chambers straight from the train was not registered or given a number at Auschwitz. None of the forms matched with the numbers of bodies, and before long the head of the dental unit wrote to Berlin and explained the problems. Their solution was to send an SS Sergeant Körfer to Auschwitz and his big idea was to melt the gold into lumps so it could easily be sent for purification in Frankfurt.[5] This was duly put into effect and the new system was to remain in place in Auschwitz. But Körfer was greedy. He wanted to steal some of the dental gold and he decided that the best way to do this was to simply post some to his wife.

He selected three lumps of gold and packaged them inside a small cardboard box. But gold is very heavy and the package caught the attention of the customs office at the border with Germany. Because Körfer was in the SS, customs sent the package and a covering note 'For further action' to the SS courts, where it made its way to Konrad Morgen as the investigating judge at the SS and police court in Kassel.[6] When Morgen opened the package he found one lump of gold about the size of two fists, along with two much smaller lumps. This immediately got him thinking: if this were dental gold and had been extracted from the teeth of Jews who had been gassed at Auschwitz – and assuming that not every Jew who entered the gas chambers had a gold filling – then the gold in the package must have come from the mouths of 20,000, 50,000 or even 100,000 dead bodies.

When Morgen was relating this at the 1963–5 Frankfurt Auschwitz trial of former SS officers and guards, he paused at this point in his narrative before saying, 'A shocking thought.' He went on to say:

> For the first time I realised that this Auschwitz, which at that time was little-known and whose geographical location I had to look up with some difficulty on the map, must have been one of the biggest human extermination sites the world had ever seen. [Pause] I could have dealt with this matter of the confiscated gold package very easily. The current evidence was very convincing and I could have had the perpetrator arrested and charged and that would have addressed the facts of the matter. But after my deliberations, which I described to you briefly, I absolutely had to go and see for myself. And so I travelled as quickly as I could to Auschwitz so I could lead the investigations there and then.[7]

From this, it sounds as if what was happening at Auschwitz came as a complete surprise to him, but the sequence of events around this time in early November 1943 indicates that Morgen knew more about Auschwitz than his testimony suggests. We know that Morgen was in Lublin just after 3 and 4 November, where he arrived to investigate the mass shootings of Jewish prisoners at Majdanek and its sub-camps. It was there that Wirth had talked to Morgen about SS Colonel Rudolf Höss, the commandant of Auschwitz. We also know that Morgen visited Auschwitz in early November 1943 because in his 1964 testimony he describes meeting Rudolf Höss on his first visit. Höss left Auschwitz in early November and was replaced by SS Colonel Arthur Liebehenschel.

Morgen may have simply become confused over dates and the order in which events happened. Or he may have been deliberately suggesting to the court that Auschwitz was a total surprise to him on that first visit when the evidence suggests that it was not. We can only speculate as to the reasons why he might have done this. Unfortunately, no record survives of the actual date when Morgen and his team arrived in Auschwitz – I asked the Auschwitz Memorial and Museum if they had any documentation about this but sadly they did not. There were other issues with Morgen's testimony at Auschwitz and these are set out in Chapter 9, which discusses the trial in detail, and in Chapter 10.

The exact date is unknown, but sometime in early November, Morgen's investigating team – consisting of three Gestapo officers, SS Lieutenant Colonel Reimers, SS Captain Bartsch and SS Captain Fischer – arrived at Auschwitz while Morgen was at Lublin. The intercepted gold package must have arrived at Morgen's office around this time too, and he set off for Auschwitz straight away. A reminder was issued to the SS at Auschwitz on 16 November that all money, jewellery, clothing and other valuables taken from prisoners belonged to the Reich and that anyone caught stealing had committed an offence that would lead at the very least to expulsion from the SS.[8]

Having investigated the mass shootings at Majdanek and spoken to Wirth, Morgen knew about the extermination programme which he was likely to find when he arrived at Auschwitz. But this time, when he got there he would be able to do something about it, instead of arriving too late as had been the case at Majdanek.

ARRIVAL AT AUSCHWITZ

On his arrival at Auschwitz Konrad Morgen got out of the train and looked around.* He spent some time looking for a sign, something that indicated that this was where terrible things happened. But there was nothing to be seen. Instead, he saw trains coming and going, troop trains, hospital trains, goods trains and ordinary passenger trains; he saw people disembarking and he saw prisoners from Auschwitz, in their uniforms, being put on trains departing for somewhere else.

With nothing out of the ordinary to be seen at the station, Morgen made his way to the camp. From the outside it looked like other camps he had seen, with high walls, watchtowers, barbed wire and patrolling guards. He reported to SS Colonel Rudolf Höss, whom he described as stocky, very reserved and monosyllabic, with his face set in stone. There may have been a reason for Höss's taciturn behaviour: in his autobiography, written in prison after the war, Höss said, 'In Auschwitz where I found my so-called colleagues

* This section is based on Morgen's testimony at the 1963–5 Auschwitz trial. One of the defendants, Franz Hofmann, testified that he was Morgen's guide at Auschwitz. Morgen does not give his name during his own testimony.

constantly going behind my back and where each day I suffered fresh disappointments, I began to change. I became distrustful and highly suspicious and saw only the worst in everyone.'[9]

Höss is one of the most notorious concentration camp commandants in the Second World War. His autobiography is the work of a fanatical Nazi. When describing the Holocaust he said, 'There was no doubt in the mind of any of us that Hitler's order had to be obeyed regardless and that it was the duty of the SS to carry it out.'[10] Historian Tom Segev describes in his book, *Soldiers of Evil*, how he met Fritz Hensel, Rudolf Höss's brother-in-law, in 1975. Hensel once stayed with the Höss family at their house in Auschwitz for four weeks. He was a German Army artist and he told Segev how he was able to wander around Auschwitz freely and even once drew a picture of a pile of dead bodies. He described to Segev that one evening he and Höss were talking over a glass of wine. Hensel asked Höss about the term *Untermensch*, or sub-human, and Höss replied:

> Look, you can see for yourself. They are not like you and me. They are different. They look different. They do not behave like human beings. They have numbers on their arms. They are here in order to die … Here you are on another planet. Don't forget that.[11]

Morgen had already sent a telex informing Höss of his arrival and now he told him face to face that he was here to carry out his investigation. Höss replied by telling Morgen that they had been given a very difficult task at Auschwitz and that not everyone was up to the job. He asked Morgen how he would like to proceed, and Morgen told him that first of all he would like to look around the camp.

Höss looked at the staff rota for the day, picked up the phone and summoned SS Captain Franz Hofmann to show Morgen around, with instructions that Hofmann was to take him wherever he wanted to go.

Morgen decided that first he would like to visit the place at Auschwitz-Birkenau that was the starting point for the final journey of the people who arrived: the ramp. To Morgen it looked like any ramp at a normal railway yard, so he asked his guide to explain the process. Hofmann explained to Morgen that the train station at Auschwitz would telephone the camp to tell them that a transport train containing Jews was due to arrive shortly. Once this call came in, a well-rehearsed routine swung into action. A security team blocked off access to the railway yard and the ramp. When the train pulled in and stopped, the Jews were told to climb out and place their suitcases on the ground. Then the men were sent to join one line and the women and children a second line.

The first part of the selection process involved identifying rabbis and other 'important' Jews. They were taken off to the camp where they were forced to write letters and postcards to people in the outside world to remove any suspicion that there was anything untoward happening at Auschwitz. The second part of the selection process involved identifying anyone who had a particular skill that was needed in the various factories linked to the camp. Finally, Jews who could work were pulled out, leaving behind those who couldn't. The people who had been selected as workers were then forced to walk to the camp while those unfit for work were taken by truck straight to the gas chambers. Hofmann also described what happened when time was short or when there was no doctor available to select those fit for work – then the SS simply told the Jews that anyone who didn't think they could walk the few kilometres to the camp could take the trucks instead. Anyone who climbed into the trucks was taken straight to the gas chambers.

Hofmann then took Morgen to the gas chambers at Birkenau. He noticed the way the road went downhill and out of sight as the Jews were taken to the undressing room. He saw the Kanada camp, where the Jews' possessions and valuables were sorted. There was a huge pile from the previous transport still being sorted. When Morgen and Hofmann were walking in the yard they were surrounded by Jewish Kapos – from the *Sonderkommando* – who circled them, waiting for orders. Morgen observed to Hofmann that they behaved like a pack of dogs waiting for orders. Yes, said Hofmann, and he told Morgen how important it was that newly arrived Jews were reassured by the presence of other Jews – the aim always being to prevent mass panic breaking out. Morgen saw the undressing rooms, the gas chambers with the signs pointing to them saying 'To the showers' and the crematoria. These were all spotlessly clean, he noticed.

Until now, Morgen had not met any members of the SS who operated this machinery of death and now he asked Hofmann if he could meet some of them. Hofmann took him to the SS guard room and Morgen was astonished by what he saw. He was expecting a typical spartan German guardhouse with little furniture and a desk with a telephone. At Auschwitz, he found a room with sofas and SS men lounging about on them, mainly lower-ranking non-commissioned officers with pretty young Jewish women, who were clearly prisoners but who were dressed in normal clothes and serving them food. To Morgen, the SS men looked like they had been drinking before their arrival but even so he expected that as SS officers, their presence would have been acknowledged by the SS men in the guardroom. But they ignored Morgen and Hofmann. What surprised Morgen even more was that the Jewish prisoners and the SS men were addressing each other as 'Du', equivalent to being on first-name terms with each other.

For an English-speaking audience, this revelation has far less resonance than for a German audience. In German, there are two ways of addressing someone: formally one uses 'Sie' and informally one uses 'Du'. Even today, this can be a minefield for anyone trying to navigate a conversation with someone in Germany, as it remains a country where formality is still very important. In 1964, this revelation would have had a big impact in the courtroom and the judges, lawyers and public who were present would have known instantly what a grave breach of rules and protocol this would have been. Morgen turned to Hofmann, who shrugged his shoulders and said to excuse their behaviour, 'They have had a hard night; they had to process a couple of transports.' Morgen relayed his reaction to the Frankfurt courtroom: 'That meant that during the night, while I was standing on the train to Auschwitz, several thousand people, several trainloads, were gassed and incinerated and of these thousands of people there was nothing left, not even a speck of dust on an oven fitting.'

After his visit to the guardroom, Morgen toured the rest of the camp with Hofmann. They saw what Morgen described as the 'carefully chosen' prisoners' barracks – the inference being that he was being shown only the prisoners' accommodation which the camp SS wanted him to see – the hospital, the cell blocks, as well as the so-called *Schwarze Wand*, the Black Wall, where executions were carried out. Prisoners were stood against this wall and shot.

By now it was late afternoon and Morgen decided it was time for his investigations to begin. He ordered the SS staff at the crematorium to assemble for a locker inspection. There he found a variety of jewellery and money in different currencies, gold rings, necklaces and pearls, which the SS men had clearly stolen from the Jews who were being sent to their deaths. He was astonished to find in one locker the genitals of freshly slaughtered bulls and the owner sheepishly told Morgen he used them as an aid to sexual potency.

That night, Morgen retired to his accommodation with his mind in turmoil. For the second time in his career as an SS investigating judge, he faced a crisis of conscience. The first time had been as a judge in Nazi-occupied Poland when he was overwhelmed by the scale of the criminality which he had encountered. His response to this had been to ask for a transfer to a quieter corner of the Reich but instead he had been sent to the Eastern Front as an ordinary soldier in the Waffen SS. But now what he faced was on a completely different level: the mass killing of millions of Jews. He had arrived in Lublin too late to stop the mass shootings there but in Auschwitz he could at least try to do something to stop the almost daily slaughter. The question was, what?

KONRAD MORGEN'S DILEMMA

In his testimony at the 1963–5 Auschwitz trial, Morgen set out at length what was going through his mind that first night he was in Auschwitz. He had been in a number of concentration camps and seen what was happening there but nothing like what he had encountered at Auschwitz-Birkenau. What were the practical steps which he could take? Morgen very carefully set out the legal situation in the Reich, which confronted him in navigating his way to a solution. He did this for the benefit of the lay assessors who sat alongside the professional judges.

Firstly, he talked about what would normally have happened in Germany. Investigating judges couldn't just go around arresting people; instead the public prosecutor would have determined if an arrest could have been made on application from a judge, and for someone important, like a member of the government, the application would have had to have been referred upwards for approval to the chief prosecutor or the Ministry of Justice. As an SS judge, Morgen's options were even more limited than this. The SS and police court were military courts and derived their authority from the commander in chief of the SS and police, *Reichsführer*-SS Heinrich Himmler, and above him, Hitler himself. Therefore, in order for Morgen to arrest either of these two he would have had to apply for an arrest warrant against themselves, which clearly wasn't going to be granted.

Given these problems, Morgen's mind then turned to the possibility of an attempt on Hitler's life. But he knew first-hand the security which surrounded Hitler as he had once been at Hitler's headquarters – the Wolf's Lair in Gierłoż, near Kętrzyn, in what was then East Prussia and what is now part of modern-day Poland – to give a lecture for Himmler. There had been any number of security checks and different buildings. Morgen would have needed to have been in a position where he was in the same room as Hitler for an attempt to work. And that, for Morgen, was not going to happen – although this was the way a group of Wehrmacht officers did try (and fail) to kill Hitler on 20 July 1944.

Morgen's next thoughts were to consider the possibility of leaving the Reich and alerting the Allies about what was happening in

Auschwitz and what had happened at Majdanek. He had previously had a discussion with a detective inspector who had served on the Swiss border and had told Morgen about the way the border went straight through people's houses, so you could go through the front door in Germany and out the back door in Switzerland. This would be easy enough for Morgen; he had a pad of blank military travel permits, which he simply filled in himself when he had an urgent investigation.

He got as far as getting into his car and setting off. But then Morgen wondered to himself what the Swiss authorities would make of his story. And he also thought about abandoning the family who had supported him and the comrades he had fought with on the Eastern Front. He had been part of the SS Wiking Division and had served alongside many Danish, Dutch, Belgian and Norwegian volunteers who had told him they weren't Nazis but that they were there to fight for Europe against the Bolsheviks.

He came to the conclusion that crossing the border to Switzerland wasn't the answer, and he resolved instead to fight even harder within the system to bring murderers and criminals to justice. He outlined his approach to the court in Frankfurt:

> Where the highest legal principle, life itself, is worth nothing and is trampled into the dirt and destroyed, then all other legal principles, whether they be around property, loyalty or something else, must also collapse and lose their value. And therefore – and I had already convinced myself of this – these people, to whom these tasks had been assigned, were set on a path to criminality. And my instructions and the criminal code gave me my duty to

> prosecute these crimes, namely crimes which were not covered by official orders. And that's exactly what I did.

He drove straight to Berlin and reported the bare facts of what he had found at Auschwitz to his police boss, SS General Arthur Nebe in the Reich Security Main Office. He emphasised the locker inspection and the stolen property he had found in twenty lockers and briefed his new investigative team, who were working in Auschwitz.

Morgen told the court in Frankfurt that the reason for this was that he was hoping to conduct a very wide-ranging investigation but he did not want at this point to reveal his true intentions. Although we only have Morgen's word for what he did and what he thought, it is likely that this is correct. Nebe would have expected a purely factual report which detailed only Morgen's official purpose at the camp – namely, to unearth corruption.

THE MURDERS IN BLOCK 11

Morgen's investigation quickly focused on the cell block, or bunker, which in Auschwitz was called simply Block 11. One of his team, SS Captain Helmut Bartsch, heard about the murders of prisoners taking place there, and Morgen opened an investigation into both the bunker and SS Lieutenant Maximilian Grabner, head of the Gestapo and political section at Auschwitz. According to SS Corporal Pery Broad, who worked with him:

> Grabner had become the most outstanding man in Auschwitz thanks to his unscrupulous brutality, his morbid ambition, his

> need for self-assertion and his proverbial double dealing. Even the commandant, SS Colonel Höss who was his equal in sadistic cruelty and unscrupulousness, avoided wherever he could, being at cross purposes with this experienced Gestapo man.[12]

Morgen's initial focus was on reports he heard about so-called 'enhanced interrogations'. The method which was used was known as the 'Boger swing' after SS Lieutenant Wilhelm Boger, who invented it as a means of obtaining confessions from prisoners. Two tables would be placed about a metre apart and the prisoner forced to sit between them and cross his hands (which were then handcuffed) in front of his knees, which he had to draw up. A bar would then be passed through the gap between the prisoner's elbows and knees and the ends of the bar placed on the two tables. This action lifted the prisoner from the floor and left him hanging with his head downwards and his backside and the soles of his feet presented to the torturer. Boger would then use a bull-hide whip to flog the prisoner, with the blows delivered so strongly that the prisoner would rotate and each blow would be delivered on each rotation. If the prisoner's cries became too loud, Boger would put a gas mask on their head, which would only be removed to ask if they wanted to confess anything.

Prisoners usually only lasted fifteen minutes before losing consciousness but when they did, they were revived with hot water dripped into the nose. Once the prisoner had agreed to sign the confession, they would be flogged again if they did not stand up to come to the table to sign. Usually, Boger had difficulty in removing the handcuffs as the prisoner's hands would by now have swollen up. After using this method for some time, it was found that the bar was moving too much and the prisoner often fell to the floor because of the violence of the blows. The prisoner workshop was forced to make two wooden frames with a moveable steel bar and this was found to be more reliable as a means of increasing the prisoners' torments.

Alongside these 'enhanced interrogations', the Gestapo at Auschwitz was also organising its own killings. Once or twice a week, Grabner would review the prisoners in Block 11 in order to make space for more prisoners. Along with SS Captain Hans Aumeier, and other SS officers and guards, he would visit the cells, and between them, Grabner and Aumeier would decide who would live and who would be taken out and shot. Some prisoners were in the cells for minor infringements of camp rules, for example smoking a cigarette when they were supposed to be working. These prisoners might be flogged or sent to a punishment work party. Others who had committed more serious offences, for example escape, were instead condemned to death by Grabner.

Once Grabner had finished in the cells, he and Aumeier would walk out into the yard. There was a black wall at one end, against which the prisoners were shot. First, they were ordered to undress, then they were taken to the wall to be shot at close range with a small-calibre pistol. One of the prisoners, chosen for his strength, would grab the first two prisoners to be shot and force them to stand facing into the wall. The SS officer or guard doing the shooting would then shoot the prisoner in the back of their neck. If the prisoner said or shouted anything then the executioner would beat them before shooting them, aware that other prisoners on the other side of the execution wall might be listening and take heart from what was happening. Once the prisoners had been shot, their bodies would be loaded on to stretchers and piled up at the back of the yard by other prisoners. Another prisoner would scatter sand on to the execution place to cover up the blood from the bullet wounds. While this was going on, the executioner would reload his pistol and the process would start again. Once all the prisoners had been shot, Grabner would eat a big breakfast.

Morgen very quickly identified that these executions were not legal; they had not been authorised by an order from Hitler, Himmler or any other officers who had delegated authority. Having established this, Morgen immediately issued an order for the arrest of Grabner.

This prompted an immediate reaction from the Gestapo. Grabner's boss, SS Colonel Rudolf Mildner, had been the local Gestapo chief in Katowice, and he was already on Morgen's radar because when questioned, Grabner had said, 'I'm just a poor little man carrying out my orders.'[13] Mildner was a notorious figure at Auschwitz as he held regular sessions of the police summary court there, which he chose as a location deliberately so that executions could be carried out immediately. According to Pery Broad, Mildner was 'one of the most blood-thirsty butchers that existed in the Third Reich'.[14] He used this court to pass death sentences on Poles and Germans who had committed political offences – for example, talking about enemy radio broadcasts or suspected membership of the Polish resistance movement – and criminal offences such as black-marketeering.

Each court case usually lasted a minute for Mildner to pronounce the prisoner guilty and then prisoners would be taken out and shot almost immediately. Usually, the evidence in the form of a confession had already been obtained, but on one occasion in 1943, the

Gestapo organised a special session of the court where the prisoners were interrogated using the Boger swing and confessions obtained. Then they were put in front of the court, sentenced to death and shot.

Morgen's investigation represented a threat to the Gestapo at Auschwitz, and Mildner complained to the Reich Security Main Office in Berlin after Grabner had been arrested.* Morgen was summoned to see SS General Heinrich Müller, head of the Gestapo, at his office in Prinz-Albrecht-Straße in Berlin.† As soon as Morgen entered the room, Müller started shouting at him about what he had done and how he had no understanding of the duties of the Gestapo. Morgen remained calm. 'General,' he replied. 'I am not a Gestapo officer. I am an SS judge, sworn to uphold the law. At the end of the day, we live in a constitutional state and there are limits which even the Gestapo has to adhere to.'

Müller went as white as chalk. He jumped up and shouted at Morgen. What right did he have to speak to him like that, he a general in the SS and Morgen a lowly lieutenant, a *Würstchen* – literally a little sausage. He would soon prove that to Morgen. 'Get out!' he shouted, and he literally threw Morgen out of his office.

Morgen found himself in the corridor outside Müller's office. He stood and thought about his situation. On his way in he had had to fill in a visitor's form, which he had had to hand in when he left the building so he wouldn't be able to leave without being accounted for. He thought that Müller, in his anger, might well have called the

---

* Mildner was transferred to Denmark in the autumn of 1943 but Morgen was clear that the complaint to the Reich Security Main Office had come from him.

† In his testimony to the 1963–1965 Auschwitz trial, Morgen says the office he visited was the former Kaiser Friedrich Museum, but in fact he would have been to see Müller in Prinz-Albrecht-Straße, which was the headquarters of the Reich Security Main Office, including the Gestapo.

guard downstairs to have Morgen arrested and put in one of the cells in the basement. He stood and thought for a few minutes and then he made a decision. He had to put things right with Müller and this meant he had to go back into the lion's den and talk to him again.

He turned and went into Müller's outer office again and told the secretaries that he had an important message for General Müller and please could he be let back in to see him? To his surprise, the door of Müller's office opened, and he had calmed down. Morgen launched straight into an apology for his unseemly and unmilitary behaviour. 'General, I've really come here to ask for your advice and orders for further investigations.' Müller was transformed immediately,

'But of course,' he replied. 'I am at your disposal.' He gestured and invited Morgen to sit down. 'Kamerad Morgen, please do have a seat.'

'General,' Morgen said. 'It is the case that in every personal file of a concentration camp commandant and head of the political department there is a statement that is signed by the person concerned, which states that it is the Führer who makes decisions about the life of an enemy of the state.'

'*Ja*, that's right,' agreed Müller.

Morgen continued, 'I am also correct in saying that this authority has been delegated to you as head of the Gestapo and to no one else.'

'*Jawohl*, that is right,' agreed Müller again.

'What would be your verdict if someone far below you in rank were to kill prisoners on his own initiative without reporting to you first?' asked Morgen.

'No, that's impossible. That wouldn't happen,' replied Müller.

'Look, General,' said Morgen. 'Your authority is being abused in the concentration camps. That's what Lieutenant Grabner did and that's why I arrested him.'

'That's different,' agreed Müller, 'I didn't look at it like that.' He thought for a while and then told Morgen a story. 'You know, now you've told me that, I recall a few things which made me think at the time. For example, there was someone important, a priest or someone who had been arrested and the relatives turned to me. I looked into the case and promised them that I would have the prisoner released. I sent a telex ordering the release and I naturally assumed that this happened. But after a few weeks they got in touch again to say that the person concerned had not yet arrived at home. I immediately called the camp on the telephone and asked, "Why hasn't the prisoner been released in accordance with my instructions?" The response was, "Yes, the prisoner has an infectious disease and is in the camp hospital. The doctor's orders are that he has to be free of disease before he can be released." A few weeks later, I received a message to say that the prisoner had died as a result of his illness. That was strange, but if I cannot rely on a doctor's report, who should I believe?'

'Look, General,' replied Morgen. 'I make it my business to prevent this.'

'Carry on what you are doing,' said Müller, 'but talk to the local Gestapo regional office in, I don't know, Kattowitz [now Katowice] or Gleiwitz [now Gliwice] and find out from them about the specific tasks of the Gestapo in the concentration camps and local regional office there.'

Morgen decided not to follow Müller's instruction to talk to the

Gestapo regional office, as he didn't want to fetter his discretion to act as he saw best. Instead he kept Grabner in custody and charged him with 2,000 counts of murder.[15] Alongside the investigation into Grabner, he also opened investigations into Höss and Aumeier for perjury and one count of attempted murder.

THE CASE OF ELEONORE HODYS

What Morgen and his investigative teams had needed was a reliable witness who could testify to what was happening in Auschwitz and specifically in Block 11. And very quickly, Morgen found one. Eleonore Hodys was a political prisoner from Austria who had been initially sent to an ordinary prison at Hamm near Dortmund for defaming the state and for high treason. Having served her sentence, she was then sent to the concentration camp at Ravensbrück and from there she was sent to Auschwitz in 1942.

When Morgen found her, she was being held in one of the four so-called 'standing cells' in Block 11. These cells were designed as a form of torture for the prisoners who were held there. They were only one square metre wide and the only air in the cell came from a grill which was 5 centimetres by 5 centimetres wide. Entry was through a hatch, which was set low in the wall. Four prisoners were put into each cell and were forced to stand in these cells for as long as the SS decided, which in Hodys's case was for days on end. She had been confined to one of these cells because the commandant of Auschwitz, Höss, had made her pregnant and now he wanted to murder her. He had given the bunker staff specific instructions that she was to be left in this cell to die of starvation but when Morgen found her, the SS guards had been keeping her alive against their orders by occasionally giving her something to eat and drink.

Höss could, of course, have simply had her shot, but by starving her to death he would have been able to record her death as being from natural causes, which would have meant that he would have escaped scrutiny. However, Morgen found her and immediately had her released. Unsurprisingly, after all that she had been through in Auschwitz she was very poorly and Morgen eventually took her out of Auschwitz and to a hospital in Munich run by nuns where over time, during October 1944, he coaxed a statement out of her.

Höss had noticed her from the time she had arrived at Auschwitz, when the call had gone out for anyone with skills and she had put herself forward as a pharmacist. Instead of sending her to the hospital, he ordered her to report to his wife Hedwig at their house. When Hodys arrived, Hedwig Höss asked her if she could repair a carpet for her and this was the start of a relatively privileged life for Hodys. She made tapestries, blankets and cushions – anything which Hedwig found for her to do.

She worked in the Höss house by day and returned to the camp at night. Because she was working in the Höss house she was able to eat the same food as the Höss family, which she compared in her statement to Morgen as similar to food you would expect to find in a large hotel: typically a starter of soup, followed by meat and vegetables, and then pastries, cakes, fruit salad and coffee to finish it all off.[16] She worked alongside two other seamstresses, both Jews, and together they lived this life of relative luxury when compared to the lives of other prisoners in the camp.

It wasn't long before the other prisoners noticed that Höss was paying her particular attention. He would call in to see her if they were both in the camp together, and when Hodys told him she shared a room with four other prisoners, he instructed Aumeier to move her into her own single room in Block 4, which she was allowed to decorate herself and find her own furniture for. In addition, Höss allowed her out of the camp to visit the town of Oświęcim at night and she was even able to stay out for the night in the SS accommodation. Höss allowed her to smoke and even organised a birthday party for her in his house.

Then one day when Hodys was working at the Höss house and Hedwig was out, Höss came to her and kissed her. Surprised and frightened, she ran to the toilet and locked herself inside. That was the end of her visits and work at the Höss house. Hodys told Morgen that she actually liked Höss as a person but that the gulf between them both, she the political prisoner, he the concentration camp commandant, was too great.

After rejecting Höss, Hodys was promised a job as a pharmacist at the SS hospital in Auschwitz, but instead she was sent to the cell block. Her detention conditions were still better than those of the other prisoners in the bunker – she had her own cell with her welfare being watched over by Aumeier and Grabner. They told her that the commandant himself was in charge of deciding what happened to her. Due to her incarceration in the cell block, Hodys was able to provide Morgen with details of individual prisoners who were subjected to the regular 'clearing-out' sessions in the bunker and who were executed. These details then formed the basis of the charges against Grabner. On one occasion, Hodys herself was taken out to be shot but when Grabner and Aumeier saw her being taken out, she was immediately sent back inside again. Later, Grabner told her it had been a joke on the part of one of the SS guards.

Then, one night, Höss came to see her in her cell. He told her that he had been ill but he had come to visit her at the first opportunity he had. Hodys was confused. She had written to him to ask to be released; why hadn't he answered? She would be released, he said, and again he tried to kiss her. Hodys, remembering how she had been taken out to be shot, backed off but Höss told her that he would return. When he did return a couple of nights later, he asked her if he should leave but this time she said 'No' and they had sex. This turned into a routine. Over the course of the next four days, Höss would visit her at night for sex. On one occasion he had to hide naked behind the door of the cell because the guard did his rounds and looked through the spy hole into the cell where they were.

Despite the risks, Höss was never caught. After four nights, he stopped coming to see Hodys and after a while, she became sick with regular vomiting. One of the camp doctors examined her and told her she was eight weeks pregnant. When the doctor asked her who the father was, she refused to name Höss. She obtained some drugs for an abortion but these did not work. The next thing she knew, she was confined in one of the standing cells in the bunker. This time the SS had orders to let her die, but through occasional gifts of food from individual guards she stayed alive for the nine weeks she was in the cell. Sometimes she was on her own and could kneel down. When she was first put into the standing cell she shared it with a dead body, which she only found out about because she could feel it in the darkness of the cell.

At this point in her statement, Morgen made a note that she

became emotional, owing to the terrible time she had endured. She then told Morgen that after her release, and before she had been transferred to Munich, she had had an abortion in the camp hospital. She also told Morgen that one of his colleagues, SS investigating judge Sergeant Gerhard Wiebeck, had interviewed her in her room in the presence of Höss. When Hodys told Wiebeck that Höss must have known who was in the cell block with her, Höss, clearly rattled, put his hand on the bed to steady himself. He maintained that she was in the bunker for her own protection and that he hadn't known about her being in a standing cell.

After she left the camp hospital, still struggling with illness, Morgen had had her transferred to hospital in Munich, where he took her statement in the autumn of 1944. Morgen was delighted that she had talked to him. He had Grabner imprisoned the whole time and this was just what he needed to bring him, Höss and others at Auschwitz to court. On 9 October, he wrote to his fiancée Maria to tell her that he had been in Munich for the past two days: 'I now have new evidence in my possession which will bring the slow moving Weimar trials to a just end and which will prove I have been right.'[17] In his next letter, two days later, he had nothing further to report, and then on 13 October he wrote again:

> This afternoon I am going to Munich again to visit my prisoner whom I already wrote to you about. I am hoping for a big success for my efforts and for the scalps of a large number of dangerous criminals. Apart from that she is in every way a remarkable personality, she is charming and feminine in a Viennese way, she has had an academic education and has travelled extensively to

> Abyssinia, Africa, Palestine and Italy. She is a pharmacist and bacteriologist and she is sophisticated and intelligent … but not an intellectual, an artist of the needle whose hands must have crafted amazing tapestry works. On the other hand she is a convicted political criminal, divorced and she has been ill for a year. This lady is a phenomenon of willpower, it is unbelievable what she has endured without affecting her character or looks.[18]

Morgen's sessions with Hodys had a great impact on him and he clearly cared deeply about her. On 15 October, he had a marathon ten-hour interrogation session with her where she described her imprisonment to him. Emotionally exhausted, Morgen wrote the next day to Maria, 'I was so drained that I couldn't do anything productive before my train left. I walked up and down at the Munich-Ost railway station for nearly an hour … I thought so longingly of you.'[19]

On 22 October, Morgen had his last session with Hodys. With his other letters, he had always told Maria about Hodys after talking about other things but in this letter, he launched straight into telling her about his last two days with her:

> Darling, this afternoon I returned from Munich. For two days I have been in the orthopaedic hospital where my prisoner now resides … Small children, teenage girls with amputated legs dragging themselves along, wounded soldiers, they are all looked after by the Catholic sisters in their white nun's headdresses. They are female enough to appreciate friendly words and gestures. There is a good atmosphere in this building and I was thinking that amid

> the general decline in standards we still care for the helpless, the disfigured and disabled with compassion and without excluding anyone. At noon the air raid sirens sounded for a long time, I was in the cellar with all the patients. Suddenly the nuns and the children started to pray the rosary, 'Blessed art thou amongst women, and blessed is the fruit of thy womb … now and at the hour of our death.' Does it always have to be like this? My prisoner was very awkward and was feeling unwell. Me too. So we didn't achieve anything on the first day. I went to bed at 5 p.m. in the afternoon completely done in and woke up the next morning at 9.30. The next day we caught up and I am glad to have finished this awful chapter. I'm sorry I can't do more to help this unfortunate woman. Even if the case is clear-cut everything can get bogged down in bureaucracy without someone influential to help. Who will take an interest in her when I am no longer running the case? Only her enemies. Perhaps one day she will be made to suffer for giving me her trust. She realised that as we finished, she was in despair. I could only offer her my goodwill but what is that worth to a woman who has been let down so often?[20]

Morgen's fears were well founded but in the end, Eleonore Hodys survived the war. After the war, while Morgen was imprisoned by the Americans and giving testimony at the various Nuremberg trials, he asked Maria to find out Hodys's whereabouts, presumably so he could check how she was doing. The police in Leipzig replied that she was registered there.[21]

Actually, Hodys had been taken into police custody in Leipzig for one month between March and April 1945 as a former concentration camp prisoner. She had been married in 1927 to an Italian,

Pietro Mattaliano, and she had become an Italian citizen.[22] This marriage lasted until 1952.[23] The 1963–5 Auschwitz trial in Frankfurt was interested in Hodys and the judge asked if she was still alive. He was informed that the prosecution team's information was that she was still living in Leipzig until a couple of years before the trial started.[24]

* * *

The year 1943 had been one of success for Konrad Morgen. He had survived a winter on the Eastern Front and the fierce fighting against the Soviet Army. He had been recalled from the front, reinstated into his old officer rank and promoted. He had had success in Buchenwald and Auschwitz. But in 1944, his enemies were circling again, determined more than ever to frustrate his efforts. One sign of this came in Auschwitz itself, when a fire destroyed the office where Morgen and his investigative team stored their evidence and their official investigation files. Another came in his efforts to arrest Höss, who was protected by Morgen's old enemy SS General Oswald Pohl.*

But Morgen wasn't finished, not at all. As he said in his letter to Maria, he had evidence to move forward the slow-moving Auschwitz trial against Grabner and the court was still to hold the Weimar trials of SS Colonel Karl-Otto Koch from Buchenwald and SS Major Hermann Florstedt from Majdanek. As the war moved into its final stages, Konrad Morgen still had all to play for.

---

* SS Sergeant Körfer, who had started off the chain of events by trying to steal the dental gold, was sent to prison for twelve years.

CHAPTER 8

THE INVESTIGATIONS INTO ADOLF EICHMANN AND OTHERS

DAY UNKNOWN, JANUARY 1942

SS Lieutenant Colonel Adolf Eichmann is in Kulm (Chełmno) in Nazi-occupied Poland on a fact-finding mission. He is under orders from his boss, Gestapo chief SS General Heinrich Müller, to observe how the SS kills Jews in Kulm and report back to him at the Reich Security Main Office with his findings and observations. Müller isn't with Eichmann on this trip; he prefers to stay in the background at his desk in Prinz-Albrecht-Straße where he works long into the night and without holidays in order to ensure the security of the Reich and the success of the Final Solution.

When he arrives at the designated place where the killings are scheduled to take place, Eichmann observes naked Jews climbing into a large van. Once they are all inside, the doors are closed and locked and Eichmann notices that the exhaust pipe is fed back into the van. A doctor in a white coat invites Eichmann to look through a peephole in the side of van and observe the deadly effects of the exhaust gas on the Jews inside.

Once they are all dead, the driver of the van leads the convoy and Eichmann follows the van in his car down a forest track to a meadow where a pit has been excavated. The van lines itself up, the doors open and the naked bodies fall out into the pit. Before they are burned, a civilian moves among the bodies, opening their mouths and pulling out any gold fillings with pliers.

The next stop on Eichmann's killing tour is Minsk in the Nazi-occupied Soviet Union. The weather is bitterly cold and Eichmann is well wrapped up in a long padded coat and a plentiful supply of red wine, which he prefers to spirits. He is late arriving at Minsk and misses the first day of killing, but the next morning he is in time to witness the last group of Jews being killed. He can hear the sound of the machine guns as he approaches the pits where the Jews are being shot and he and his driver arrive in time to witness the shooting of a Jewish mother with a small child in her arms. Eichmann is standing so close to the pit that when the bullets hit the child in the head, his driver immediately sets about cleaning Eichmann's coat, which has been spattered with bits of the child's brain. They get back into the car and Eichmann tells his driver to take him to Berlin. Along the way, he consumes large quantities of schnapps and he thinks about his own children.

When they arrive back in Berlin, Eichmann reports to Müller and asks to be relieved of his position. Müller tells him, 'The soldier at the front cannot choose where he would like to fight. But he has to do his duty where he is placed.'[1] With this in his mind, Eichmann continues with his planning and organisation for the mass deportations of Jews to their deaths.

On Friday 10 July 1942, with the deportations of the Jews underway, Eichmann receives a memo from Paris asking about what should happen to 4,000 Jewish children who have been identified as stateless. He asks for advice within the Reich Security Main Office and is told the children are to be deported. He passes the instruction back to Paris and, once again, thinks about his own children.[2]

Auschwitz was accustomed to receiving transports of Jewish families, but occasionally a transport containing only Jewish children arrived. In October 1944, a Jewish member of the *Sonderkommando*, Zalman Lewenthal, witnessed the arrival of a Jewish child transport containing 600 boys wearing rags and with clogs on their feet:

> When the children saw the clouds of thick smoke, they realised at once that they were being taken to their death. They began to run in all directions within the courtyard, mad with fear, pulling out their hair and not knowing how to save themselves. Many of them began crying in terror and they all started to howl. The [SS] *Kommandoführer* and his assistants beat the children savagely in order to make them undress ... The SS men chased them, rushing and whipping, until they took control of the situation and finally shoved them inside. They [the SS] were unimaginably happy. Were none of them ever fathers?*[3]

* * *

* Zalman Lewenthal wrote one of the 'Scrolls of Auschwitz'. These were personal accounts by members of the *Sonderkommando*, who knew they would not survive Auschwitz because members of the *Sonderkommando* were routinely killed after a few months. They wrote their accounts down and buried the manuscripts in the hope that they would be found and the world would discover their stories.

Having found out the extent of the mass killings at the extermination camps, Morgen made further enquiries into the operation of the system that had resulted in millions of people being deported to the extermination camps. Morgen subsequently identified Adolf Eichmann and his staff as being key to the process of deporting these people to their deaths and he decided to go after Eichmann in order to disrupt the system. Eichmann worked for SS General Heinrich Müller in Group IV B of the Reich Security Main Office. Eichmann had previously been a part of the security police apparatus, but this position now gave him the authority to issue orders to all Gestapo offices to ensure that his deportation programme could proceed as smoothly as possible.

Morgen interviewed Eichmann, who told him about his work managing the deportations of the Jews and how he negotiated with local administrations and authorities about deadlines and the transfer of Jewish assets to those administrations.[4] In this way, Eichmann told Morgen, he won over the local authorities, especially in the wider Reich, who might otherwise have resisted the deportations. Once he had their support, he would liaise with local police officials and also demand from the local Jewish communities the names of a minimum number of Jews who could be 'resettled' by being sent to the extermination camps in Nazi-occupied Poland. Eichmann would promise the Jewish leaders exemption from resettlement if they cooperated with his demands. Eichmann also told Morgen that he organised the transport of the Jews as military transport trains so that the departure and transit railway stations did not know the final destinations of these trains.

By mid-1944, Morgen had assembled enough evidence against Eichmann to ask the SS Court in Berlin to carry out an investigation into him. As with his previous investigations, Morgen started building his case with an inquiry into corruption; in Eichmann's case, it was diamonds. Morgen had found out about a pouch of diamonds in a safe in the headquarters of the secret police that was connected to Eichmann's department and launched his investigation. However, because Morgen's jurisdiction was limited to the concentration camps and Eichmann was a part of the Reich Security Main Office in Berlin, he had to ask his colleagues in the SS court in Berlin for an SS judge to investigate on his behalf. They appointed a Dr Bachmann, an SS judge, to do this.

The SS court in Berlin sent two police detectives from the Reich Central Detective Office to talk to Eichmann. They asked him about a pouch of precious stones and Eichmann told them what he knew. Bachmann then summoned Eichmann and he was interrogated, with a police sergeant taking notes. Unsettled, Eichmann set his staff to do more research and they found correspondence between SS General Heinrich Müller, head of the Gestapo, and SS General Richard Glücks, inspector of concentration camps, about a pouch of diamonds in a safe in the Reich Security Main Office.

Meanwhile, SS judge Bachmann had issued a warrant for the arrest of Adolf Eichmann. This warrant went to SS General Ernst Kaltenbrunner, head of the Reich Security Main Office, for action. Bachmann later told Morgen that this arrest warrant against Eichmann resulted in what he called 'rather dramatic incidents'. Kaltenbrunner immediately consulted SS General Heinrich Müller, head of Office IV, the Gestapo, which included Group IV B, Eichmann's office. Bachmann was informed by Kaltenbrunner that Eichmann would not be arrested as he was carrying out a secret task of the utmost importance for the Führer.

At the same time, Eichmann took the letters he had found about the diamonds to his boss, Müller, who told him that the arrest order against him had just been turned down. Eichmann told Müller he felt he had been treated very badly by the SS court and he asked that the SS judge Bachmann should come and apologise to Eichmann in front of his staff for putting him through a criminal investigation, which he did. Morgen's attempt to put Eichmann out of action by organising an investigation through the SS court in Berlin had failed. After the war, Eichmann managed to escape to Argentina where he was eventually found and taken to Israel by Mossad agents. He was tried by a Jerusalem court and hanged in 1962.

* * *

Konrad Morgen's workload was extraordinary. His investigation into Eichmann was carried out alongside his main activities in concentration camps. He installed investigative commissions into a number of camps, despite opposition from SS General Oswald Pohl, head of the concentration camps in Berlin.

One concentration camp which Morgen investigated personally, without any assistance, was Herzogenbusch concentration camp at Vught in the Netherlands. Early in 1944, a small group of Dutch women prisoners had fallen out and when the SS demanded to know the names of the women involved in the quarrel, twenty-three stepped forward, far more than had been involved. The camp commandant, SS Major Adam Grünewald, was incensed at this act of solidarity and he ordered the guards to imprison as many as possible in a single cell in the bunker. Seventy-four women were forced into a cell designed to hold only two or three prisoners. When the prisoners were released, ten were dead.

When Morgen investigated, SS General Pohl told him, 'What do the lives of ten women matter in view of the thousands of German women dying every night in the air raids?'[5] However, Morgen was undaunted. He arrested Grünewald, who was sent swiftly for trial, probably because the news had leaked out – not at Morgen's court in Kassel but at an SS and police court in the Netherlands. Grünewald was demoted and sent to the Eastern Front, where he was killed. The resistance from Pohl and the concentration camp commandants was sustained and a real risk to Morgen and his team.

Morgen sent his investigative team into Sachsenhausen concentration camp to investigate the previous commandant, SS Senior Colonel Hans Loritz, for corruption and murder. Loritz had been transferred out the previous year and sent to Norway. He had been born early enough (1895) to have served in the First World War, after which he had joined the Augsburg police. However, his use of violence saw him removed from the police and the city found him a new job, as it was obliged to do, as a debt collector for the gasworks. When the Nazis came to power, Loritz applied to run a concentration camp. He was described by one prisoner at Esterwegen concentration camp where Loritz had previously been commandant as a 'beast in human form'.[6] When he ordered the shooting of Soviet political prisoners, Loritz was credited with inventing a new method of execution. The prisoner was invited in for a medical check and when he was having his height measured, an SS guard shot him in the neck through a hole in the wall.

Alongside enriching himself personally, Loritz also used concentration camp prisoners for his own purposes. He had them build a boathouse, bowling alley and a game park, which he lamely suggested were for the use of the SS at the camp.[7]

Unlike Buchenwald, where Morgen had carried out his investigations against Koch with the cooperation of his replacement, Pister, at Sachsenhausen he had to contend with a hostile camp commandant, SS Colonel Anton Kaindl. On one occasion, one of the witnesses at the camp, a man called Rothe, was about to be hanged after Pohl requested an order from the Reich Security Main Office under false pretences – really as an example to other inmates not to cooperate with Morgen and his team. Luckily, one of Morgen's team heard about it at the last minute and was able to prevent it from happening. Sachsenhausen was also where Morgen pioneered the use of new technology. Due to the reluctance of the prisoners to come forward with information after the episode with Rothe, he brought potential witnesses among the prisoners together and then used SS listening devices to record their conversations through the walls of the office when they thought they were alone.

Loritz would ultimately evade prosecution following Morgen's investigation. He committed suicide in Soviet custody after the war.

* * *

Two other camps where investigations were initiated by Morgen resulted in the arrests of the commandants. Both were in Warsaw, one in Warsaw concentration camp where an investigation into corruption led to the arrest of SS Captain Nikolaus Herbet and one in Kraków-Płaszów concentration camp, where the commandant was the notorious SS Captain Amon Göth. He had taken over the camp in February 1943 and immediately introduced a reign of terror over the prisoners, who tried to avoid him because of his habit of picking inmates at random and beating them to death. He had two dogs and would set them on prisoners. On one occasion, one of his dogs, Rolf, killed one of the inmates for no other reason than Göth ordered him to. He held frequent roll calls and barrack searches so that he could further terrorise the prisoners, and on one occasion he lined up a group of young naked prisoners, walking up and down and looking at them before shooting several at random. The brutality wasn't just confined to Göth – his officers and the SS Ukrainian guards were also noted for their cruelty.

Shortly after arriving at Kraków-Płaszów, Göth was given the job of clearing the Jewish ghetto at Kraków. This involved bringing up to 10,000 Jews to the camp as well as the bodies of 2,000 Jews, which were buried in a mass grave. Once the Jews were imprisoned in the camp it was much more difficult to escape, especially since Göth shot ten prisoners for every one who did manage to escape. In September 1943, Göth oversaw the clearing of the Jewish ghetto at Tarnów as well.[8]

Morgen's investigation of Göth centred on corruption, especially the way in which he helped himself to Jewish valuables, money and possessions from the clearing of the ghettos and accepted bribes from Oskar Schindler, who was paying money to protect individual Jews – a relationship that meant he became a suspect in the corruption enquiries as well. In the end, although Morgen arrested Göth, he escaped justice from the SS and was still awaiting trial when the war ended. The Americans turned him over to the Polish authorities, who tried and executed him near to the camp which he had commanded.

With all of these investigations going on, Morgen felt that the special court in Kassel which he had been working for was not sufficient to meet the challenges he was now facing.[9] For a start, he could only investigate crimes in the concentration camps and he wanted to be able to investigate crimes wherever he found them without having to involve local SS courts and police. Morgen's idea was based on the main Wehrmacht court – he wanted a single central SS court based at Munich, where the SS judiciary was, and with Morgen as the main investigator.

Himmler agreed with Morgen and a new central SS court was set up in Munich with its own investigative office, under the leadership of SS judge Lieutenant Colonel Kurt Mittelstädt, in early May 1944. But there were immediate challenges. All the files from Morgen's cases were moved across to Munich; there were no tables and chairs and there was no team in place to make sense of it all. Soon, Mittelstädt felt they were being overwhelmed. 'It'll never work,' he said to Morgen in despair. 'Stop your work in the concentration camps and come and sort this out, the place isn't functioning.' And worse was to come: the SS judiciary building in Munich was hit in an air raid and burned down. They moved to Prien, but the relationship between Mittelstädt and Morgen started to deteriorate.

SS General Oswald Pohl of the SS Main Economic and Administrative Office had chosen this moment to start agitating against Morgen and his work again. At first, he told Morgen that he welcomed his investigations and that he wanted to work closely with him and that Morgen would be very welcome to visit him and report so they could work together. When Morgen stayed away, Pohl started to criticise him again. Things came to a head when Pohl wrote to Morgen, 'My dear Morgen, I am now doubting your common sense. In your reports you have said X and Y about my enterprises. Sit yourself down and write to everyone you have informed about these false reports and tell them they are false [reports]. Don't do it again'.[10] Morgen wrote back a very flowery response but this now caused a rift with Mittelstädt, who was caught in the middle between his determined investigator and Pohl.

At the same time, Morgen received new orders from *Reichsführer* Heinrich Himmler to go to Hungary and investigate corruption, an investigation which went nowhere but which was to cause Morgen problems after the war when allegations were made by Mittelstädt that Morgen had drawn up a leaflet encouraging Jews to take their valuables with them when they were deported. Morgen denied them and nothing came of them.

Pohl then adopted new tactics to rid himself of the troublesome Konrad Morgen. Further investigations, he told the Reich Security Main Office, would unsettle the concentration camps. Office V of the *Reichskriminalpolizeiamt*, the Central Police Detective Office of the Reich, where Morgen was attached as a police official, told Morgen they were now caught between Pohl and SS General Kaltenbrunner on the one hand and Morgen, backed by Himmler, on the other. With a worsening situation in Germany's war, Himmler ordered that Morgen's unit stop taking on new cases and work only on existing ones.

One of those cases that was still pending was the Buchenwald trial, which still had not taken place. Himmler wanted to use the trial, assuming that Koch was going to be found guilty, to make an example of Koch. He planned to invite all the SS concentration camp commandants to Buchenwald where Koch would be hanged in the evening firelight, and while Koch was hanging, Himmler would make a speech to all the commandants telling them that they now had the opportunity to confess anything they had done wrong. If they confessed, they would be forgiven, but if they didn't confess and were later found guilty of something, they would be shot. Morgen argued against this plan, saying that such a spectacle 'would not be a punishment and would have no effect on this gang of criminals'.[11] But before any of this could happen, the trial needed to take place.

Pohl continued to increase the pressure on Morgen. Through SS Lieutenant Colonel Kurt Schmidt-Klevenow, head of the legal department at the SS Main Economic and Administrative Office under Pohl, he peppered the Reich Security Main Office with complaints about Morgen and even tried to cut off Morgen's direct channel to SS Senior Colonel and judge Horst Bender, who was on Himmler's staff and who was the liaison between Himmler and the SS judiciary. Pohl issued instructions that no member of the SS judiciary was to be allowed to enter a concentration camp without his permission.

Then Pohl talked to SS General Heinrich Müller and together they came up with a plan. Müller and his boss, SS General Ernst Kaltenbrunner, head of the Reich Security Main Office, went to see Himmler to discuss Morgen. According to Morgen, they told Himmler, 'He has worked really hard; he has cleared up a lot of things and has had huge success. But now justice has been served. Any further investigative work in the concentration camps will lead to disorder and the discipline of the prisoners will be put at risk.' They added that security could not be guaranteed; work in the concentration camps was being obstructed and guarantees could no longer be made to the arms industry, which relied on prisoner labour. Pohl added that he would resign from all his positions if Morgen didn't disappear.

Why was Pohl so afraid of Morgen? SS General Richard Glücks, inspector of the concentration camps, told Morgen that it was because he was a thorn in Pohl's side. Through his investigations, Morgen had a direct reporting line to Himmler, who found out from him things about the concentration camps that he hadn't learned from any report that Pohl had sent through to him. Pohl was starting to worry about his job and Glücks told Morgen that Pohl came out of every meeting with Himmler 'with wobbly knees'.[12] According to Morgen, Pohl's main worry wasn't really about his job; instead it was about losing access to the wealth he was accumulating personally through his position running the concentration camps.

With all this going on, Morgen's boss, Mittelstädt, said to him, 'In order to achieve the best outcome it might be best if you are no longer personally involved. We have enough people we can use, just stay in the background and supervise.'[13] Morgen was suspicious of Mittelstädt and suspected him of double-dealing. Morgen heard from Bender, who was on Himmler's staff, that Mittelstädt was going behind his back and telling Himmler that he wasn't a good investigator.[14] Whatever behind-the-scenes conversations were going on, several things now happened to Konrad Morgen all at once.

Since he started work investigating the concentration camps, Morgen had had a dual line of reporting. He was both an SS investigating judge responsible to the SS judiciary in Munich and he was also a police official reporting to the *Reichskriminalpolizeiamt*.

After a request from the SS judiciary, Himmler now removed the reporting line to the Central Police Detective Office and Morgen was now back to being an SS investigating judge, as he had been at the start of his SS judicial career.

The result of the last whispering campaign against Morgen had been that Himmler demoted him and sent him to the Eastern Front as a member of the Waffen SS. This time, in response to Pohl's campaign, Himmler decided to award Morgen a promotion to SS major and a three-week holiday. In doing this, he was sending mixed signals: on the one hand he was thanking Morgen for his work and on the other he was removing him from his investigative duties and giving his enemies a break from him. And lastly, Morgen was to be transferred back to the SS court at Kraków, away from his troublesome boss. But before Morgen could take up his holiday and his new position, there were trials to be conducted where Morgen was a key witness.

THE CONCENTRATION CAMP TRIALS

The setting for the trial of the concentration camp personnel who had been investigated and indicted by Morgen was Kranichfeld Castle, about nineteen miles from Buchenwald as the crow flies. In September 1944, the SS court assembled here for cases including those of SS Colonel Karl-Otto Koch, Ilse Koch, SS Captain Dr Waldemar Hoven and SS Sergeant Martin Sommer from Buchenwald concentration camp and SS Lieutenant Maximilian Grabner, former head of the Gestapo and political section at Auschwitz. Others including SS Major Hermann Florstedt, former commandant of Majdanek extermination camp, were probably brought here to be tried, although there is no documentary evidence for this or for anything at all pertaining to Florstedt after his arrest and return to Buchenwald. However, Morgen and other SS judges were very clear that he was tried and shot.[15]

At the trials, Morgen came face to face with his old enemy, SS Lieutenant Colonel Kurt Schmidt-Klevenow, who attended the trial on behalf of Pohl. Because of the importance of this event for the SS, other senior figures were also present, such as SS General Richard Glücks and a number of observers from the SS, including SS Senior Colonel Hermann Pister, commandant of Buchenwald after Koch, who was there to represent Buchenwald concentration camp.[16]

Morgen found the atmosphere in the court hostile. One of Morgen's colleagues, SS Lieutenant Gerhard Wiebeck, told him that he had heard from the chief of police in Weimar that an arrest warrant had been made out for Morgen. When Wiebeck told them that Morgen could not be arrested and accused while he was testifying in the trial, they said they would wait until it was over. Morgen also heard the same story from an SS Captain Jansen from the Security Police Training Academy in Berlin, who was there because he was a friend of Waldemar Hoven. As Morgen remarked later, 'The real trial was not against the accused but against me as the investigator and attorney.'[17] Another one of his colleagues who had been talking to Glücks reported to Morgen that Glücks had said to him, 'Are you still with Morgen? I think he's done for.' When his colleague had asked why, Glücks simply repeated his line: 'Just listen to me, his number's up.'

As the trial got underway, the hostility increased. After each day, Schmidt-Klevenow and the others would go out for meals together, where they would talk about Morgen behind his back.

Schmidt-Klevenow told the court that Morgen had exaggerated the facts and sent false reports through to Himmler. He said that Morgen had brought the SS into disrepute and disrupted the work of the concentration camps. In setting out this line of attack, Morgen was clear that Schmidt-Klevenow was asserting the validity of the whole concentration camp system:

> In saying this Schmidt-Klevenow was affirming the way concentration camps committed murder and accused me as investigator and representative of the prosecution of turning against this system. On the other hand I relied on the legal system which was still in force, namely the murder paragraphs [in the normal German legal code] and also on the orders which were issued by the *Reichsführer* and the Führer in respect of concentration camps, namely, 'The Führer himself makes decisions about the life of an enemy of the state.' That meant these cases were excluded and they could not rely on any (legal) power to kill prisoners.[18]

In advance of the trial, Himmler had directed that the death sentence should be passed against Koch and Hoven, but Pohl and Schmidt-Klevenow wanted to get them off. There were two lines of attack. For Koch, Schmidt-Klevenow persuaded the court to separate out the murder charges from the corruption charges. He argued that Koch should not face murder charges and instead a new trial should take place to consider the corruption charges only, with Himmler's approval. Schmidt-Klevenow told the court that the order that only the Führer could make a decision about the life of an enemy of the state was open to interpretation. Then SS Colonel Dr Werner Heyde from the Reich Security Main Office told the court that in respect of Hoven, doctors like him had been given free rein to operate; he had acted in good faith and was, at worst, a borderline case.[19]

Schmidt-Klevenow was in his element. According to Morgen, he was effective because he didn't recognise the independence of the SS court. For Schmidt-Klevenow, the court was part of the SS like everything else and subject to orders from above, especially from him.

On 12 September, while the trial was going on, Morgen wrote to Maria with the news that he had been given the three-week holiday by Himmler, but before then he had to face the courtroom again. 'Instead of having a relaxing day, I must return to the fight for justice so I can validate honour through my own being.'[20]

Thanks to Schmidt-Klevenow and Heyde, doubts arose in the minds of the judges, especially the chief judge, SS Lieutenant Colonel Ende. Koch then introduced a new defence, which was that SS General Ernst-Robert Grawitz, the chief Reich physician, had told the doctors at Buchenwald to carry out the commandant's orders to kill prisoners and that this then meant that Koch, as commandant, had the legal power to order the killings.

As a result, the trial was postponed. For this first trial, Morgen had had the status of an attorney and as such was a part of the court, but with his transfer, he returned to the second trial as a witness only. The final verdict in the case of SS Colonel Karl-Otto Koch, in this continuation of the trial, was that he was found guilty of corruption but not of murder. As Morgen remarked:

> The court had no courage to judge about the murders. The only sentence awarded was for the frauds and for those Koch was

> condemned to death and his wife acquitted because of the lack of evidence ... Koch was the test case for the SS jurisdiction. I tried to make it easy to be a success with the formulation of my bill of indictment which had to be [drawn up] in accordance with Nazi law. But it was only a half success, because all the others didn't dare or didn't want to change the system and to establish in this test case, that the life of man is holy.[21]

In the end, Himmler's plan for a grand execution ceremony for Koch came to nothing. With the end of the war in sight, in 1945 Koch was taken out of his cell at Buchenwald and shot by order of SS General Prince Josias of Waldeck. After the war, Ilse Koch was arrested by the Americans and sentenced to life imprisonment, which was later reduced to four years. Morgen had given evidence at her trial and had refused to cooperate with the Americans when they wanted him to testify that she had made lampshades out of human skin. He told the American historian John Toland that the Americans had threatened to kill him if he didn't but he refused.[22] While she was in prison, Ilse became pregnant and her son Uwe Köhler, born in 1947, was taken away from her and given to the Bavarian authorities. He only found out who his birth mother was when he was nineteen. After she was released by the Americans, she was given a life sentence after a third trial in Germany and she committed suicide in prison in 1967. Her son had got in touch with her and was visiting her on a regular basis when she died.[23]

In the case of SS Captain Dr Waldemar Hoven, the court was similarly indecisive and deferred its decision. He was released towards the end of the war. However, justice caught up with him in the form of the American authorities, who charged him with war crimes and crimes against humanity relating to his work on the euthanasia programme and medical experiments using prisoners, as well as with membership of a criminal organisation, the SS. The Americans also convicted him of murdering prisoners in the same way as Morgen had uncovered.[24] He was hanged in 1948.

SS Sergeant Martin Sommer also escaped justice from the SS. Despite his being charged, there is no record of a verdict against him. He was sent to the front line after the trial, where he was badly injured when a shell hit the tank he was driving. Captured by American soldiers, his life was saved – had they known who he was, he would probably have been tried and sentenced to death. Eventually, he was sentenced to life imprisonment by the German authorities in 1958 for the murders which he committed. He was released into a nursing home in 1971.

In between the gaps in the Buchenwald trial in Kranichfeld, the SS court also tried SS Lieutenant Maximilian Grabner from Auschwitz, who had been charged with 2,000 counts of murder. This court had a different chairman, SS judge Werner Hansen, and Morgen took time before the trial to give him the background to what was happening at Auschwitz in terms of the extermination programme. Hansen later recalled:

> Doctor Morgen described these mass killings to me and was horrified and outraged by these measures which were being carried out by the highest authorities. And he said that it should now be our job to at least stop it somehow, as far as we can, and to pursue what measures we could.[25]

At the trial, Grabner put forward a similar defence to that put forward in the Buchenwald trial, namely that he was acting under orders when he killed these prisoners. The problem for him was that there was no proof that these orders ever existed. Hansen asked the SS judiciary headquarters to carry out a search to see if these orders did in fact exist, but all they could turn up was an order from Himmler stating that no prisoner was to allowed to be killed or mistreated. It was the same story at the Reich Security Main Office: they couldn't find any orders covering the people Grabner killed, only orders from Himmler forbidding prisoners to be killed or mistreated.

Grabner himself had been in Gestapo detention for nearly a year and, according to SS Lieutenant Wilhelm Boger, had become a 'living corpse'.[26] Rudolf Höss turned up at Weimar to support his officer and struck an arrogant pose, telling the court, 'What is it you actually want? You have no idea what's going on here!'

'Tell me, what's going on here?' replied Hansen. Höss told him about the transports and how the selection process worked, whereupon Hansen asked him, 'Were the prisoners taken to the cell block?'

'No,' said Höss.

'So why are you telling me this?' replied Hansen. 'It has nothing to do with the indictment.'

These exchanges went on for some time and Hansen had the same reply for each: 'What you are saying does not excuse the 2,000 murders which are the subject of this indictment.'

When Hansen was repeating all this to the courtroom in Frankfurt at the 1963–5 Auschwitz trial, the trial judge asked him about this conversation. 'So if I understand correctly, he [Höss] wanted to get across the point that what were 2,000 people when entire transports were being killed there on orders from above?'[27]

'That's exactly how it was,' agreed Hansen, who went on to tell the court that every time Höss used this argument he refuted it and eventually Höss gave up and left the courtroom. Hansen then found him outside the courtroom shaking hands with Grabner and criticising the court, which Hansen interrupted and told him off.

The trial was adjourned and the next thing that Morgen heard was that the Reich Security Main Office had transferred Grabner to Berlin and released him in March 1945. He was outraged and told Hansen, 'When we lose the war, you'll be the first to be hanged!'[28]

The 1963–5 Frankfurt Auschwitz trial finally brought Wilhelm Boger to account for his actions in Auschwitz. He was found guilty of complicity in at least 1,000 murders and of complicity in the joint murders of ten further people. The court sentenced him to life imprisonment with an additional five years' hard labour. He died in prison in 1977.

After the war, the Polish authorities had no hesitation in bringing Maximilian Grabner to justice. He was arrested in Vienna and sent to Poland, where he was tried in December 1947. The court sentenced him to death and he was hanged on 28 January 1948. At the same trial, Arthur Liebehenschel, who succeeded Höss as commandant at Auschwitz, was also sentenced to death and hanged the same day. So was Hans Aumeier. In total, forty-one former Auschwitz staff were convicted of crimes in relation to the atrocities which were committed there and of these, twenty-four were executed. SS Colonel Rudolf Höss, commandant at Auschwitz, was arrested by the British after the war, gave evidence at Nuremberg and was then transferred to Poland to stand trial. Such was the interest that the trial itself was held in the Polish Teachers' Union building in Warsaw, which held 500 people, mainly former Auschwitz prisoners. The trial lasted three weeks, from March 1947 into April, and Höss was hanged at Auschwitz in the grounds of the concentration camp he once commanded.

THE END OF THE WAR

At the end of 1944, Konrad Morgen took up his new position at Kraków, the place where he had started his SS judicial career. On 12 December, he wrote to Maria about his arrival. He said that he was pleased that his reputation as the *Blutrichter*, bloodhound judge, had preceded him and told her, 'Things are going really well for me.'* Morgen was in a reflective mood in his letter:

> What lies ahead for me in the city this time? As the train emerged from the rain clouds towards Kraków, we could see the city towers below under clouds and fog. As the clouds parted, a bright light illuminated the valley like the silver mirror on the surface of a lake. It was enchantingly beautiful and unreal. Let us see it as a sign that much will be uncovered here.[29]

In later letters he suggests to Maria that she could join him there but, wisely, in the end they decide against it.

On 15 January, Morgen wrote to tell her:

> The Russians are outside Kraków. The main defences have been overpowered either because they were too weak or simply weren't

* Some commentators translate *Blutrichter* as 'hanging judge', as was the case for some Nazi judges, but in his interview with John Toland (see the introduction to this book), Morgen links it to the word 'bloodhound'.

> in place. Someone has messed up again and now things have turned out differently. Right now it's late in the night or early in the morning, whichever you prefer. I have had our files and typewriters packed up and today I will send them back to the Reich. My suitcase is also ready, destination Tarnowitz [now Tarnowskie Góry] in Upper Silesia where the court has a couple of rooms. We are staying here and waiting for the Russian tanks, either to destroy them or to be destroyed ourselves. I'm very relaxed and calm; I'm not thinking about the worst that can happen.[30]

Morgen also told Maria about a speech that Himmler gave to the Wehrmacht back on 25 July 1944 and which was read out to the staff at Kraków:

> It is still having a considerable effect on us and it has impressed us deeply. He talked about the virtues of an officer and about how un-German we have become and the speech was delivered with a frankness which we have not previously seen. The *Reichsführer* came across as a great person with a sensitive heart and was practical when it came to things which affected the troops which was unexpected.[31]

In the end, Morgen left Kraków when the Germans abandoned the city to the advancing Soviet Army. He drove south, constantly avoiding the advancing Russians. He finished up in Breslau (Wrocław), where he was in early May when the Czechs captured him amid another Russian advance and forced him to hand over all his files.[32] His letters to Maria show his destinations as he stopped using the military field post number of his location on his letters; he wrote to her from Bielitz (Bielsko-Biala) and Teschen (Cieszyn). Eventually he made his way back to Prien am Chiemsee and from there he went north into the Sudetenland – now part of the Czech Republic. He then walked westwards to Seckenheim in Baden-Württemberg, a distance he later estimated at over 1,000 kilometres.[33] From there, hearing that the US Army was looking for him, he went to Mannheim in order to give himself up to the Americans.

The war was over for Konrad Morgen. Ahead lay court appearances and interrogations, this time not as an investigating judge but, initially, as a suspect and as a witness.

CHAPTER 9

AFTER THE WAR: NUREMBERG AND OTHER TRIALS

WEDNESDAY 8 FEBRUARY 1950

At Landsberg Prison in Bavaria, a church ceremony is taking place. Oswald Pohl, former SS general and head of the SS Main Economic and Administrative Office in Berlin, is today being received into the Roman Catholic Church in a ceremony presided over by the Bishop of Augsburg. He is wearing the scarlet red jacket that denotes a prisoner condemned to death. It is the culmination of a conversion process that has come about through the ministry of Karl Morgenschweis, a Roman Catholic priest who has ministered to the inmates of Landsberg Prison from the time of the Weimar Republic, through the Third Reich and now in post-war West Germany.

Morgenschweis is delighted to welcome Pohl into the Roman Catholic Church and hopes that other senior Nazis will follow his lead. Because of the importance to the church of Pohl's conversion,

Morgenschweis sponsors a 76-page booklet written by Pohl, with a foreword by Morgenschweis, which sets out his road to Damascus. Called *My Way to God*, it is the product of Pohl's time in Landsberg. According to Morgenschweis, Pohl lives like a monk in his cell, praying, working and studying. He describes him as someone who is every inch an officer, upright and truthful, 'full of love towards Christ and the Church'.[1]

This love does not seem to extend to those whose lives he destroyed when he was an SS general. Pohl even describes himself in his booklet as ex-Waffen SS General Pohl, probably to encourage people to think he was a simple soldier, a member of the combat branch of the SS, the Waffen SS. He certainly had the Waffen SS element as an honorary title but Pohl was too busy with the concentration camps to do any front-line fighting. He denies everything: 'I did not kill anyone, nor did I ask or encourage others to do so. I was demonstrably energetic about inhumanity when I became aware of it. But did that absolve me of guilt?'[2]

US High Commissioner John J. McCloy isn't taken in by Pohl's conversion, nor does he take any account of the intensive German, American and church lobbying to save Pohl's life. Instead, in his official communication, he confirms the death sentence on Pohl, avoiding mentioning his name, and reminds everyone about his work running the concentration camps and his personal role in the destruction of the Warsaw Ghetto, when 56,000 Jews were killed or deported.[3] On 8 June 1951, Oswald Pohl is taken from his cell and hanged.

* * *

Two years after the end of the war, in 1947, Konrad Morgen and Kurt Schmidt-Klevenow both took part in another court case, this time in the trial of former SS general Oswald Pohl at Nuremberg. He had been indicted by the Allies for crimes against humanity, war crimes and membership of a criminal organisation (the SS). Their last meeting had been at the Buchenwald trial of SS Colonel Karl-Otto Koch nearly three years earlier. At that trial, Schmidt-Klevenow had worked hard to try and discredit Morgen but now, with Pohl on trial for his life, Morgen had a chance to settle old scores.

Schmidt-Klevenow was called first and gave his evidence on 3 June 1947.[4] He told the trial that his former boss, Pohl, was determined to crack down on corruption and that he took a great interest in the work of the SS courts because he wanted to make sure that everyone in his department understood that they couldn't break the law. In fact, said Schmidt-Klevenow, after the von Sauberzweig case – the SS captain sentenced to death after an investigation by Morgen – Pohl had even written an essay about the case, which had been published in the in-house SS magazine.

After Schmidt-Klevenow had talked for some time about what a great leader Pohl had been, prosecution lawyer James R. Higgins asked him:

> You stated that the defendant Pohl was greatly interested in curbing corruptions which existed in concentration camps, and he went out of his way to see that such things would not occur. And you stated also that Pohl had gotten along exceedingly well with everyone who worked with him. Was he a particularly good friend of Dr. Morgen – Konrad Morgen?[5]

This question prompted Schmidt-Klevenow to launch into a character assassination of Morgen. He was just getting into his stride, proclaiming, 'Morgen was a man who, according to his entire nature and in his behaviour, was scarcely popular with any superior. Morgen was not only—' But he was interrupted by the president of the tribunal, Robert M. Toms, judge of the Third Judicial Circuit Court of Michigan, who told him to stick to the question.[6] This provoked a more factual response: 'The relationship was not good at all.'

Higgins then read out an affidavit sworn by Morgen, in which he talked about the Sauberzweig case and how Sauberzweig had looted and stolen from Poles and sent a couple of trucks full of loot to Pohl in Berlin. Schmidt-Klevenow said he knew nothing about this; at the time he hadn't known Morgen and it was nothing to do with him.

Undeterred, Higgins pressed on but Schmidt-Klevenow was giving nothing away. He had just been a visitor at the Buchenwald trial and he knew nothing or very little about the other Morgen cases that Higgins mentioned to him. Dr Alfred Seidl, Pohl's lawyer, then asked Schmidt-Klevenow about the relationship between Pohl and Morgen. Schmidt-Klevenow launched into a full-scale attack on Morgen, and this time the tribunal allowed him to say what he wanted. Morgen had, according to Schmidt-Klevenow, done a good job on the von Sauberzweig case but thereafter had not.

In the case of the Buchenwald trial, he told the tribunal that Morgen had not prepared properly, especially when it came to the question of whether Koch's orders to kill prisoners were legal or not. And it wasn't just Kurt Schmidt-Klevenow who thought that: everyone else who attended the trial thought so too. In fact, once the verdict of death for Koch had been announced, there had been no one keener than Pohl to see it carried out. As for Pohl stopping SS investigating judges, police officials and officers entering concentration camps, well, he had never heard of such an order and he would have done if one had existed.

On 21 August, Morgen was called to the witness stand. As a defence witness, he was first questioned by Dr Karl Hoffmann, defence lawyer for Rudolf Scheide, who had been in charge of transport under Pohl. In his responses, Morgen talked about the concentration camp accommodation, the hospital facilities and then he moved on to the abuses that he had encountered there. The president of the tribunal, Robert M. Toms, took issue with some of Morgen's answers in respect of concentration camps when they contradicted what the Allies had found after the war, especially in respect of Dachau and the gas chamber and crematorium there.

Morgen set out his investigations into concentration camps and related how some senior officials had been surprised when confronted with his descriptions of the extermination programme. Others, including SS General Heinrich Müller, had not been – in fact, Müller had said to Morgen, 'Why don't you arrest me?'[7] When asked why he didn't, Morgen then explained how the legal system in Germany meant that he would have needed an arrest order signed by someone very high up, which he did try to get for Eichmann. After several long answers, which ended with Morgen telling the tribunal how disgusting he found the practices in concentration camps, Judge Tombs told the lawyer questioning Morgen, 'Don't let the witness get away from you. Go ahead with your question. Unless you ask him questions quickly, he starts on a ride of his own. So keep the questions "popping" at him.'[8]

Morgen was then asked by Seidl, defence lawyer for Pohl, about the investigations that Pohl had hampered. He quoted Morgen a memo dated 16 May 1944 from Pohl to all staff, telling them about the new central court which had been set up and that they must cooperate with it. Morgen replied by saying that it was a normal Pohl ploy: 'It is one of the typical examples of the behaviour of Obergruppenführer Pohl that he used big words and so he would put on the veil of protection of law and discipline, although he, in reality, did exactly the opposite.'[9]

A battle then ensued between Morgen and Seidl. Seidl would put a point to Morgen about an investigation and cast doubt on the way in which Morgen said that Pohl and Schmidt-Klevenow impeded it and Morgen would refute it. Eventually, it got to the stage where the president of the tribunal intervened: 'This cross examination has assumed the proportions of a brawl or a quarrel between the witness and Pohl on matters that do not concern the Tribunal at all. Unless you confine it to matters relating directly to charges in the indictment, we'll stop the cross examination forthwith.'[10]

Seidl then tried to discredit Morgen by accusing him of taking part in medical experiments at Buchenwald and quoted two sources. The first was the diary of former SS major Dr Erwin Ding-Schuler, one of the Buchenwald doctors, which talked about an experiment where Morgen was present. Seidl also quoted an affidavit by Dr Eugen Kogon, who said that Morgen had been present at medical experiments where prisoners had died. Morgen flatly denied this and said that Kogon had this information third-hand and that it was untrue. Tombs asked him if he had been questioned about it and charged? Morgen replied that the prosecution lawyers had questioned him about these claims and no, he had not been charged.

Ultimately, the tribunal's death sentence for Oswald Pohl was given to him for organising the concentration camps with all the atrocities which were committed there and for his role in destroying the Warsaw Ghetto. In his concurring opinion on the verdict, judge Michael A. Musmanno said:

> The German people must know the SS scale of values. Concentration Camp Inspector Morgen, in bringing charges against one Standartenführer Koch, commandant of Buchenwald concentration camp, listed his offences as; first, embezzlement and disloyalty; and second, murder. To the SS hierarchy human life was not as important as money and what it stands for. It was this type of gross presumption which placed SS men outside the doors of the Quedlinburg Cathedral to charge an entrance fee and in recompense hand the visitor a booklet, containing a speech by Himmler.*[11]

Morgen would probably have agreed with this assessment; after all, the way he operated was to go after corruption first, in line with his orders, and then he would investigate murder as well. Morgen does not give us his reaction to the death sentence passed on Pohl but he must have been pleased. The running battle between the two SS officers through the course of the war and again during Pohl's trial had culminated in Pohl being convicted, sentenced to death and executed for crimes against humanity, war crimes and for being a member of the SS.

* Himmler requisitioned Quedlinburg Cathedral from church authorities because of his fascination with Heinrich der Vogelfänger (Henry the Bird Catcher), first king of a unified Germany who died in 936 and who was thought to have been buried there. The SS removed all Christian symbols, installed Nazi ones instead and charged people an entrance fee.

THE SS TRIAL

After the war, Morgen's first stop in American custody had been Dachau, where he came across some of the SS officers he had himself investigated. One of these was Hermann Hackmann, whom he had investigated in Buchenwald and Majdanek and arrested. Hackmann had escaped the full force of SS justice and had been sent to a penal unit instead. He was imprisoned until 1955 and then was again tried and sentenced to a further ten years in the 1980 Majdanek trial in Germany.

By November 1945, Morgen was in Offenbach near Frankfurt. From here he got his first chance to send a letter to Maria since his arrest.[12] He told her that he was well apart from some minor health issues, which the American doctors were looking after. He told her that apart from the loss of liberty, which was the hardest thing to bear, he was being treated well, the gardens were nice and he had access to a library. More importantly, the Americans were looking after him and one officer in particular was friendly and engaging in conversation.

Morgen had been marked as a possible suspect on his initial detention document as well as a witness.[13] Once the Americans discovered the extent of his knowledge about the concentration camps, the SS court and activities in Nazi-occupied Poland, his prisoner file was marked so that all interrogations were to be transcribed and turned into briefing documents for submission to the Allied forces. But before these detailed interrogations began, Morgen was summoned to appear as a defence witness in the main Nuremberg trial.

In the summer of 1945, the Allies had convened a conference in London to decide how the Nuremberg Trials would work. The US, Soviet, British and French all had different legal systems and the plan was for them to come to a consensus as to how an agreed legal process would be applied to senior officers and officials in Nazi Germany. In the end, the conference agreed on three new crimes: crimes against peace, involving planning and waging a war of aggression which violated international agreements; war crimes, involving the murder or ill treatment of civilian populations and prisoners of war and wanton destruction of towns and cities; and crimes against humanity, involving murder, enslavement and other mistreatment against ordinary people, including persecutions on racial, religious or political grounds even if domestic law in the country allowed this.

This last point was important. In Nazi Germany, the Holocaust had been legal because the Führer had ordered it, which had prevented Morgen from using the SS courts to stop it directly. Now the Allies were saying that under these new universal laws, any country which tried to do what the Nazis had done would find themselves in an international court because that country had broken international law. The agreement in London had not been arrived at easily – in particular, the Soviet government had had reservations but eventually signed up to the protocol.

In his report to the US president after the London conference, the chief American delegate Robert H. Jackson discussed what would happen if an organisation such as the SS or Gestapo was found to be criminal, which he anticipated the tribunal would do. In these cases, he reported:

> Findings in the main trial that an organisation is criminal in nature will be conclusive in any subsequent proceedings against individual members. The individual member will thereafter be

allowed to plead only personal defences or extenuating circumstances, such as that he joined under duress.[14]

With Morgen's arrival into custody, other former senior SS officers spotted an opportunity. Morgen had been an investigating judge in the SS and police courts, so who better to defend the SS in the forthcoming Nuremberg trial when the tribunal was going to consider if the SS was a criminal organisation? He could tell the court that he followed a legal process and this, the others hoped, would convince the tribunal that the SS wasn't as bad an organisation as had been suggested.

Morgen made his first appearance at a Nuremberg trial on 7 August 1946. In his responses to the initial questioning, Morgen emphasised that his route into the SS had not been a voluntary one; instead he had been drafted in through the Reich Committee for Youth Fitness. This, he hoped, would protect him from prosecution if the SS were to be judged to be a criminal organisation. He also emphasised to the tribunal that technically he had been an SS major of the reserve rather than a full member of the SS. He told the tribunal about his work as an SS investigating judge, and when asked about the conditions in the concentration camps, he told the tribunal about his arrival at Buchenwald: 'The camp is situated on wooded heights, with a wonderful view. The installations were clean and freshly painted. There was much lawn and flowers. The prisoners were healthy, normally fed, sun-tanned, working.'[15] At this point, the president, Sir Geoffrey Lawrence, mindful that the Americans had found appalling conditions at the end of the war in Buchenwald, interrupted and asked Morgen when it was that he was describing. Morgen answered that it was 1943.

Morgen then proceeded to describe his work as an SS investigating judge and police official. He suggested that SS Major Christian Wirth, whom he had met in Lublin, was not a member of the SS (he was) and instead was a police officer. When Morgen was asked to describe the bad elements of the concentration camps, he then launched into an attack on both the concentration camp system and Oswald Pohl. At this point, Thomas Dodd, one of the prosecution lawyers, interrupted: 'It seems to me that what we are hearing here is a lecture on the Prosecution's case, and I do not see how it in any sense can be said to be a defence of the SS.'[16]

One of the defence strategies was to suggest that the SS had not run the concentration camps and some rather farcical exchanges took place in the tribunal where Morgen was shown pictures of camp staff in uniform and asked to say if they were SS uniforms or not. However, Morgen did get the opportunity to run through his career and some of the cases that he had investigated. When he started talking about Auschwitz, he referred to Birkenau, the extermination camp, as 'Monowitz', which was incorrect, and he later corrected this in subsequent trials and interrogations. Some commentators have used this to accuse Morgen of lying, but he did correct himself and use the correct name in subsequent trials – for example, in the Pohl trial. One of these is historian Kevin Prenger, who has stated that Morgen 'did not hesitate to lie, for instance by claiming that Monowitz was an extermination camp not supervised by the SS'.[17]

As was often the case with Morgen's testimony, he talked about what was important to him and his wartime work rather than what might have been useful to the trial where he was appearing as a witness. At one point, SS defence lawyer Dr Horst Pelckmann asked

Morgen what actions he took when he realised that mass killing was taking place in Lublin and at Auschwitz-Birkenau. Morgen launched into a long description of the ways in which he tried to disrupt the killings by investigating the people involved. Pelckmann asked him, 'Witness, were you in danger of your life in all these investigations?'

Morgen replied:

> It was clear that the discovery of these horrible crimes was extremely unpleasant to those responsible for them. I knew that a human life meant nothing to these people and that they were ready for anything. As proof, I may cite the following: after I had arrested Grabner, the chief of the political section in Auschwitz, and the investigating commission—

He was suddenly cut off by Lawrence: 'You aren't forgetting that you said you were going to take forty-five minutes with this witness, are you, Herr Pelckmann?' After Pelckmann apologised, Lawrence said, 'It seems of very little importance whether this man was in danger of his life or not.'[18]

Pelckmann persuaded Lawrence to let Morgen continue and he talked about his efforts to inform the senior SS officers in the Reich Security Main Office about what was happening. He talked about his investigation into Herzogenbusch concentration camp in the Netherlands, when seventy-four women had been forced into a small cell designed to hold two or three people and, as a result, ten women had died. Morgen told the tribunal that when he had reported this to Pohl, he told him that the lives of ten women did not matter in view of the thousands of German women dying every night.[19]

After further cross-examination by other defence lawyers, Lawrence asked Sir David Maxwell-Fyfe, prosecution lawyer, if the prosecution wanted to question Morgen. He told the tribunal that the prosecution did not accept what Morgen had set out regarding the good conditions he observed at the concentration camps because they had so much other evidence about appalling conditions there. This abrupt dismissal of Morgen's evidence by the prosecution meant that they had concluded that Morgen had done the defence no favours by his glowing description of Buchenwald. In addition, there was pressure on time and the prosecution did not want to take more of it by engaging in arguments with Morgen, who was proving very adept at sparring with the lawyers. In the end, Morgen's evidence was of no help to the former members of the SS, as the SS was judged to be a criminal organisation by the court.

Morgen also appeared as a witness in the trial of Prince Josias of Waldeck, where he recounted the events surrounding his investigation at Buchenwald. Once again, the question of how the law operated in the SS came to the fore. Charged alongside Waldeck was Koch's successor as Buchenwald commandant, Hermann Pister.

This trial was noteworthy because of an exchange between Morgen and Dr Wacker, lawyer for the defence, about the legality of the orders which came through from Berlin to execute individual prisoners. Morgen told Wacker that these orders had to be agreed by SS General Heinrich Müller, head of Office IV at the Reich Security Main Office, who would approve them. Wacker then asked Morgen, 'How finally came the execution order to Buchenwald?'

'Through letter,' replied Morgen.

'In your opinion was such written execution order based on German law legal?' asked Wacker.

'Technically yes,' replied Morgen.

'What do you understand by that – technically right?' asked Wacker.

'That it's technically right means it doesn't have to be really right,' replied Morgen.

After some legal argument among the lawyers, Wacker asked Morgen, 'Dr Morgen, please explain to the court why you use the term "technically legal".'

'The same way as a court can make a mistake in its sentence, the police can make mistakes in its decision but sentences based on a mistake are still legal sentences and no matter whether the sentence was legal or not they were still legal sentences,' replied Morgen.

Wacker asked another question: 'Dr Morgen, in its investigation did the police have to consider only the evidence against the accused or also the evidence in his favour?'

'The position of the German police and the German legal system is entirely different to the Anglo-Saxon one,' replied Morgen. 'In accordance with German law, the Police and the public prosecutor have to clear the entire case already through the preliminary investigation as much as possible and have to consider to the fullest extent all evidence in favour of the accused as well as the evidence against the accused. Legally nothing has changed in this respect under the Nazi system.'[20]

Exchanges like these did not help Pister's defence. The court decided that quoting superior orders was not a defence and he was sentenced to death – although he died in custody shortly after the trial.[21] In respect of Waldeck, ultimately the tribunal decided that although Morgen and another SS judge had testified about the investigations at Buchenwald and Waldeck's support for them, Waldeck's actions in taking over the running of Buchenwald as the war drew to a close meant that he was personally involved in the events at Buchenwald that led to such terrible tragedies (see Chapter 4). As a result of Waldeck's involvement in Buchenwald, he was convicted and sentenced to life imprisonment. He was released due to ill health in 1950 and died in 1967.

After the trial, Morgen was interrogated for the first time. These interrogation sessions were lengthy and went back and forth over his wartime career and activities. They started on 30 August 1946 and the last one took place on 22 March 1948. By April 1947, Morgen was getting fed up with the endless questioning and he asked about his status: was he a prisoner or a witness? As a prisoner he was under suspicion but as a witness he was not. He asked his interrogator, Mr Dobbs, about it: 'I don't know why I should be in prison, as I was never a criminal but have investigated war crimes like you are doing now.'

'I shall order to have you reclassified as a witness so you can stay in your witness wing of the prison,' replied Dobbs.[22]

But Morgen was still useful to the Americans and they continued to question him. Morgen had asked them to let him out on leave to visit Maria who was in hospital, but they refused, saying that she wasn't ill enough to merit a visit from Morgen. However, the Americans did let him out to see her later on and they eventually provided supporting documentation to enable Morgen to complete the marriage formalities. They were married in 1948.[23]

In his final interrogation, Morgen wanted to have a few digs at the Americans for their repeated questioning. He pointed out, 'My nature is not suited to saying anything which contradicts the truth. I testified both for and against the prosecution based on my knowledge and observations.'

Victor Singer, his interrogator, replied:

> I am aware of your actions as an SS judge. I know that you tried to bring these people who are now in the dock to justice for these crimes back then to bring to court things that were described as crimes at the time and which today do constitute crimes.

'Because of that, I've been sitting here for two years now. Is that justice?' asked Morgen.[24] Singer had no answer for him but he did make some calls and told Morgen that there was nothing standing in the way of his release to the German authorities for de-Nazification.

DE-NAZIFICATION

From Nuremberg, Morgen was moved to the internment camp at Ludwigsburg while the German authorities completed their enquiries into him. The Americans had already investigated him and found no grounds for any charges, while the German proceedings were designed to ensure that Nazi criminals were not released into public life. The Allied Control Council, which was the governing body of the Allied zones of occupation, set out five categories into which de-Nazification tribunals would place individuals like Morgen who had been SS officers and party members. If a tribunal found someone to be a major offender then the penalty was life imprisonment or death, someone who was an activist would get up to ten years in jail, lesser offenders would be placed on probation, Nazi followers would be given a fine and surveillance, and exonerated individuals would be let off entirely.

Going into the tribunal, the odds were stacked against Morgen. He had been a member of the Nazi Party and a middle-ranking officer of the SS, which was now a criminal organisation after the Nuremberg judgment. But everything that had been a problem for him in his dealings with the Nazi Party and the SS was now a point in his favour. The tribunal noted that Morgen had refused to vote in 1934 to give Hitler ultimate power in Germany and had been persecuted by the party as a result, that his 1936 book *War Propaganda and War Prevention* had annoyed the party to the extent that they had tried to ban it, that in 1939 he had been fired as a judge in a political case, and that as an SS judge he had been demoted and sent to the front by Himmler because he upset the wrong people.

However, the tribunal did want to look into Morgen's wartime career in depth and they obtained official documents and sifted through the material in order to establish how they should assess Morgen's record. One thing that particularly concerned the tribunal was a book which had been written by a former prisoner at Buchenwald, Eugen Kogon, *Der SS-Staat: das System der deutschen Konzentrationslager*. In the book, Kogon stated that Morgen had been present at a medical experiment designed to find out which poison had killed one of his key witnesses, SS Sergeant Rudolph Köhler. Their initial enquiries to Kogon about this elicited no reply. Morgen flatly rejected the accusation in the book. To assist the tribunal, he said he would be happy if they obtained a sworn statement and they could settle the matter in writing instead of in front of the tribunal.

A lawyer was sent to speak with Kogon, who backed off from his claims. He set out in his statement that the story had come from Dr Ding-Schuler and others second-hand and that his book was intended to inform readers about the system of terror in concentration camps:

> I do know and I have written this in my book that Dr Morgen was determined to investigate the lawlessness which prevailed, the abuse of the law, the outrageous killings and corruption in Buchenwald and to paralyse the guilty through all the legal means he had at his disposal.[25]

In the final sentence of his statement he said, 'When writing the passage in question in my book *Der SS-Staat*, namely about the psychology of the prisoners, I had no intention of telling the public anything that could have been incriminating for Dr. Morgen.'[26]

Morgen was also helped in his defence by a former political prisoner at Buchenwald, Alfred Miller. He told the tribunal how he had been imprisoned in the bunker since his arrival at Buchenwald in 1942 and had initially been sceptical when Morgen came to Buchenwald looking for evidence of the murders there. However, Morgen had gained his trust and eventually his release. Miller told the tribunal:

> Faced with Dr Morgen the SS were shaking. Dr Morgen was seen as the devil himself … The bunker in Buchenwald was no longer allowed to hold prisoners, [instead] Dr Morgen filled the bunker with the SS. Since there was no longer enough space there, SS men were imprisoned in Weimar.[27]

The tribunal also collected supporting statements from friends and others, who told them that although Morgen had joined the Nazi Party, he had never been a National Socialist. One surprising intervention on Morgen's behalf came from former Waffen SS General Hans Jüttner, former head of the *SS Führungshauptamt* (Waffen SS headquarters). Jüttner sent through an affidavit in which he stated that, although he didn't know Morgen personally, he could testify that:

> He was widely known and feared by the troops because of his calling to take action in respect of all SS transgressions against people and their possessions in the occupied territories even those committed by higher ranks. He was energetic and impartial and because of all this he got into frequent conflicts with the offices at headquarters especially with General Pohl who was his sworn enemy.[28]

Morgen himself made an impassioned final plea to the tribunal:

> If I had kept myself away from these things I could have had a really nice life. I scrutinised the high ups and I stood up for those who were suffering and who were being punished. In doing so I was playing with fire and I did more than my duty. I stood against violence, against injustice, against despotism and I fought against the guilty. I wasn't a follower but right from the start of my career in public service I have swum against the tide.*[29]

* One of the official categories that the tribunal could have placed Morgen into was *Mitläufer* (literally translated as 'fellow traveller'), used to describe people who passively supported the Nazi regime without directly committing atrocities. When Morgen makes this final statement, he uses the official term as a verb: *Ich bin nicht mitgelaufen*, literally I did not follow the others.

On 21 April 1948, the Allied Chief of Counsel for War Crimes confirmed that they were no longer interested in Morgen. Then, on 24 June, the tribunal reached its decision. Konrad Morgen was formally exonerated and he was free. The judgment, written by the tribunal president Meyer, praised Morgen. After listing the cases Morgen investigated, he wrote:

> It could not be shown that in carrying out his duties he was guilty of perverting justice or suppressing the law. On the contrary he pursued SS men for prosecution and brought them to justice. He has therefore followed the ethics of a Judge in search of the truth to its utmost extent and has fulfilled the duties of a conscientious representative of the law.[30]

With a clean record, Morgen was able to move to Prien where Maria was living. Free at last, they could both start to think about the future. Except there was a problem. When the verdict of the tribunal reached the Ministry for Political Liberation, they weren't impressed. How could a major in the SS be exonerated? On reading through the judgment, the ministry came to a different conclusion to the tribunal. They decided that Morgen's SS career had simply been an internal SS cleansing process. There was no evidence, in their eyes, that Morgen had actively resisted the regime and so, in order to prove the correctness of their point of view, the ministry ordered a second tribunal to sit in judgment on Morgen.

A private detective named Feichtinger was dispatched to Prien to dig up some dirt on Morgen. However, he struggled to find any. He talked to a Dr Rupert Dorrer, who recalled that Konrad and Maria had both been at the hospital before the war ended. The air raid alarms had gone off and they had all gone to the air raid bunker in the cellar. Dorrer had been surprised that Morgen had been critical of the Nazi government, even though he hadn't known Dorrer's politics, which could have been dangerous for Morgen as the Gestapo was always looking for people criticising the regime. Dorrer hadn't expected to hear such views from an SS officer and Morgen made a very good impression on him, the more so as he had pitched in and helped at every opportunity.

Feichtinger went to the police station and the town hall, neither of which could tell him anything about Morgen. He then called on Maria, Morgen's fiancée, who naturally spoke of him in glowing terms. Feichtinger was interested in their struggle to obtain permission to marry from the SS and how it was never forthcoming. He noted that although Maria was on the radar of the German authorities (she had been implicated in a treason trial in 1934) and the SS refused permission to marry, Morgen never gave up on her and was always there for her. Finally, Feichtinger found a Frau Wally Stadler, who was the cashier at the hotel Bayerische Hof. She had worked for the SS officers' mess in Prien and remembered Morgen as a very decent person. She had nothing bad to say about him and recalled that he was away travelling a lot and didn't do anything in public life in Prien. Feichtinger had found nothing incriminating at all.

Morgen put up a spirited defence of his actions to the new tribunal, which sat in 1950 under a Dr Wedlich. He told them:

> If it is correct that the concentration camp system formed the core of the regime of tyranny then I attacked that core head on. My actions were not the fulfilment of a National Socialist duty

> but the fulfilment of all those moral and legal standards which the Nazis trashed. The ministry claims that my commitment to the rule of law was a 'cleansing operation' in the spirit of the SS and Nazism. By saying this it postulates that the Nazi state was a constitutional state. In other words: the concentration camp crimes were not in keeping with the will of the Nazi leadership at all. They must therefore have been pure when they cleansed themselves of the criminals in their ranks.[31]

In the end, the new tribunal concluded that Morgen wasn't a keen supporter of the Nazi regime. In fact, his support for the party was negligible, and as an SS judge he hadn't been working in Nazi courts as the SS was a military jurisdiction like the Wehrmacht. In the end, they reclassified Morgen as a *Mitläufer*, literally 'fellow traveller', a passive supporter – one level up from exonerated. This had no impact on Morgen, as the lower classifications of de-Nazification were by now irrelevant owing to a new law which removed the differences between the lower categories. He was now free to get on with his life.

While the de-Nazification proceedings were ongoing, Morgen had been unable to resume his professional career as a lawyer. Now, at last, he could, and from the early 1950s to the end of his life he practised law in Frankfurt. The only interruptions to his legal career were to come in the form of trials and other legal proceedings relating to the war and the events he had participated in and witnessed.

THE 1963–5 AUSCHWITZ TRIAL

By the mid-1960s, West Germany had become settled as a member of the international community and ordinary Germans were set on making the most of their position as citizens in a modern, prosperous and democratic Germany. But there was a dark side to West Germany. Former Nazis occupied key positions at every level in West German society and while many had gone through the de-Nazification process and had formally been cleared to resume their former careers, others had not, especially former members of the SS who had reason to cover up their wartime records. The worst of these tried as best they could to live quiet lives without attracting attention.

Generally, public opinion supported them in their endeavours. For example, Wilhelm Boger, who had invented the 'Boger swing' at Auschwitz, lived openly in his local community where everyone knew who he was. Even when former SS men and women were reported to the authorities, those authorities were themselves full of former party comrades who could ensure that investigations proceeded either very slowly or not at all.

One notable exception to this was Frankfurt where the state attorney Fritz Bauer, who himself had been in a concentration camp before the war, pursued former Nazis with unrivalled zeal and dedication. When Bauer had information about Adolf Eichmann's whereabouts in Argentina, he passed that information on to the Israelis directly. He knew that if he gave the information to the German authorities, someone would tip Eichmann off.

The best chance of any action being taken against a former Auschwitz guard or officer was if two things happened: firstly, if they were recognised by a former prisoner at Auschwitz and secondly, if the report was actually acted upon. This is exactly what happened to Wilhelm Boger. In 1958, a prisoner in Bruchsal called Adolf Rögner wrote to the state prosecutor in Stuttgart complaining about a lack of medication.[32] In the same letter, he set out how Wilhelm Boger, inventor of the 'Boger swing' and whom he had come across when he was a prisoner at Auschwitz, was now living and working in West Germany. This started an investigation, which was given added impetus when, out of the blue, a man called Thomas Gnielka sent state attorney Fritz Bauer an envelope full of documents.

These documents consisted of Auschwitz records of prisoners who were shot 'while trying to escape' and had been retrieved from the SS and police court in Breslau, which had been set on fire at the end of the war. They showed the prisoners' names and numbers as well the name of the guard that shot them and the signature denoting which SS officer signed off on these shootings.[33] Bauer passed these documents along to the Central Office of the State Judicial Administration in Ludwigsburg for solving Nazi crimes, which in turn sought advice from the federal courts. Eventually, it was decided that these Auschwitz crimes would be investigated and brought to trial in Frankfurt rather than in Stuttgart.

Alongside Boger, the investigations had led the authorities to other former SS personnel at Auschwitz and in the end twenty-four were charged. One of the limitations of this trial was that it only prosecuted the lower levels of the SS; higher-up Nazis who had actively assisted the Third Reich were perceived to be untouchable because they had friends in high places. One of the defendants at Frankfurt, Oswald Kaduk, was found guilty of ten counts of murder and jointly guilty for the murder of more than 1,000 people. Kaduk attracted attention because he had been a notoriously sadistic guard at Auschwitz who had literally trampled a person to death, and yet when he went to work at a hospital in Berlin after the war, he was so popular that his patients called him 'Papa Kaduk'.

He told the public prosecutor:

> The thing is that the people who sent us into this misfortune, the majority of them [are] free, running around like Globke … And the fact that we, the henchmen, are sitting in the dock today hurts us terribly, Mr. Public Prosecutor.[34]

Hans Globke was a lawyer who became one of West German Chancellor Konrad Adenauer's closest advisers, despite the fact he had played a key role in the Nazi race laws and later in the government of the Third Reich.

The trial opened in December 1963. However, there was a key difference between the way in which this trial would work and the post-war Nuremberg trials. At Nuremberg, the Allies had used the new charges of crimes against peace, war crimes and crimes against humanity to hold defendants retrospectively to account for crimes they had committed during the Third Reich before these new crimes had even been drafted, agreed and adopted. West Germany, however, had not adopted these new crimes and instead the Frankfurt authorities had to rely on the standard German penal code, which made it necessary for prosecutors to prove individual participation in and motive for individual acts of murder. In addition, there was no retrospective application of German law so individuals could only be tried on the basis of the law in force at the time the offence was committed.

By the time Morgen was called as a witness, the trial had already been in session for twenty-four individual court days. He was a key witness from the ranks of the SS as he had been at Auschwitz and had investigated crimes there. He took the stand on 9 March 1964. In a sign of the differences between the German legal system and other countries, the presiding judge at the trial, Hans Hofmeyer, kicked off the questioning of Morgen. Later, his fellow judges joined in before the lawyers, as well as the defendants themselves, got their chance to ask him questions.

After Morgen had set out a very lengthy description of his career in the SS and the investigations he led at Auschwitz, Hofmeyer came straight to the point: 'Witness, here we are primarily interested in the experiences which you had with the individual defendants. During your questioning by the investigating judge, I read constantly that you mentioned Boger's name. Please could you tell us if and how you remember this defendant?'

'Today, after twenty years, I can only remember individual cases vaguely, if at all,' replied Morgen. 'I think that any one of you, as judges, would find yourselves in a similar position if you had not seen the case files for twenty years.'[35]

Hofmeyer continued to press Morgen about Boger but Morgen was not forthcoming with the details that the judge was looking for. However, as Hofmeyer pointed out, Morgen had given more details in his pre-trial questioning about Boger, and it seemed from the discussion between Hofmeyer and Morgen that he was reluctant to repeat them in open court. Morgen was one of many SS witness who had given lots of detail in the pre-trial questioning by an investigating judge, only to become much less forthcoming on the witness stand. Hannah Arendt, the famous political theorist who wrote *Eichmann in Jerusalem: A Report on the Banality of Evil*, wrote about these discrepancies:

> Behind them one can sense public opinion, which the witnesses had not faced when they testified *in camera*. Almost every one of them would rather admit that he is a liar than risk having

> his neighbours read in the newspapers that he does not belong among the Germans who "stick together".[36]

This is an important point to consider because the Auschwitz trial was given extensive coverage in the German press. There were 933 articles in four major German newspapers – *Die Welt*, *Frankfurter Allgemeine Zeitung*, *Frankfurter Rundschau* and *Süddeutsche Zeitung* – during the course of the trial.[37] Professor Devin O. Pendas has collected nearly 1,400 articles from seventy different newspapers during the trial, which shows that coverage by the press was almost universal.[38] However, this blanket coverage by the German press was not universally welcomed by their readers. Emmi Bonhoeffer, widow of Klaus Bonhoeffer, who had been executed because of his part in the plot to kill Hitler, wrote:

> Naturally the Auschwitz trial is unpopular. This makes it all the more peculiar that almost the entire press corps provides daily coverage, if not always very thoroughly. They write stories that nobody actually wants to read, certainly not those in need of it.[39]

In his analysis of the trial, Pendas writes:

> The trial encountered a degree of pre-existing hostility on the part of Germans who were unable or unwilling to confront their past. To the extent that the public in 1965 had an agenda for dealing with Nazism, it was largely to forget about it. To their credit, certain judicial actors (Hessian Attorney General Fritz Bauer, above all) did not allow that to happen.[40]

This problem of memory reached its extreme when one of the defendants at the trial, former SS captain Franz Hofmann, was allowed to talk directly to Morgen on the witness stand. Hofmann told Morgen that he was the officer who had showed Morgen around Auschwitz and he had also been to the trial of Maximilian Grabner. He told Morgen:

> The trial was scheduled to take place in a room, where I can no longer say. Shortly before or right at the beginning of the proceedings the air raid alarm went off and all the judges, defendants, witnesses, everyone we had to relocate above the Goethe House. The reason I remember this is because I worked in Weimar in 1930/31, that's how I knew Weimar. We waited above the Goethe House and then a police truck came and we all had to get in. Former SS General Prince Waldeck was sitting in a Kübelwagen and we all drove off to a castle somewhere.[41]

But Morgen still maintained he could not remember Hofmann, nor could he remember the air-raid alarm. Given that Hofmann himself was volunteering these details, it is, of course, possible that Morgen genuinely could not remember them as it would have been unlikely that his fellow Germans would have held it against him if he had been able to remember.

In his speech delivering the opinion of the court, Hofmeyer referred to this problem of the memory of the witnesses. The problem for the court was that there was no actual physical evidence of murders at Auschwitz because it had all been destroyed long ago. All the court could rely on to establish guilt or innocence were witness statements. He said:

> Even the ideal witness who wishes to speak only the truth and tries hard to search his memory is sure to suffer lapses after twenty years ... The very fact that the witnesses were asked questions they could not answer proves how unbelievably difficult it is to ascertain and define specific incidents after twenty years.[42]

Although Morgen's memory was not always as forthcoming as the court would have liked, he did engage with Hofmeyer and the other judges and lawyers about the nature of law in the Third Reich in general and in the SS in particular. The problem for the court was that it faced a similar problem to that which Morgen himself had faced: namely, how to make charges of murder stick under the laws that were in operation in the Third Reich. The prosecutor, Joachim Kügler, referred back to a question asked by one of the defendants at the trial and put it again to Morgen: 'Why do you want to accuse us of a few shootings when a couple of thousand Jews were killed every day in Auschwitz. Surely that means we did nothing wrong?'

'Well, no,' replied Morgen, 'there is a subtle but important difference. Whenever gassings or executions were ordered any personal initiative was out of the question. There was an order and it was carried out. But in the case of the other shootings then the defendants were not covered by an order and they did it because they decided to for personal reasons.'[43]

Towards the end of Morgen's time on the witness stand, one of the defence lawyers, Gerhard Göllner, asked him, 'Herr witness, from your experience as a prosecutor or as a judge in the former SS and police courts, can you tell the jury about proceedings which were concerned with the disobeying of orders?'

Morgen replied:

> The motto of the SS was '*Meine Ehre heißt Treue* – for me honour means loyalty'. Anyone who did not follow orders and refused to obey them could not expect any leniency. And because the SS judiciary generally gave out harsh sentences, the troops were repeatedly threatened with the SS court. And that had a moral effect.[44]

Hofmeyer interrupted and asked Morgen about Section 47 of the Military Penal Code. This section allowed a soldier in Nazi Germany not to follow an order that involved committing a crime.

In response, Morgen started talking about the war in the East and told Hofmeyer that because there was a non-aggression pact with Soviet Russia, which Germany later broke, then any soldier attacking the Soviet Army could have been committing murder: 'If an order comes from the relevant superior officer and it is clearly made as part of official or war business, then he must carry it out without objecting. And that's what the courts ruled at the time.'

Hofmeyer came straight back with a real-life situation from elsewhere in the trial:

> Yes. Doctor Morgen, what you have just described is an appropriate subject for discussion. But what is not for discussion is the question of whether a soldier is allowed to or is required to carry out an order to throw innocent little children into a fire. I don't think any soldier could have the slightest doubt that this order was a crime, could he?

'You are absolutely right, Herr Direktor,' replied Morgen. 'I mean, I have read about that but I can't picture it. And I would like to hope that it didn't happen because that would have gone against all the rules.'[45]

Morgen gave his evidence on the twenty-fifth day of the trial. Over a year later, when Hofmeyer was setting out the reasons behind the judgment on the 183rd day of the trial, many more stories like this had been heard in the courtroom. At the end of the trial, seventeen defendants were found guilty and sentenced to varying terms of imprisonment or imprisonment with hard labour. These included Franz Hofmann, who received a life sentence. So did Wilhelm Boger.

Morgen's testimony had been important to the court because it prompted discussions about the nature of law in the Third Reich and the extent to which the defendants could rely on it. Although the Frankfurt court had not had access to the Nuremberg crimes of crimes against peace, war crimes and crimes against humanity and had instead relied on the standard German law in place at the time, the court did decide that orders issued by Hitler were not legal when they clashed with normal German laws in place. In other words, the court ruled that the so-called 'prerogative state' identified by Ernst Fraenkel, which constituted a parallel legal system to the normal legal system (the 'normative state'), would have no impact on this Auschwitz trial.

This was set out by Hofmeyer in his final ruling:

> The German Federal Republic because of the continuity of identity is the successor of the German Reich. This state has been in existence from 1871 to the Weimar Republic to the Federal Republic and has always had the same penal code. Under this penal code murder has always been a punishable offence. National

> Socialism did exercise all-embracing power in Germany but this did not give it the right to turn wrong into right. In particular, it could not determine that a deed bearing all the earmarks of a punishable offence was not an injustice because it had been ordered by a specific person – even though that person may have been the sole ruler of the country. National Socialism was also subject to the rule of law. This holds true in particular on the question of the 'final solution of the Jewish problem'.[46]

After the Auschwitz trial, Morgen once more focused on his legal practice. But the demands on his time to talk about his SS career and the cases he investigated did not reduce. In October 1971, he talked to John Toland for material about Toland's biography of Adolf Hitler, and towards the end of the 1970s he was contacted by the court in Düsseldorf about appearing in the trial of Hermann Hackmann, whom he had investigated in Buchenwald and Majdanek.

However, by this time Morgen's health was failing. Too ill to travel to attend the court, in January 1980 Morgen was instead visited at his home in Frankfurt by two of the judges and a doctor in order to collect his witness testimony for the court. He followed the trial through newspaper clippings, which he carefully removed and preserved.[47]

He died on 4 February 1982.

CHAPTER 10

KONRAD MORGEN: A FINAL WORD

Looking back on Morgen's career, we can see that it falls into three distinct phases. First, there was his career as an SS investigating judge and police official, then after the war there was a second phase when Morgen talked about his SS career, either as a defendant or as a witness. And now, after his death, there is a third phase where Morgen has attracted the interest of historians and academics, who discuss his wartime career and what Morgen said about that career after the war.

It was John Toland who kicked off this third phase towards the end of Morgen's life with his interview in 1971 and his judgement that Morgen was one of the good guys. As highlighted in the introduction to this book, Toland describes Morgen as 'the man who did the most to hinder the atrocities in the East', and his work as 'one man house-cleaning', as well as a 'lonesome attempt to end the Final Solution'.[1]

What is interesting about Morgen is that he attracts the attention of several different academic disciplines. He is of interest to historians because of the extraordinary nature of his wartime career and he is of interest to moral philosophers and legal academics because of the moral choices he made, as well as the fact that his SS career brings to life abstract ideas about the nature of law and our relationship to it.

One of the most important academic analyses of Morgen is a very thoughtful 2015 study by philosophy professors Herlinde Pauer-Studer and J. David Velleman called *Konrad Morgen: The Conscience of a Nazi Judge*, which they characterise as a moral biography of Morgen. This is a very well-written and well-researched book and essential reading for anyone with a serious academic interest in Morgen. It weaves moral and philosophical themes into the narrative to give the reader continual food for thought.

While the authors are careful to balance their analysis, at times judgements from the distance of the twenty-first century do intrude into their assessment of Morgen's actions. Morgen called himself a *Gerechtigkeitsfanatiker*, a fanatic for justice, and one of the criticisms made by Pauer-Studer and Velleman is that 'Morgen's antenna for justice was tuned only to the criminal variety; social and political justice were not on his radar'.[2] This is an unfair criticism. Morgen had a full-time job pursuing criminals within the SS and he put himself in danger in doing so. Overtly pursuing social and political justice could easily have landed him in big trouble in the Third Reich; others who did so lost their lives in the concentration camps. It is also worth pointing out that by pursuing criminal justice from within the SS, he was pursuing social and political justice in the only way that he could: by applying the law literally and bringing murderers, sadists and thieves in the SS before the courts. By staying alive and using the only powers available to him within the system, he was far more effective than he would otherwise have been if he had been neutralised through detention, and probably execution, in a concentration camp.

Pauer-Studer and Velleman's final conclusion does give credit to Morgen:

> Despite his allegiance to the SS, he was a thorn in the side of its hierarchy, and in the end, he used his powers against some of its foremost perpetrators, at considerable risk to himself. Morgen was no saint, not by a long shot, but neither was he evil. He was … an exercise in moral complexity.[3]

Professor Charles Fried has written a very balanced review of this book and discusses some of the abstract ideas around an individual's relationship with the law in a way that is very accessible for the general reader. He writes:

> The law says we must or may not do this or that, but must we really? We may be legally obligated, but are we morally obligated? The connection between legal and moral obligation is the signature issue of legal philosophy.[4]

Fried goes on to question, 'I am driven to ask: what would I have done in Morgen's shoes? What should I have done?'[5]

In terms of a judgement on Morgen himself, Fried considers the vast number of middle-level officials like Morgen: 'What kind of people are these, these ordinary mid-level bureaucrats? … How do we know by what processes, moved by what confrontation, what realization, some may change from being guilty time-servers to being heroes of resistance – or like Morgen something in between?'[6]

Fried does not say exactly where he would place Morgen between the two extremes, but he is right to highlight that he is somewhere in between. When it comes to Morgen, we do know the process by which he came to move away from being a time-server towards active resistance – he saw at first hand the way the Nazis were operating: first in Nazi-occupied Poland where, alongside rampant corruption, he was confronted by the atrocities committed by Oskar Dirlewanger's unit, then in the concentration camps where he pursued individual members of the SS for murder and other atrocities. As he told the Frankfurt court, he identified a way of doing it, by applying the law literally.

Professor Joel Marks, Emeritus Professor of Philosophy at the University of New Haven, has written an informal four-star review of the Pauer-Studer and Velleman biography. He writes that he learned about Morgen from Toland's biography of Hiter and goes on to say:

> Morgen is subjected to critical examination and still turns out to have been, if anything, more extraordinary than I had already thought him to be. He appears to have been a one-person anti-Holocaust crusader, yet he was a member of the Nazi administration. His impetus came from both legal principles and gut humanitarian instincts, but also from allegiance to a certain ideal of professionalism and honour as an SS judge. As such he would seem to have been a living contradiction. But the contradictory aspects, while certainly contributing to the wow factor, are the

> least of his story, as far as I am concerned. For me his story is that of a human being who, single-handedly, took on a monstrous institution and succeeded to a remarkable degree, motivated by noble intentions and guided by strictly rational thinking. He displayed great courage, perseverance, and competence.[7]

Marks adds, 'I do, however, have one major reservation to express (hence my four stars). No doubt it comes with the territory of their (and my) field of ethical philosophy, but I found their treatment of Morgen to be heavy-handed.'[8]

This is certainly true of a number of academics. The problem is that it is all too easy to criticise Morgen from the safety and freedom of a modern academic environment, whereas Morgen was living in a world where he was faced with impossible choices on an almost daily basis.

In their concluding chapter, Pauer-Studer and Velleman write, 'Perhaps he would have been equal to the moral challenges of other times, but for his own times, his moral range was certainly inadequate.'[9] In response to this argument Marks writes:

> Konrad Morgen was the perfect person for his time and place. Anyone with an 'adequate' moral sentiment would have been less effective or dead. All that stood in the way of Morgen's greater effectiveness was the unfortunate timing of his return to judicial duty after serving on the front. He was just a little too late to attempt to forestall the worst of the Holocaust.[10]

Marks is right. Morgen was the right person in the right time and the right place. He chose to work against the Nazi state and the SS from within because he judged that to be the most effective way to disrupt the activities of the SS. Had he been someone with an 'adequate' moral range and taken a publicly moral stance against the Third Reich he would have put himself at risk of arrest and execution, which is precisely what happened to a number of other Germans.

Another study of Morgen is one by Dutch historian Kevin Prenger: *A Judge in Auschwitz: Konrad Morgen's Crusade against Corruption and 'Illegal' Murder*, first published in Dutch in 2017 and in English in 2021. This book adds additional details to the Pauer-Studer and Velleman biography, especially regarding Morgen's activities after the war, and tries to bring something new in its criticism of Morgen. The final paragraph concludes, 'Although Morgen's intentions were probably well-meant in principle and he was not a corrupt or bloodthirsty villain, he was after all a servant of the law in the wrong place at the wrong time.'[11]

Actually, Morgen was a servant of the law who was in exactly the right place at the right time. He was stubborn, he was prickly, he had a highly developed sense of personal honour and he was fearless: exactly the qualities which he needed to bring justice to the victims of the SS and to take on criminals in the ranks of the SS. Prenger also accuses Konrad Morgen of lying during the Nuremberg trials, writing, 'He did not hesitate to lie, for instance by claiming that Monowitz was an extermination camp not supervised by the SS.'[12] The problem with this accusation is that Morgen corrected himself after he gave this testimony in a later American interrogation with a Dr Halle, when he told him that he should have been referring to Birkenau.[13]

THE IMPORTANCE OF LAW

Alongside these two biographies, Morgen appears in other books about the Third Reich, where he is also subject to critical analysis. Two of these books are by historians Nikolaus Wachsmann and Rebecca Wittmann. In his *KL: A History of the Nazi Concentration Camps*, Wachsmann writes an authoritative study of the concentration camps and the concentration camp system. But when it comes to Morgen and the Buchenwald investigation, Wachsmann describes him as arrogant.[14] He says:

> Morgen testified against some former Camp SS men, portraying himself as a tireless campaigner for law and order. Several historians have fallen for this pose, as did some judges. But his postwar testimony was self-serving, riddled with omissions and brazen lies … During his investigation of Koch, he condoned RSHA executions, the killing of prisoners in medical experiments, and the murder of supposedly sick and infectious inmates. His main aim was not to stop prisoner abuse but to root out corruption … Morgen was no champion of ordinary decency, but a crusader for Himmler's peculiar brand of SS morality.[15]

The problem with this analysis is that Wachsmann gives Morgen no credit at all for his work investigating murder in concentration camps. There is no recognition of the fact that Morgen's modus operandi was to use corruption investigations as a way in to start murder investigations. In order to understand why Wachsmann might be so critical and write a one-sided analysis of Morgen's wartime career, we need to investigate further. There is an endnote at the end of the sentence about historians and judges falling for

Morgen's pose, which refers the reader to Rebecca Wittmann's *Beyond Justice*. Wittmann's book is a very readable and accessible study of the 1963–5 Auschwitz trial in Frankfurt and it is also very critical of Morgen.

In her book, Wittmann criticises Morgen for forgetting the name of Franz Hofmann, who had shown him around Auschwitz, and for not recalling the trial of Maximilian Grabner in 1944, describing this forgetfulness as implausible. She does highlight the assistance that his testimony provided to the court in its deliberations, as well as his work at Buchenwald and Auschwitz, including his investigations of Maximilian Grabner and Adolf Eichmann. Wittman concludes:

> Despite these seemingly noble pursuits, I contend that Morgen presented himself in a much more positive light after the fact, to avoid investigations into his own activities. His reluctance to state anything specific about the defendants on the stand in Frankfurt (despite his having investigated Boger and the injections) demonstrates that he was not willing to provide specific pertinent information to the court.[16]

Wittmann is correct about Morgen's reluctance to provide specific information to the court. But when it comes to avoiding investigations into Morgen's own activities, Wittmann does not set out what those investigations might have found. The Americans had already interrogated and investigated Morgen for three years after the end of the war, and Morgen had been subject to more investigations as part of the de-Nazification process and even more investigations as the years went past. None of them found any evidence of any wrongdoing and Morgen was never convicted for anything he did during the war.

Why are these historians so critical of Morgen? Apart from their criticism of Morgen, is there anything else which their analyses have in common? The answer to this question is yes and that is their approach to the law in Nazi Germany. A crucial factor in understanding Morgen's wartime SS career is in acknowledging the legal situation in Nazi Germany.

After the war, the Nuremberg trials judged senior Nazis according to laws drafted by the Allies as the war came to an end: crimes against peace, war crimes and crimes against humanity. But, and this is a crucial point, Nazi Germany itself did not have any laws like this. Instead, the Third Reich had the standard German penal code dating from 1871 and it also declared that orders issued by the Führer personally were to be considered lawful. What this means is that, under Nazi law, the killings in the extermination camps were legal. We all agree, of course, that these killings were horrific and rightly judged by the Allies as crimes against humanity after the war, but this does not alter the situation under Nazi law, which was that at the time, right up to the point when Germany was defeated, these killings were legal. Historians and other academics need to understand and acknowledge this fact in order to make sense of how the Third Reich in general and Morgen in particular operated.

A very important analysis of the career and the legal environment in which Morgen operated is set out in Professor David Fraser's academic paper 'Criminal Law in Auschwitz: Positivism, Natural Law, and the Career of SS Lawyer Konrad Morgen'. This paper should be essential reading for anyone researching and writing about Morgen because it provides effective counter-arguments to historians who fail to understand the legal situation in Nazi Germany, it highlights the legal environment in which Morgen operated and as a result it provides a thoroughly credible and balanced academic analysis of his wartime career.

Fraser writes, 'It is not possible to situate the juridical activities and criminal investigations carried out by Morgen within the camps without understanding the system as one that was legally constituted.'[17] Yet some historians do not understand this vital point. When it comes to Wachsmann's very critical analysis of Morgen, Fraser writes, 'Wachsmann uses the term murder to describe what Morgen carefully analyses and compares in his treatment of the difference between legal and illegal killings in the camps. Wachsmann decides to ignore the distinction.' Fraser goes on to say that using the word murder in a legal sense is very unhelpful when it comes to socio-legal study and that in using this term, Wachsmann does not give Morgen any credit for the way he operated. This is an important point because Morgen's whole approach is to make a distinction between what was legal and what was illegal in Nazi law. At the very least historians should acknowledge this.[18]

Wachsmann also misses the point when he criticises Morgen for focusing on corruption rather than on prisoner abuse. Morgen's official role was always to root out corruption but then he always exceeded his official orders and went after individuals in the SS for murder, abuse of prisoners and other offences too.

It is a similar situation when it comes to Wittmann's book. As set out in Chapter 9, this trial struggled with the question of the legality of the killings in Auschwitz under West German law at the time of the trial. For the historian, this should mean treading carefully in order to highlight the legal issues at stake. Fraser points out that

Wittman is morally outraged when she describes Auschwitz as a 'place of murder' but that this was the central point at issue during the trial.[19]

As Fraser shows, historians need to be careful with their language when discussing Morgen and the role he played in the SS. Prenger uses the word 'murder' in the title of his book: *A Judge in Auschwitz: Konrad Morgen's Crusade against Corruption and 'Illegal' Murder*. This is problematic because first, murder is, by definition, illegal and second, when a historian uses the word murder, the question arises as to how murder is defined. Even today, different countries define murder differently and historians risk confusion and error if they use the word and assume that everyone understands what they mean. As Fraser highlights, murder is a crucial and technical legal term and historians cannot get away with using it without providing context, explanations and other arguments.[20]

In his thoughtful paper 'The Ethics of a Truth-Seeking Judge: Konrad Morgen, SS Judge and Corruption Expert', Raphael Gross examines the question of whether Morgen can be accurately described as an active resistance fighter when set against his work in the SS and his post-war testimony.[21] He compares Morgen to former SS officer Kurt Gerstein who tried to alert the outside world to what was happening in the extermination camps. His conclusion is that more academic study is needed, a call which is also echoed by Fraser. He calls for more study into the legal world of the Third Reich and these issues of lawful and lawful killing which Morgen embodied.

In his very interesting and accessible study of judicial opposition to the Nazis, particularly in Norway, Professor Hans Petter Graver highlights the cases of two judges who tried to persuade police and executive commanders to change their practices. While noting that their actions fell into the category of dissent, he writes:

> Konrad Morgen is different. Although he did nothing ostensibly illegal, he had a secret strategy guiding him in his actions. Had he openly declared that his aim was to stop the mass exterminations and to get at those responsible for it, his efforts would immediately have been put to an end. Apart from the fact that he was acting alone, his actions could have been regarded as an instance of judicial resistance.[22]

This is an important point, and Gross also discusses the question of whether Morgen was an active resister before calling for more study. Perhaps a more accurate term to describe his wartime activities is that of a disrupter: after all, he actively sought to use the law of the Third Reich to interfere with the administration of the Holocaust and concentration camp system by targeting key individuals like Eichmann, Koch, Florstedt and other camp commanders and officials, arresting them and charging them with corruption and murder.

Which brings us back to John Toland. There is one key difference between Toland's analysis of Morgen and many of those who have come after him and judged Morgen. While Toland's research into Morgen was not as extensive as that carried out by others, since his book was ultimately about Hitler, he did have an immediate grasp of the historical reality confronting Morgen: namely that there were laws and a legal system in Nazi Germany. At one stage in his discussion with Morgen in 1971, Toland said to Morgen, 'It says something that in German law there were people like you carrying on a legal process.'

'And why not,' said Morgen animatedly. 'After all, the government may have changed but the judges didn't turn into criminals!'[23]

Toland's grasp of the legal situation in Nazi Germany may have been instinctive but it was historically correct. Other historians have not recognised the legal reality in which Morgen worked and this has led to a flawed understanding of what Morgen was trying to achieve. We need to acknowledge that there were two legal systems operating in Nazi Germany at the same time, the normative system, similar to other European countries, and the prerogative system, which gave Hitler power to issue orders which were then legal. We also need to acknowledge that Morgen's pursuit of justice involved applying the law literally in order to disrupt the Nazi occupation of Poland and the work of the concentration camps. Once we acknowledge the legal situation in Nazi Germany and how Morgen used the law, then we come much closer to Toland's assessment of Konrad Morgen as 'the man who did the most to hinder the atrocities in the East'.

THE VALUES OF THE SS

Wachsmann, in his conclusions about Morgen, writes, 'In short Morgen was no champion of ordinary decency, but a crusader for Himmler's peculiar brand of SS morality.'[24] In their biography, Pauer-Studer and Velleman also talk about Morgen and SS values. They write that after his loyalty to his parents and his comrades in his SS regiment *Germania*, his second loyalty was to the values of the SS.[25] They go on to state that 'Morgen's loyalty was rather to an ideal SS of his own envisioning, an elite corps marked by secular virtues such as honesty and integrity'.[26]

Books and academic papers that cover Morgen often mention his allegiance to the values of the SS without actually setting out what those values are. If you are to claim that Morgen was loyal to SS values or SS morality, then it would surely help the reader to understand exactly what those SS values were or what that morality was.

So, what precisely was the SS morality that Wachsmann mentions and the value system of the SS highlighted by Pauer-Studer and Velleman? In his detailed and definitive biography of Heinrich Himmler, Peter Longerich sets out the virtues of the SS:

> Himmler in numerous speeches to SS members worked his way through a positive 'catalogue of SS virtues.' Central to it were the concepts of loyalty, obedience and comradeship, and he frequently emphasised bravery, honesty, hard work, and fulfilment of duty. But he demanded repeatedly, and above all, one thing from his SS men – decency.[27]

Longerich goes on to discuss each of these in turn. Loyalty meant total submission to the Führer and obedience was the way in which individual SS officers and men demonstrated their loyalty, through Himmler as the head of the SS, to the Führer himself. Disloyalty was therefore a very serious breach of SS values, which could have been treated as treason, and Himmler looked beyond individual cases of disobedience to establish if the person concerned was still loyal. Thus, when Himmler demoted Morgen to the ranks of the

SS and sent him to the Eastern Front with the Waffen SS, he must have satisfied himself that Morgen was still a loyal member of the SS.

The next virtue, comradeship, was one which Himmler uncharacteristically had very little to say about. But when it came to the most important virtue, decency, Longerich writes, '"Decency" was omnipresent in Himmler's world.'[28] Decency for the SS meant behaving in a chivalric way towards the 'right' enemies. Longerich also points to the fact that Himmler maintained that anyone the SS killed should be eliminated 'decently' and highlights the contradiction in the way that the SS did not behave at all decently when it came to the way they tortured and killed people. He sets out the explanation for this, as discussed in Chapter 5: 'Decent treatment could be expedient, but there was always the danger of treating enemies too well and thus doing damage to one's own cause – and that was morally reprehensible. Accordingly, it was decent not to treat one's enemies decently.'[29]

So how does Morgen's own behaviour measure up against the virtues of the SS? When it came to loyalty and obedience, Morgen was in trouble with the SS. He exceeded his orders to stick to investigating corruption and, on his own initiative, he investigated murder as well. He refused to be intimidated by senior SS officers and as a result he was punished with a spell on the Eastern Front. He certainly did value comradeship and talked about it specifically in reference to his time on the front line, but his actions in investigating corruption and murder and in trying to interfere with the Holocaust do not fit with Himmler's ideal of what 'decent' SS behaviour should look like. However, while he steered very close to the wind, he usually managed to stay just on the right side of Himmler, who could have stopped his activities very quickly, if he had chosen to.

So, was Morgen, as Wachsmann suggests, 'a crusader for Himmler's peculiar brand of SS morality'? Was his second allegiance, as Pauer-Studer and Velleman argue, to the values of the SS? The answer to both questions is no. If we look at the values of the SS and compare them to Morgen's behaviour, he was neither a crusader for Himmler's brand of SS morality nor was he loyal to the value system of the SS.

What about the idea put forward by Pauer-Studer and Velleman, that his 'loyalty was rather to an ideal SS of his own envisioning, an elite corps marked by secular virtues such as honesty and integrity'? The problem with this statement is that integrity does not form part of the value system of the SS; so while Morgen's personal values included justice, which for him was far more important than the SS, and integrity, these were not the values of the SS. Therefore, he was not loyal to an ideal SS that he made up himself, he simply acted in accordance with his own personal set of values.

THE TESTIMONIES OF KONRAD MORGEN

Two of the main criticisms of Morgen relate to his testimony at the Nuremberg Tribunals and the 1963–5 Frankfurt Auschwitz trial. His stated personal mission during the Second World War was to investigate and arrest SS criminals for breaches of the law and in this way interfere with the operation of the concentration camps. In addition, he also sought to remove units like those operated by Oskar Dirlewanger, which routinely committed atrocities.

He continued this after the war when he used his interrogations and testimony to pursue Oswald Pohl. However, in the trial of the SS he was criticised for appearing to stick up for the SS. He famously talked about Buchenwald in positive terms from his first visit: 'The camp is situated on wooded heights, with a wonderful view. The installations were clean and freshly painted. There was much lawn and flowers. The prisoners were healthy, normally fed, sun-tanned, working.'[30] He said this in spite of the fact that when the Americans had liberated Buchenwald, they had found appalling conditions (see Chapter 4).

Critics use this testimony to suggest that Morgen was a stout defender of the SS but this is a simplistic approach. When asked about the negative aspects of concentration camps as a defence witness during the SS trial, Morgen was so critical that he was interrupted by one of the prosecution lawyers: 'It seems to me that what we are hearing here is a lecture on the Prosecution's case, and I do not see how it in any sense can be said to be a defence of the SS.'[31] When talking about his first positive impressions of Buchenwald, he must have known about the American liberation of Buchenwald and what they found. He must have known that his testimony would have gone down like a lead balloon in court. He could easily have kept quiet, but he didn't. What if he were deliberately highlighting his own first positive impressions at Buchenwald in order to deliberately discredit his own testimony as a defence witness for the SS? We will never know the answer to this question but it is a valid one to consider.

Another problem with Morgen's testimony was that he suggested that SS Major Christian Wirth was not a member of the SS but a member of the police and therefore outside the command structure of the SS when he was organising the extermination camps in

Nazi-occupied Poland. Wirth had been a police officer before the war but he was certainly a member of the SS when Morgen met him in Lublin.

This testimony given by Morgen led Wachsmann to write of Morgen, 'His postwar testimony was self-serving, riddled with omissions and brazen lies.'[32] Unfortunately, Wachsmann does not provide specific examples of these, but we can look at each in turn. Of course, Morgen was treading carefully with his testimony; he was a middle-ranking officer in the SS and understandably he did not want to face charges himself for being a member of the SS, which was declared to be a criminal organisation. His testimony did omit a lot of material, but in his subsequent interrogations with the Americans, Morgen did supply a vast amount of extra information and he corrected errors he had made, for example mistakenly describing Auschwitz Monowitz as an extermination camp when he meant Auschwitz Birkenau.[33]

At the 1963–5 Auschwitz trial, Morgen pleaded memory loss when asked about individuals who were on trial. As set out in Chapter 9, this may have been due to the atmosphere in West Germany at the time, when there were still many ex-Nazis and ex-SS who were still around and occupying many positions in official life and in industry. Perhaps Morgen feared for his legal practice if he were seen to be helping the trial too much. Perhaps it was that with the war long since over, and like most Germans, Konrad and Maria Morgen simply wanted a quiet and comfortable life without attracting criticism from neighbours and clients.

CORRUPTION

In his book, Wachsmann writes about Morgen, 'His main aim was not to stop prisoner abuse but to root out corruption (and other cases of insubordination).'[34] As set out in Chapter 2, *Reichsführer* Heinrich Himmler gave a speech to his senior SS officers in 1943 about the rules concerning wealth taken from the Jews:

> I have given a strict order, which SS General Pohl has carried out, that these riches shall be diverted to the Reich, without exception. We have taken none of it. Individuals who failed were punished according to an order given by me at the beginning: he who takes even one mark of it, that will be his death. A number of SS men – not very many – have violated that order, and that will be their death, without mercy.[35]

As stated earlier, Morgen's official job within the SS was indeed to root out corruption, but he always exceeded his orders and used corruption as a way to start investigations for murder and other crimes as well. Wachsmann misses this point. A more useful debate might be around the corruption in the SS itself and to ask what any of us would have done in Morgen's shoes. The money and valuables that Morgen saved went into the Reich's coffers and were used to pay for the war and to fund the government of the Third Reich, including the SS, as well as more normal state activities. Was that better than allowing the money and valuables taken from the Jews to be stolen by individual SS officers and men? There is no easy answer to this question. One of the interesting things about Morgen is that he challenges us with difficult questions. As Fried highlights, we should ask ourselves: what would I have done? What should I have done? One part of the answer might come from another question – how many families in Germany and elsewhere are wealthy today because of Jewish wealth stolen by a relative who was in the SS?

Morgen himself was clear about the moral and legal need to investigate and prosecute cases of theft and corruption. In 1964, he wrote:

> I certainly made sure (although I delegated this more to my colleagues) that the executioners did not enrich themselves from their victims but were harshly punished for what they did. Even today I still feel a certain sense of satisfaction about that. There is no legal system or legal theory in the world that allows robbery and corpse-scavenging.[36]

CONCLUSION

Whatever else anyone may say about Morgen, the fact remains that he was an SS investigating judge and police official who used the law as he found it in the Third Reich to bring SS criminals to justice. Crucial to our understanding of Morgen is the simple fact that Nazi Germany had laws and a legal system in which both the normal German laws, as well as orders issued by Hitler, were recognised as legal and lawful. Any historian or academic who ignores this historical and legal reality will inevitably lack credibility by producing a flawed and uninformed analysis of Morgen and his SS career.

At the very outset, we must recognise that Morgen embodied a number of contradictions. He spent his wartime career trying to frustrate the work of the concentration camps and the Final Solution and yet at the end of the war, he wrote to Maria praising Himmler as 'a great person with a sensitive heart'.[37] At the 1963–5

Auschwitz trial, he came across as someone who cared more about improper relationships between the SS and female Jewish prisoners and the familiar forms of address they used than about the Holocaust. Added to this, he claimed he had forgotten important details about those in the dock when asked. A question mark hangs over some of his post-war testimony at Nuremberg.

But whatever feelings Morgen may have had for Himmler himself, they did not extend to the rest of the SS. Morgen roamed the Reich in his SS uniform as a menacing, fearless and threatening figure to the SS, a reputation which he himself enjoyed and encouraged. Buchenwald prisoner Alfred Miller said, 'Faced with Dr Morgen the SS were shaking. Dr Morgen was seen as the devil himself.'[38] Another prisoner, Stefan Heymann, said, 'Morgen was extraordinarily feared and hated by all SS officers in Buchenwald.'[39]

Although Morgen was a member of the Nazi Party, he always said he joined the party for opportunistic reasons only and nothing he said or did contradicted that. He refused to vote in the 1934 referendum to give Hitler ultimate power in Germany, he crossed swords again with the party with his book *War Propaganda and War Prevention* and he was fired as a judge in 1939 for failing to support a party-inspired case. Later, he stopped his fiancée Maria from joining the Nazi Party when she suggested it as a means for them to marry.

As an SS investigating judge in the General Government, Morgen's main focus, apart from the atrocities committed by Oskar Dirlewanger and his unit, was on corruption cases. Here he made powerful enemies, including Oswald Pohl who succeeded in getting him demoted and removed to the Eastern Front. As a result of his experiences on the front line in a Russian winter and spring,

Morgen became a battle-hardened combat veteran of the Waffen SS – to the extent that when he was reinstated into his former rank and position, he showed no fear in investigating and arresting concentration camp commandants and other SS officers for corruption and murder. Nor did he hesitate in confronting senior SS officers with evidence of what was happening in the camps.

Having found out about the extermination camps, Morgen resolved to work even harder to use the legal system in Nazi Germany against the SS. By the end of the war, Morgen had conducted 800 investigations into crimes committed by members of the SS, with 200 brought to trial. Alongside his attempt to go after Adolf Eichmann, he personally arrested five concentration camp commanding officers and two were executed after their trials.[40]

What about John Toland's assessment of Morgen as, 'the man who did the most to hinder the atrocities in the East' and his work as 'one man house-cleaning', as well as a 'lonesome attempt to end the Final Solution'?[41] When we look at the evidence and consider the arguments of Morgen's critics, Toland was right in making these three statements. Toland uses the word 'hinder' to describe Morgen's work and that is exactly what Konrad Morgen did; he was a disrupter of the Nazi killing machine and he used laws in place in the Third Reich to do it.

Konrad Morgen did indeed carry out a one-man house-cleaning and he did what he could to try and stop the Final Solution. Realistically, however, neither he nor anyone else could have stopped the Holocaust on their own. In the end, it took the combined might of the Allied armies to invade Germany and put a stop to the Holocaust and the killings. It is also interesting that no other SS investigating judge attracts the level of criticism which Morgen attracts – but then, of course, no other SS investigating judge was investigating and arresting SS criminals not just for corruption but for murder.

Today, you won't find many references to Morgen in Germany outside the academic world. This is a shame because whatever your views about Morgen, his SS career certainly prompts meaningful discussions about the nature of the law and our relationship to it, as well as questions like those asked by Fried about Morgen: 'How do we know who we are, what we would be in such times?'[42]

This lack of interest in Germany is disappointing because the fact remains that the very first person to carry out a successful criminal investigation into a concentration camp commandant was a German and he did it before the end of the war.

Before and during the war, Konrad Morgen was a prickly, stubborn and awkward character. He was quick to take offence and he fell out with colleagues and with his bosses. On the other hand, he was loyal and dedicated to his fiancée Maria. He was a thoughtful lawyer who was determined to do the right thing, and since he lived in the Third Reich, doing the right thing for him meant coming into conflict with the SS by pursuing criminals within its ranks and trying to put a stop to the killings. His ultimate loyalty was not to the SS but rather to his own values and sense of justice, and he worked non-stop to live up to both of these.

As set out in the Introduction, both Philip Kerr's fictional police detective Bernie Gunther and Konrad Morgen faced the same challenge: how do you stay alive in the Third Reich and perhaps even prosper without selling your soul to the devil? Everything to do with the Nazis was a Faustian bargain. In return for jobs, economic stability and prosperity, the German people gave Hitler the keys to the Reich and in return he made them accessories to the Holocaust. For Morgen, his Faustian bargain was that he could develop his legal career as an SS judge in return for what was supposed to be his help in cleansing the SS of corruption. As part of the deal, he was given access to the darkest secrets of the Third Reich, but he quickly broke the agreement by exceeding his orders and going after SS criminals for murder. Ultimately, only defeat by the Allies released Germany and Morgen from their pacts.

While we puzzle over Morgen's contradictions, it is worth remembering that these contradictions have yet to be resolved in the academic world as well. Part of the problem is that Morgen defies some of the labels that academics like to attach to people, especially when it comes to legal philosophy. As set out earlier, Fried sums up the two sides of the argument very neatly when he says, 'The law says we must or may not do this or that, but must we really? We may be legally obligated, but are we morally obligated? The connection between legal and moral obligation is the signature issue of legal philosophy.'[43]

Simplistically, those who say that we must obey all laws and set aside any moral considerations are labelled as legal positivists and those who say that we must only obey laws that have a moral foundation are labelled as natural law theorists. Because Morgen recognised the validity of both the normal set of laws in the Third Reich (the normative state) as well the legal validity of orders issued by the Führer (the prerogative state), he is often described by academics today as a legal positivist.

However, Morgen does not fit into the box marked 'legal positivism'. He certainly recognised the legal validity of both systems of law in Nazi Germany: the laws in place in the normative state as well as orders issued by Hitler under the prerogative state. But Morgen also recognised the immorality of the orders issued by Hitler under the prerogative state, orders that the SS carried out and which led to mass killings, atrocities and to the Holocaust. In order to actively hinder the work of the Nazi prerogative state, Morgen weaponised the laws that were part of the normative state and used them against the SS, which was the agent of the prerogative state and responsible for carrying out Hitler's orders.

Simply describing Morgen as a legal positivist does not therefore adequately capture the contradictions which he displayed. Existing academic frameworks appear to be inadequate when it comes to Morgen. Fraser is right when he says that when it comes to writing a socio-legal history of Morgen, 'Positivism is only a somewhat insignificant first step. It does not, nor can it, provide us with a basis upon which to ground moral or ethical critiques of Morgen, Nazi law, or any substantive legal norm.'[44]

It is, of course, part of the job description for an academic to explore the individual actions and motivations of noteworthy historical figures and to come to a judgement on them, but academics do need to avoid falling into the trap of making superficial judgements about Morgen. Equally, Professor Joel Marks is right to highlight that when criticism goes overboard in the case of Morgen then academics open themselves up to a charge of heavy-handedness. When studying Morgen, academics and anyone else who is interested in his story need to think about his situation and ask themselves the questions posed by Fried: 'What would I have done in Morgen's shoes? What should I have done?'[45]

The last word in this book belongs to Morgen himself, from a letter which he wrote after the war, in which he asked his own questions about his wartime career. As set out in Chapter 9, the first de-Nazification tribunal exonerated Morgen but the Ministry for Political Liberation refused to accept this judgment for a major in the SS and so they convened a second tribunal. As a result, on 3 January 1950, Konrad Morgen wrote to the ministry and argued his case:

> It is undisputed that I took action against this regime of tyranny and its exponents. Not through whispering campaigns, not through theoretical conspiracy plans, not through treason but through the most direct and effective means, by calling out crimes, murder, criminals, by accusing the culprits of their misdeeds and sending them to prison and to the execution squads. What more and what better could I have done?[46]

APPENDIX: WHAT HAPPENED NEXT?

What happened to the main characters in Morgen's story has been set out in the main chapters of this book. Others who appeared in the narrative are listed here.

Reichsführer-SS Heinrich Himmler

Captured by British forces on 23 May 1945, Himmler distinguished himself from other Nazi fugitives by announcing who he was to the British duty officer at Lüneberg Civilian Interrogation Camp, Captain Thomas Selvester. Although the British searched Himmler, they were careful to avoid his mouth as they presumed he had a cyanide capsule concealed there. He was in good humour and cooperative. However, when he was transferred to the headquarters of the British 2nd Army in Lüneberg, the doctor examining him started to look in his mouth, at which Himmler bit down on his hand then bit into the cyanide capsule he had concealed there. After his death, his body was photographed by the British to prove that he had died.[1]

SS General Heinrich Müller

Müller had a central role organising the Holocaust and was in charge of Office IV, the Gestapo, in the Reich Security Main Office. Adolf Eichmann worked in Office IV B, Jewish Affairs, under Müller. Müller was last seen alive at the end of April or early May 1945 in Hitler's bunker in Berlin, and his subsequent whereabouts have been the subject of years of speculation. Immediately after the war the Allies searched for him, but their search was hampered by the fact that Heinrich Müller was and is a very common German name. In the 1960s, the German authorities started looking again with no success, followed by a CIA investigation also with no success. The most likely explanation is that he died in Berlin in 1945.[2]

SS General Odilo Globočnik

In May 1945, Globočnik was captured by the 4th Hussars, a unit of the British Army. An informer had told them there was a group of former SS men hiding out in the mountains in Carinthia, Austria, and he very nearly convinced his captors that he wasn't important. However, he was picked out by another informer and a British officer, Major Ramsay, called out his name, at which his head moved fractionally. As he was being taken into custody, he bit into his hidden cyanide capsule and died. In 1983, the historian Gitta Sereny was contacted by someone claiming to have evidence that Globočnik had not, in fact, died and that the photograph the British took of his body was a fake. Sereny investigated these claims and tracked down Major Ramsay's widow in Vienna. She had a much clearer picture of Globočnik's body in her possession and Sereny was able to conclude that he had definitely died when the official reports said he did.[3]

SS Colonel Rudolf Mildner

After leaving Auschwitz, Mildner was transferred to Denmark as head of the Gestapo. There he was tasked with deporting Denmark's 8,000-strong Jewish population, but they managed to escape to Sweden after the deportation plans were leaked by the German naval attaché, Georg Duckwitz. At the post-war trial of Ernst Kaltenbrunner at Nuremberg, Mildner claimed that he had flown to Berlin to try and stop the deportation. After this, he was posted to the Reich Security Main Office where he was Adolf Eichmann's boss during the period Eichmann was arranging the deportation of Hungary's Jews to Auschwitz. Finally, he was posted to Vienna as head of the Gestapo. He was captured by Allied forces in May 1945 and cooperated with his American interrogators. The British, Danish and Polish governments all requested his extradition, but Mildner had provided useful information to the Americans about the workings and structure of the Gestapo and so they kept him detained. In 1949, he escaped to Argentina.[4]

SS Captain Franz Stangl

After working under Christian Wirth, Stangl was given command of Treblinka extermination camp. He had previously been the commandant of Sobibor, another extermination centre. As commandant, he was in the habit of riding into camp in a white riding coat and the prisoners nicknamed him 'White Death'. After the camps were liquidated, Stangl was posted to Trieste with other senior officers from the extermination programme. After the war, he escaped to Brazil. He was hunted down by the Nazi hunter Simon Wiesenthal in 1967 and extradited to Germany, where he was sentenced to life imprisonment. While in prison, he was interviewed by the historian

Gitta Sereny and these conversations were published. They talked about his life and she asked him on a number of occasions about facing up to what he did. In their last conversation, just before he died of heart failure in prison, Sereny asked him again and he started talking about guilt: 'Once again, as so often when he tried to come to grips with the impossibly difficult question of his guilt, the sentence trailed off. "My guilt," he started again, "is that I am still here. That is my guilt."'[5]

NOTES

Most of the documents in the sources are written in German. All translations of original documents from the German are by the author.

INTRODUCTION

1 Konrad Morgen interview tapes, FDR Presidential Library and Museum, series 2, C-47 and C-48
2 *Adolf Hitler* by John Toland. Doubleday, 1976, p.761 and p.774
3 *The Dual State* by Ernst Fraenkel. OUP, 1941, p.xiii
4 Ibid.
5 Konrad Morgen interrogations, 19 September 1946, US National Archives, record group 238, microfilm 1019, roll 47
6 'Tape recordings of the Auschwitz trial (1963–1965): Witness Konrad Morgen', 9 March 1964, *Fritz Bauer Institut*, https://www.auschwitz-prozess.de/zeugenaussagen/Morgen-Konrad/
7 United States Holocaust Memorial Museum, 'Nazi Camps', *Holocaust Encyclopedia*, https://encyclopedia.ushmm.org/content/en/article/nazi-camps
8 Ibid.
9 'Nuremberg Trial Proceedings Volume 20: One Hundred and Ninety-Seventh Day, Wednesday; 7 August 1946', The Avalon Project, Yale Law School, p.488, https://avalon.law.yale.edu/imt/08-07-46.asp

CHAPTER 1: BEGINNINGS

1 *Encyclopedia of Camps and Ghettos, 1933–1945*, vol 1. United States Holocaust Memorial Museum, 2009
2 *Walter Krämer*, Kreisarchiv Siegen-Wittgenstein 2013, S.3-5, https://www.siwiarchiv.de/wp-content/uploads/2020/11/WalterKraemer.pdf
3 *Der SS Staat – Das System der deutschen Konzentrationslager* by Eugon Kogon. Heyne Verlag, 1988, p.324
4 'Kraemer Walter', *Yad Vashem*, https://collections.yadvashem.org/en/righteous/4015823
5 *The Buchenwald Report*, translated by David A. Hackett, Westview Press, 1995, p.123
6 Kogon op. cit.
7 *USA v. Josias Prinz zu Waldeck et al.*, case 000-50-9, United Nations War Crimes Commission, trial transcript at p.2749 onwards, https://www.legal-tools.org/doc/5b740c/
8 'Tape recordings of the Auschwitz trial (1963–1965): Witness Konrad Morgen' op. cit.
9 Hackett op. cit., p.341
10 *USA v. Josias Prinz zu Waldeck et al.* op. cit., p.2750
11 *Entnazifizierung* Konrad Morgen, Landesarchiv Baden-Würtemburg, EL903/3, 1 Bü
12 'Tape recordings of the Auschwitz trial (1963–1965): Witness Konrad Morgen' op. cit.
13 *Official Results of the Investigation into Buchenwald*, 11 April 1944, via University of Connecticut Digital Library, NARA, NO-2366/597043
14 *USA v. Josias Prinz zu Waldeck et al.* op. cit., p.2753
15 'Tape recordings of the Auschwitz trial (1963–1965): Witness Konrad Morgen' op. cit.

16 *Official Results of the Investigation into Buchenwald* op. cit.
17 *Who's Who in Nazi Germany* by Robert S.Wistrich. Routledge, 1995, p.271
18 *USA v. Josias Prinz zu Waldeck et al.* op. cit., p.2739
19 Konrad Morgen interrogations, 30 August 1946 op. cit.; *Entnazifizierung* Konrad Morgen op. cit.
20 Konrad Morgen interview with John Toland, *John Toland Papers*, FDR Presidential Library and Museum, series 2, C-47 and C-48
21 Konrad Morgen interrogations, 4 September 1946 op. cit., pp.2–3
22 'Oral history interview with Konrad Morgan' [*sic*], United States Holocaust Memorial Museum Collection purchased from the Imperial War Museum Collection, https://collections.ushmm.org/search/catalog/irn510178
23 Ibid.
24 Quoted in *Heinrich Himmler* by Peter Longerich. OUP, 2012, p.114
25 *Who's Who in Nazi Germany* op. cit., p.271
26 Longerich op. cit., p.127
27 *Entnazifizierung* Konrad Morgen op. cit.
28 *The Order of the Death's Head* by Heinz Höhne. Ballantine Books, 1986, p.153
29 *Encyclopedia of Camps and Ghettos, 1933–1945* op. cit., p.xxxiii
30 Ibid., p.47
31 Longerich op. cit., p.153
32 *Entnazifizierung* Konrad Morgen op. cit.
33 Konrad Morgen interrogations, 4 September 1946 op. cit.
34 Konrad Morgen interview with John Toland op. cit.
35 Via the University of Melbourne's historical currency converter: https://canvasresources-prod.le.unimelb.edu.au/projects/CURRENCY_CALC/ and the Bank of England's inflation calculator: https://www.bankofengland.co.uk/monetary-policy/inflation/inflation-calculator. The Deutsche Bundesbank uses an inflation factor of 4.3 applied to 1943 prices, which works out roughly the same: https://www.bundesbank.de/resource/blob/622372/21803eea8118564ea04d44592018ed60/mL/kaufkraftaequivalente-historischer-betraege-in-deutschen-waehrungen-data.pdf
36 'Nachlass Konrad Morgen', Archiv des Fritz Bauer Institut, folder 49
37 'Nachlass Konrad Morgen', folder 37
38 'Transcript for NMT 4: Pohl Case', *HLS Nuremberg Trials Project*, Morgen testimony 21 and 22 August 1947, p.6671, https://nuremberg.law.harvard.edu/transcripts/5-transcript-for-nmt-4-
39 'Oral history interview with Konrad Morgan' [*sic*] op. cit.
40 'Nachlass Konrad Morgen', folder 50
41 'Nachlass Konrad Morgen', folder 38
42 Konrad Morgen interrogations, 4 September 1946 op. cit.
43 'Nachlass Konrad Morgen', folder 38
44 *An Uncompromising Generation: The Nazi Leadership of the Reich Security Main Office* by Michael Wildt, translated Tom Lampert. University of Wisconsin Press, 2009, pp.428–35
45 *Entnazifizierung* Konrad Morgen op. cit.
46 Konrad Morgen interrogations, 31 August 1946 op. cit.
47 *Who's Who in Nazi Germany* op. cit., p.63

CHAPTER 2: INVESTIGATING CRIME IN NAZI-OCCUPIED POLAND

1 *USA v. Ernst von Weizsäcker et al.*, 24 March 1948, US National Archives, record group 238, microfilm 897, roll 5
2 Konrad Morgen interrogations, 30 August 1946 op. cit.
3 Ibid.
4 *The SS Dirlewanger Brigade: The History of the Black Hunters* by Christian Ingrao. Skyhorse Publishing, 2013, p.14
5 Quoted in ibid., p.69
6 *USA v. Ernst von Weizäcker et al.* op. cit.
7 'Nachlass Konrad Morgen', folder 39
8 Quoted in *The SS Dirlewanger Brigade* op. cit., p.108
9 Konrad Morgen interrogations, 30 August 1948 op. cit.
10 Longerich op. cit., p.145
11 Ibid., p.146
12 *The Cruel Hunters: SS-Sonderkommando Dirlewanger, Hitler's most notorious anti-partisan unit* by French L. MacLean. Schiffer Military History, 1998, pp.133–4

13 *The SS Dirlewanger Brigade* op. cit., pp.115–6
14 Konrad Morgen interrogations, 30 August 1948 op. cit.
15 'Landeskundliche Informationssystem für Baden-Württemberg' (State Information System for Baden-Württemberg) https://www.leo-bw.de/web/guest/detail/-/Detail/details/PERSON/kgl_biographien/118837419/biografie
16 *The SS Dirlewanger Brigade* op. cit., p.179
17 Konrad Morgen interrogations, 30 August 1946 op. cit.
18 *Strafvollzugslager der SS und Polizei: Himmler's Wartime Institutions for the Detention of Waffen SS and Polizei Criminals* by Stuart B. T. Emmett. Fonthill, 2017, p.30
19 'Speech [of] the Reichsfuehrer-SS at the meeting of SS Major-Generals ... at Posen', Extracts from speeches concerning the SS and the conduct of the war, *HLS Nuremberg Trials Project*, https://nuremberg.law.harvard.edu/documents/2974-extracts-from-speeches-concerning?q=Himmler+1919-PS#p.1
20 Konrad Morgen interrogations, 30 August 1946 op. cit.
21 Ibid.
22 *Entnazifizierung* Konrad Morgen op. cit.
23 University of Melbourne and Bank of England op. cit.
24 *Entnazifizierung* Konrad Morgen op. cit.
25 Konrad Morgen interrogations, 30 August 1946 op. cit.
26 *Entnazifizierung* Konrad Morgen op. cit.
27 Konrad Morgen interrogations, 30 August 1946 op. cit.
28 Ibid.
29 Ibid.
30 Quoted in James J. Weingartner, 'Law and Justice in the Nazi SS: The Case of Konrad Morgen', *Central European History*, vol. 16, no. 3, 1983, pp.276–94
31 Konrad Morgen interrogations op. cit.
32 *The Last Days of Hitler* by Hugh Trevor-Roper. Macmillan, 1947, p.87 and p.22
33 Longerich op. cit., p.320
34 University of Melbourne and Bank of England op. cit.
35 Konrad Morgen interrogations, 30 August 1946 op. cit.
36 Konrad Morgen interrogations op. cit.
37 Longerich op. cit., p.301
38 Weingartner op. cit.
39 *The Last Days of Hitler* by Anton Joachimstaler. Cassell, 2007, p.126
40 *Entnazifizierung* Konrad Morgen op. cit.
41 University of Melbourne and Bank of England op. cit.
42 *Entnazifizierung* Konrad Morgen op. cit.
43 Ibid.
44 Quoted in Weingartner op. cit., p.286
45 Konrad Morgen interrogations, 30 August 1946 op. cit.
46 Hans Petter Graver, 'Why Adolf Hitler Spared the Judges: Judicial Opposition Against the Nazi State', *German Law Journal*, vol. 19, no. 4, pp.845–77
47 *Entnazifizierung* Konrad Morgen op. cit.
48 Konrad Morgen interrogations, 30 August 1946 op. cit.
49 Ibid.

CHAPTER 3: AT WAR WITH THE WAFFEN SS

1 The opening paragraphs of this chapter are based on an article by the author: David Lee, 'Cue to a Kill', *Financial Times*, 10 February 2006, https://www.ft.com/content/0cb5ff48-9930-11da-9ffa-0000779e2340
2 *Dr No* by Ian Fleming. Pan Books, 1963, p.19
3 *The Life of Ian Fleming* by John Pearson. McGraw-Hill, 1966
4 Ibid., p.105
5 *Men Against Fire* by S. L. A. Marshall. William Morrow and Company, 1966, p.54
6 *Military Training in the British Army 1940–44* by Timothy Harrison Place. Frank Cass, 2000, p.79
7 *On Killing* by David Grossman. Little Brown, 1996
8 *Up Close and Personal: The Reality of Fighting at Close Quarters in World War II* by David Lee. Greenhill Books, 2006, p.33
9 'Nachlass Konrad Morgen', folder 16
10 Konrad Morgen interrogations, 30 August 1946 op. cit.

11 *Mein Weg zur 31. SS-Freiwilligen Grenadier-Division* by Fredo Gensicke. Nation & Wissen Verlag, 2016, pp.11–15
12 *SS Wiking: The History of the Fifth SS Division 1941–1945* by Rupert Butler. Casemate, 2002, p.26
13 'Transcript for NMT 4: Pohl Case' op. cit., p.6673
14 Ibid., p.25
15 Konrad Morgen interrogations, 30 August 1946 op. cit.
16 Quoted in Longerich op. cit., p.342
17 Konrad Morgen interrogations, 30 August 1946 op. cit.
18 *The SS-Division Wiking in the Caucasus 1942–1943* by Massimiliano Afiero. MMP Books, 2017, pp.94–100
19 Butler op. cit., p.89
20 *USA v. Josias Prinz zu Waldeck et al.* op. cit., p.2794
21 Konrad Morgen interrogations, 30 August 1946 op. cit.
22 *An Uncompromising Generation: The Nazi Leadership of the Reich Security Main Office* by Michael Wildt. University of Wisconsin Press, 2009, p.166
23 'Nachlass Konrad Morgen', folder 50
24 Bernd Wehner, 'Das Spiel ist Aus – Arthur Nebe', *Der Spiegel*, 12 October 1949. *Der Spiegel* does not name the author but Wehner swore an affidavit in 1960 that he wrote this article
25 Wildt op. cit., p.172
26 Memo from SS General Breithaupt to Reichsführer-SS, 'Nachlass Konrad Morgen', folder 50. This memo refers to Morgen as a *Hauptsturmführer*, or captain, whereas Morgen later refers to himself as being restored to his previous rank of lieutenant and officially he became a captain in November 1943
27 'Nachlass Konrad Morgen', folder 40

CHAPTER 4: THE INVESTIGATION AT BUCHENWALD CONCENTRATION CAMP, PART ONE

1 'German civilians visit Buchenwald', United States Holocaust Memorial Museum, accession number 1994.119.1, https://collections.ushmm.org/search/catalog/irn1000201
2 The *Guardian* article says there were 21,000 inmates there. The figure of 48,000 comes from the authoritative *Encyclopedia of Camps and Ghettos, 1933–1945* op. cit., p.292
3 'The horrors of Buchenwald', *The Guardian*, 18 April 1945, https://www.theguardian.com/world/1945/apr/18/secondworldwar.germany
4 'Oral history interview with Harry J. Herder', United States Holocaust Memorial Museum, gift of Mary Cook and Nita Howton, https://collections.ushmm.org/search/catalog/irn80099
5 *Weimar: From Enlightenment to the Present* by Michael H. Kater. Yale University Press, 2014, p.265
6 Ibid.
7 *Einwirkung der neueren Philosophie Sämtliche Werke nach Epochen seines Schaffens* by Johann Wolfgang Goethe. Bd. 12, 97
8 Translation of Gothe's original German provided by the author; Patrick Spottiswoode, 'Friends, Germans, countrymen: the long history of "unser Shakespeare"', *The Guardian*, 6 October 2010, https://www.theguardian.com/culture/theatreblog/2010/oct/06/german-william-shakespeare
9 'Welcome', *Deutsche Shakespeare-Gesellschaft*, https://shakespeare-gesellschaft.de
10 Kater op. cit., p.249
11 Ibid.
12 *Goethe in German Jewish Culture*, ed. by Klaus L. Berghahn and Jost Hermand. Camden House, 2001, p.xi
13 Kater op. cit., p.265
14 *Dem Täter auf dem Spur* by Bernd Wehner and Gustav Lübbe. Verlag, 1983, p.234
15 Konrad Morgen interrogations, 4 September 1946 op. cit.
16 'Das Spiel ist Aus – Arthur Nebe' op. cit.
17 *USA v. Josias Prinz zu Waldeck et al.* op. cit., p.2749
18 Affidavit by Werner Paulmann dated 11 July 1946, *Trial of the Major War Criminals before the International Military Tribunal*, IMT Blue series, vol. XLII, pp.543–50
19 *Official Results of the Investigation into Buchenwald* op. cit.
20 Ibid.
21 *USA v. Josias Prinz zu Waldeck et al.* op. cit., p.2745
22 *USA v. Josias Prinz zu Waldeck et al.* op. cit., p.2865
23 *Soldiers of Evil: The Commandants of the Nazi Concentration Camps* by Tom Segev. McGraw-Hill, 1988, p.142
24 Konrad Morgen interrogations, 4 September 1946 op. cit.,
25 *Entnazifizierung* Konrad Morgen op. cit.

26 *The Buchenwald Report* op. cit., p.123
27 Segev op. cit., p.25
28 *The Buchenwald Report* op. cit.
29 *The Buchenwald Report* op. cit., p.45
30 *Official Results of the Investigation into Buchenwald* op. cit.
31 Ibid.
32 Segev op. cit., p.133
33 *USA v. Josias Prinz zu Waldeck et al.* op. cit.
34 Affidavit by Konrad Morgen dated 13 July 1946, *Trial of the Major War Criminals before the International Military Tribunal* op. cit.
35 *The Buchenwald Report* op. cit.
36 *Official Results of the Investigation into Buchenwald* op. cit.
37 *The Buchenwald Report* op. cit.
38 Memo from SS Captain Konrad Morgen to SS General Breithaupt, 'Nachlass Konrad Morgen', folder 50
39 Memo from SS judiciary to the Reichsführer, 23 February 1944, 'Nachlass Konrad Morgen', folder 50
40 Longerich op. cit., p.343
41 'Oral history interview with Konrad Morgan' [*sic*] op. cit.
42 Konrad Morgen interrogations, 4 September 1946 op. cit.
43 *Official Results of the Investigation into Buchenwald* op. cit.
44 *Encyclopedia of Camps and Ghettos, 1933–1945* op. cit.
45 *Official Results of the Investigation into Buchenwald* op. cit.
46 Segev op. cit., p.216
47 *Official Results of the Investigation into Buchenwald* op. cit.
48 Segev op. cit., p.214
49 *Official Results of the Investigation into Buchenwald* op. cit.
50 Konrad Morgen interrogations, 4 September 1946 op. cit.
51 *USA v. Josias Prinz zu Waldeck et al.* op. cit., p.2871
52 Kogon op. cit., p.317
53 *The Buchenwald Report* op. cit. p.123
54 Konrad Morgen interrogations, 4 September 1946 op. cit.
55 'Oral history interview with Konrad Morgan' [*sic*] op. cit.
56 University of Melbourne and Bank of England op. cit.
57 *USA v. Josias Prinz zu Waldeck et al.* op. cit., p.2747
58 *Official Results of the Investigation into Buchenwald* op. cit.
59 Longerich op. cit., p.486
60 Konrad Morgen interrogations, 4 September 1946 op. cit.
61 Konrad Morgen interrogations, 18 January 1947 op. cit.
62 Konrad Morgen interrogations, 4 September 1946 op. cit.
63 University of Melbourne and Bank of England op. cit.
64 Ibid.
65 Ibid.
66 *Official Results of the Investigation into Buchenwald* op. cit.
67 'Nuremberg Trial Proceedings Volume 20: One Hundred and Ninety-Sixth Day, Wednesday; 7 August 1946', The Avalon Project, Yale Law School, https://avalon.law.yale.edu/imt/08-07-46.asp

CHAPTER 5: THE INVESTIGATION AT BUCHENWALD CONCENTRATION CAMP, PART TWO

1 'Das Spiel ist Aus – Arthur Nebe' op. cit.
2 This chapter is based on three primary sources: Konrad Morgen interrogations op. cit., 11 October 1946; *Official Results of the Investigation into Buchenwald* op. cit.; *USA v. Josias Prinz zu Waldeck et al.* op. cit., pp.2809–913
3 *Official Results of the Investigation into Buchenwald* op. cit.
4 *The Buchenwald Report* op. cit., p.60
5 *Paul Schneider: The Pastor of Buchenwald* by E. H. Robertson. Northumberland Press Ltd, 1956, p.113
6 *The Buchenwald Report* op. cit.
7 'Das Spiel ist Aus – Arthur Nebe' op. cit.
8 Wehner op. cit., p.257ff
9 *Official Results of the Investigation into Buchenwald* op. cit.
10 Konrad Morgen interrogations, 11 October 1946 op. cit.
11 Wehner op. cit.

12 *USA v. Karl Brandt et al.*, document 29, affidavit by Konrad Morgen dated 26 February 1947, HLSL 741 and 794, https://nuremberg.law.harvard.edu/documents/794-affidavit-concerning-medical-experiments
13 Konrad Morgen interrogations, 11 October 1946 op. cit.
14 *USA v. Josias Prinz zu Waldeck et al.* op. cit., p.2782ff
15 Ibid., p.2854
16 *Official Results of the Investigation into Buchenwald* op. cit.
17 *The Buchenwald Report* op. cit. p.43
18 Longerich op. cit., p.310
19 Ibid., p.375ff
20 *Entnazifizierung* Konrad Morgen op. cit.
21 *Entnazifizierung* Konrad Morgen op. cit.; 'Nachlass Konrad Morgen', folder 41
22 *Official Results of the Investigation into Buchenwald* op. cit.
23 *The Buchenwald Report* op. cit. p.126
24 *USA v. Werner Berger et al.*, 000-Buchenwald-50 https://www.jewishvirtuallibrary.org/jsource/Holocaust/dachautrial/b24.pdf
25 *Doctors From Hell: The Horrific Account of Nazi Experiments on Humans* by Vivien Spitz. Sentient Publications,, 2005 p.213
26 Konrad Morgen interrogations, 11 October 1946 op. cit.
27 Spitz op. cit., p.50.
28 *USA v. Karl Brandt et al.*, affidavit by Konrad Morgen dated 23 May 1947, HLSL 794, https://nuremberg.law.harvard.edu/documents/794-affidavit-concerning-medical-experiments
29 'Das Spiel ist Aus – Arthur Nebe' op. cit.

CHAPTER 6: THE INVESTIGATION AT MAJDANEK EXTERMINATION CAMP

1 *Majdanek: The Concentration Camp in Lublin* by Jósef Marsałek, Interpress Warsaw, 1986, p.87 and p.132
2 *Pola Braun* by Róża Ziątek-Czarnota. Adam Mickiewicz Institute, 2013, https://culture.pl/pl/tworca/pola-braun
3 *IMT: Trial of the Major War Criminals before the International Military Tribunal*, Nazi Conspiracy and Aggression, Office of United States Chief Counsel for Prosecution of Axis Criminality. United States Government Printing Office, 1948, p.1309
4 Adolf Eichmann trial transcript, 5 June 1961, session 64, Josef Reznik testimony, via Nizkor Project, https://www.nizkor.org/the-trial-of-adolf-eichmann/
5 Andrzej Żbikowski, 'Texts Buried in Oblivion. Testimonies of Two Refugees from the Mass Grave at Poniatowa', *Journal of the Polish Center for Holocaust Research*, p.90
6 Ibid.
7 Affidavit by Werner Paulmann op.cit
8 *Concentration Camp Majdanek* by Jürgen Graf and Carlo Mattogno. Theses & Dissertations Press, 2004, p.216
9 Marsałek op. cit., p.40
10 Morgen's testimony in *Trial of the Major War Criminals before the International Military Tribunal*, vol. XX, 7 August 1946
11 Wistrich op. cit., p.278
12 *The German Trauma: Experiences and Reflections 1938–2001* by Gitta Sereny. Penguin, 2001, p.106
13 Ibid., p.123
14 *Trial of the Major War Criminals before the International Military Tribunal*, vol. XX, 7 August 1946 op. cit.
15 University of Melbourne and Bank of England op. cit.
16 Konrad Morgen interrogations, 11 October 1946 op. cit.

CHAPTER 7: THE INVESTIGATION AT AUSCHWITZ

1 *Auschwitz Chronicle* by Danuta Czech. IB Tauris, 1990, pp.452–7
2 *We Wept Without Tears: Testimonies Of the Jewish Sonderkommando From Auschwitz* by Gideon Greif. Yale University Press, 2005, p.12
3 Ibid., p.301
4 Ibid., p.197
5 'Tape recordings of the Auschwitz trial (1963–1965): Witness Zdzisław Mikołajski', 25 September 1964, *Fritz Bauer Institut*, https://www.auschwitz-prozess.de/zeugenaussagen/Mikolajski-Zdzislaw/
6 'Tape recordings of the Auschwitz trial (1963–1965): Witness Konrad Morgen' op. cit.. Morgen gives the name of the SS Sergeant as Körfer in Konrad Morgen interrogations, 4 September 1946 op. cit.

7 'Tape recordings of the Auschwitz trial (1963–1965): Witness Konrad Morgen' op. cit.
8 Czech op. cit., p.527
9 *KL Auschwitz Seen By The SS* by Rudolf Höss and Pery Broad. The Auschwitz-Birkenau State Museum Oświęcim, 1995, p.35
10 Ibid., p.78
11 Segev op. cit., p.211
12 Höss and Broad op. cit., p.108. The description of the so-called 'enhanced interrogations' and weekly clearing out of the cells is also based on his account. In his account, he describes the clearing out of prisoners to be a once-weekly event; however Eleonore Hodys, who was a prisoner at Auschwitz and who gave a statement to Morgen, describes them as being twice weekly.
13 Konrad Morgen interrogations, 4 September 1946 op. cit.
14 Höss and Broad op. cit., p.112. The description of the police summary court is based on his account.
15 Affidavit by Konrad Morgen dated 10 July 1946, *Trial of the Major War Criminals before the International Military Tribunal* op. cit.
16 Eleonore Hodys statement to SS judge and major of the Waffen SS reserve, Dr Konrad Morgen in Autumn 1944, Institut für Zeitgeschichte ZS599/2. An English translation of this document also appears in a US Army booklet about Dachau concentration camp called *SS Dachau* and listed as 'Statement by E.H.'. In the Nuremberg trial against the SS, this was clarified as being Eleonore Hodys's statement to Morgen about what happened at Auschwitz by both Morgen and Günther Reinecke, who was head of legal affairs at the SS judiciary.
17 Letter from Konrad Morgen to Maria Wachter, 9 October 1944, 'Nachlass Konrad Morgen', folder 10
18 Letter from Konrad Morgen to Maria Wachter, 13 October 1944, 'Nachlass Konrad Morgen', folder 10
19 Letter from Konrad Morgen to Maria Wachter, 16 October 1944, 'Nachlass Konrad Morgen', folder 10
20 Letter from Konrad Morgen to Maria Wachter, 22 October 1944, 'Nachlass Konrad Morgen', folder 10
21 Letter from the *Polizepräsidum* Leipzig to Frau Maria Wachter, 30 September 1947, 'Nachlass Konrad Morgen', folder 42
22 '20031 Polizeipräsidium Leipzig', Sächsisches Staatsarchiv, Staatsarchiv Leipzig, PP-M 3308
23 Letter from Eleonore Hodys to Salzburg Council, 2 February 1953, Arolsen Archives 6.3.3.2/93188337, International Center on Nazi Persecution
24 'Tape recordings of the Auschwitz trial (1963–1965): Witness Gerhard Wiebeck', 1 October 1964, *Fritz Bauer Institut*, https://www.auschwitz-prozess.de/zeugenaussagen/Wiebeck-Gerhard/

CHAPTER 8: THE INVESTIGATIONS INTO ADOLF EICHMANN AND OTHERS

1 *False Gods: The Jerusalem Memoirs* by Adolf Eichmann. Black Horse Publishing, 2015, p.79, p.80, p.87, p.88.
2 Ibid., p.145
3 Greif op. cit., p.14
4 Affidavit by Konrad Morgen dated 10 July 1946, *Trial of the Major War Criminals before the International Military Tribunal* op. cit. This section also based on Konrad Morgen's testimony at Nuremberg and Adolf Eichmann trial transcript, 20 July 1961, session 105, via Nizkor Project
5 *Trial of the Major War Criminals before the International Military Tribunal*, vol. XX, 7 August 1946 op. cit.
6 Quoted in Dirk Riedel, 'A "Political Soldier" and "Practitioner of Violence": The Concentration Camp Commandant Hans Loritz', *Journal of Contemporary History*, vol. 45, no. 3, July 2010, p.556
7 Ibid., p.572
8 *Encyclopedia of Camps and Ghettos, 1933–1945* op. cit., p.863
9 Konrad Morgen interrogations, 4 September 1946 op. cit.
10 Ibid.
11 Ibid.
12 Konrad Morgen interrogations, 18 January 1947 op. cit.
13 Konrad Morgen interrogations, 4 September 1946 op. cit.
14 'Short Remarks to the Bill of Indictment against SS Standartenführer Koch, formerly commandant of the KZ Buchenwald', NARA, NO-2366/597043 via University of Connecticut Digital Library
15 See also *Das Personenlexicon zum Dritten Reich: Wer War Was Vor und Nach 1945* by Ernst Klee. Weltbild, 2008, pp.156–7
16 This section based on Konrad Morgen interrogations, 18 January 1947 op. cit.
17 'Short Remarks to the Bill of Indictment against SS Standartenführer Koch' op. cit.
18 Konrad Morgen interrogations, 18 January 1947 op. cit.
19 'Short Remarks to the Bill of Indictment against SS Standartenführer Koch' op. cit.
20 Letter from Konrad Morgen to Maria Wachter, 12 November 1944, 'Nachlass Konrad Morgen', folder 10

21 'Short Remarks to the Bill of Indictment against SS Standartenführer Koch' op. cit.
22 Konrad Morgen interview tapes, FDR Presidential Library and Museum, series 2, C-47 and C-48 op. cit.
23 *New York Times*, 7 May 1971, p.8
24 *USA v. Karl Brandt et al.*, judgment, pp.289–90, https://legal-tools.org/doc/c18557/
25 'Tape recordings of the Auschwitz trial (1963–1965): Witness Werner Hansen', 27 November 1964, *Fritz Bauer Institut*, https://www.auschwitz-prozess.de/zeugenaussagen/Hansen-Werner/
26 Ibid.
27 Ibid.
28 Konrad Morgen interrogations, 4 September 1946 op. cit.
29 Letter from Konrad Morgen to Maria Wachter, 12 December 1944, 'Nachlass Konrad Morgen', folder 10
30 Letter from Konrad Morgen to Maria Wachter, 15 January 1944, 'Nachlass Konrad Morgen', folder 10
31 Ibid. Note that the paragraph with this quote is dated 15 January 1944 but is contained within another letter which Morgen started on 7 January 1945
32 Konrad Morgen interrogations, 6 December 1946 op. cit.
33 *USA v. Oswald Pohl et al.*, p.6674

CHAPTER 9: AFTER THE WAR

1 *Credo: Mein Weg zu Gott* by General of the Waffen SS Oswald Pohl. Alois Girnth Verlag, 1950, p.13
2 Ibid., p.43
3 *US Information Bulletin*, February 1951
4 *USA v. Oswald Pohl et al.*, p.2042
5 Ibid., p.2072
6 Ibid., p.2073
7 Ibid., p.6694
8 Ibid., p.6697
9 Ibid., p.6711
10 Ibid., p.6722
11 *Trials of War Criminals before the Nuremberg Military Tribunals: The Rusha Case, The Pohl Case*, vol. V. United States Government Printing Office, 1950, p.1077
12 Letter from Konrad Morgen to Maria Wachter, 29 November 1945, 'Nachlass Konrad Morgen', folder 10
13 *Entnazifizierung* Konrad Morgen op. cit.
14 *Report to the President from Justice Robert H. Jackson, Chief Counsel for the United States in the Prosecution of Axis War Criminals*, 7 June 1945, Robert H. Jackson Center, https://www.roberthjackson.org/wp-content/uploads/2015/01/Report_to_the_President_on_the_Prosecution_of_Axis_War_Criminals.pdf/
15 *Trial of the Major War Criminals before the International Military Tribunal*, vol. XX, 7 August 1946 op. cit.
16 Ibid.
17 *A Judge in Auschwitz: Konrad Morgen's Crusade Against SS Corruption and 'Illegal' Murder* by Kevin Prenger. Pen & Sword, 2021, p.142
18 *Trial of the Major War Criminals before the International Military Tribunal*, vol. XX, 8 August 1946 op. cit.
19 Ibid.
20 *USA v. Josias Prinz zu Waldeck et al.* op. cit., p.2782
21 *USA v. Josias Prinz zu Waldeck et al.*, 'Review and Recommendations of the Deputy Judge Advocate for War Crimes Case 000-50-9', Deputy Judge Advocate's Office, 15 November 1949
22 Konrad Morgen interrogations, undated, record group 238, microfilm 1019, roll 47
23 *Entnazifizierung* Konrad Morgen op. cit.
24 Konrad Morgen interrogations, 22 March 1947 op. cit.
25 *Entnazifizierung* Konrad Morgen op. cit.
26 Ibid.
27 Ibid.
28 Ibid.
29 *Entnazifizierung* Konrad Morgen op. cit.
30 Ibid.
31 Letter from Konrad Morgen to the *Ministerium für politische Befreiung Württemberg-Baden*, 3 January 1950, 'Nachlass Konrad Morgen', folder 43
32 *Auschwitz: A Report on the Proceedings against Robert Karl Ludwig Mulka and Others before the Court at Frankfurt* by Bernd Naumann. Frederick Prager, 1966, p.6
33 Originals held in the Archiv des Fritz Bauer Institut

34 'Tape recordings of the Auschwitz trial (1963–1965): Defendants Dylewski, Kaduk, Lucas, Mulka, Schlage', 3 May 1965, *Fritz Bauer Institut*, https://www.auschwitz-prozess.de/zeugenaussagen/Befragung_der_Angeklagten/
35 'Tape recordings of the Auschwitz trial (1963–1965): Witness Konrad Morgen' op. cit.
36 *Auschwitz: A Report on the Proceedings* op. cit., p.xiii
37 Quoted in Devin O. Pendas, '"I didn't know what Auschwitz was": The Frankfurt Auschwitz Trial and the German Press, 1963–1965', *Yale Journal of Law & the Humanities*, vol. 12, no. 397
38 Ibid.
39 Ibid.
40 Ibid.
41 'Tape recordings of the Auschwitz trial (1963–1965): Witness Konrad Morgen' op. cit.
42 *Auschwitz: A Report on the Proceedings* op. cit., pp.416–17
43 'Tape recordings of the Auschwitz trial (1963–1965): Witness Konrad Morgen' op. cit.
44 Ibid.
45 Ibid.
46 *Auschwitz: A Report on the Proceedings* op. cit., p.415
47 'Nachlass Konrad Morgen', folder 46

CHAPTER 10: KONRAD MORGEN – A FINAL WORD

1 *Adolf Hitler* by John Toland. Doubleday, 1976, p.761; ibid., p.774; ibid., p.774
2 *Konrad Morgen: The Conscience of a Nazi Judge* by Herlinde Pauer-Studer and J. David Velleman, Palgrave Macmillan, 2015, p.122
3 Ibid., p.125
4 Charles Fried, 'A Conscience in Hell: Review of Konrad Morgen: The Conscience of a Nazi Judge', *The New Rambler*, https://newramblerreview.com/book-reviews/law/a-conscience-in-hell
5 Ibid.
6 Ibid.
7 https://www.amazon.co.uk/Konrad-Morgen-Herlinde-Pauer-Studer/dp/1137496940, reproduced here with the kind permission of Dr Marks
8 Ibid.
9 Pauer-Studer and Velleman op. cit., p.122
10 https://www.amazon.co.uk/Konrad-Morgen-Herlinde-Pauer-Studer/dp/1137496940 op. cit.
11 *A Judge in Auschwitz: Konrad Morgen's Crusade Against SS Corruption and 'Illegal' Murder* by Kevin Prenger. Pen & Sword, 2021, p.147
12 Ibid., p.142
13 Konrad Morgen interrogations, 13 December 1946 op. cit.
14 *KL: A History of the Nazi Concentration Camps* by Nikolaus Wachsmann. Little Brown, 2015, p.386
15 Ibid.
16 *Beyond Justice: The Auschwitz Trial* by Rebecca Wittmann. Harvard University Press, 2005, p.166
17 'Criminal Law in Auschwitz: Positivism, Natural Law, and the Career of SS Lawyer Konrad Morgen' by David Fraser, in Stephen Skinner (ed.) *Ideology and Criminal Law: Fascist, National Socialist and Authoritarian Regimes*. Hart, 2019. Also via https://www.researchgate.net/profile/David_Fraser/publication/334746074_Criminal_Law_in_Auschwitz/links/5d3efa7aa6fdcc370a69a7d4/Criminal-Law-in-Auschwitz
18 Ibid.
19 Ibid.
20 Ibid.
21 'The Ethics of a Truth-Seeking Judge: Konrad Morgen, SS Judge and Corruption Expert' by Raphael Gross, in *Years of Persecution Years of Extermination: Saul Friedlander and the Future of Holocaust Studies*, ed. Christian Wiese and Paul Betts. Bloomsbury, 2010
22 'Why Adolf Hitler Spared the Judges' op. cit.
23 Konrad Morgen interview tapes, FDR Presidential Library and Museum, series 2, C-47 and C-48
24 Wachsmann op. cit.
25 Pauer-Studer and Velleman op. cit., p.120
26 Ibid., p.121
27 Longerich, p.304
28 Ibid., p.308

29 Ibid., p.310
30 IMT, vol xx, 7 August 1946. See also Chapter 4 for Morgen's first impressions of Buchenwald
31 Ibid.
32 Wachsmann op. cit.
33 Konrad Morgen interrogations, 13 December 1946 op. cit.
34 Wachsmann op. cit.
35 'Speech [of] the Reichsfuehrer-SS at the meeting of SS Major-Generals … at Posen' op. cit.
36 Letter from Konrad Morgen to the editor of the *Deutsche Volkszeitung* 15 October 1964, 'Nachlass Konrad Morgen', folder 20
37 Letter from Konrad Morgen to Maria Wachter, 15 January 1944 (contained within a letter starting on 7 January 1945), 'Nachlass Konrad Morgen', folder 10
38 *Entnazifizierung* Konrad Morgen, Landesarchiv Baden-Würtemburg, EL903/3, 1 Bü
39 Hackett op. cit., p.341
40 'Nuremberg Trial Proceedings Volume 20: One Hundred and Ninety-Seventh Day, Wednesday; 7 August 1946', The Avalon Project, Yale Law School, p. 488, https://avalon.law.yale.edu/imt/08-07-46.asp
41 Toland op. cit., p.774
42 Fried op. cit.
43 Ibid.
44 Fraser op. cit.
45 Fried op. cit.
46 Konrad Morgen, Letter to the Ministerium für politische Befreiung Württemberg-Baden, 3 January 1950, 'Nachlass Konrad Morgen', folder 43

APPENDIX: WHAT HAPPENED NEXT?

1 Longerich op. cit., pp.1–3
2 *RG 263 Detailed Report: Heinrich Mueller* by Timothy Naftali, Norman J.W. Goda, Richard Breitman, Robert Wolfe. Interagency Working Group, https://www.archives.gov/iwg/declassified-records/rg-263-cia-records/rg-263-mueller.html
3 Sereny op. cit., p.194–215
4 *Hitler's Shadow: Nazi War Criminals, US Intelligence and the Cold War* by Richard Breitman and Norman J.W. Goda. The National Archives, 2010.
5 Sereny op. cit., p.133

BIBLIOGRAPHY

A Judge in Auschwitz: Konrad Morgen's Crusade Against SS Corruption and 'Illegal' Murder by Kevin Prenger. Pen & Sword, 2021.

'A "Political Soldier" and "Practitioner of Violence": The Concentration Camp Commandant Hans Loritz' by Dirk Riedel, *Journal of Contemporary History*, vol. 45, no. 3, July 2010, pp.555–75.

Adolf Hitler by John Toland. Doubleday, 1976.

An Uncompromising Generation: The Nazi Leadership of the Reich Security Main Office by Michael Wildt, translated by Tom Lampert. University of Wisconsin Press, 2009.

Anatomie des SS Staates Band 1 by Hans Buchheim. Deutsche Taschenbuch Verlag, 1974.

Auschwitz: A Report on the Proceedings against Robert Karl Ludwig Mulka and Others before the Court at Frankfurt by Bernd Naumann, introduction by Hannah Arendt. Frederick Prager, 1966.

Auschwitz Chronicle by Danuta Czech. IB Tauris, 1990.

Beyond Justice: The Auschwitz Trial by Rebecca Wittmann. Harvard University Press, 2005.

Concentration Camp Majdanek by Jürgen Graf and Carlo Mattogno. Theses & Dissertations Press, 2004.

Credo: Mein Weg zu Gott by General of the Waffen SS Oswald Pohl. Alois Girnth Verlag, 1950.

'Criminal Law in Auschwitz: Positivism, Natural Law, and the Career of SS Lawyer Konrad Morgen' by David Fraser, in Stephen Skinner (ed.) *Ideology and Criminal Law: Fascist, National Socialist and Authoritarian Regimes*. Hart, 2019. Also via https://www.researchgate.net/profile/David_Fraser/publication/334746074_Criminal_Law_in_Auschwitz/links/5d3efa7aa6fdcc370a69a7d4/Criminal-Law-in-Auschwitz

Das Personenlexicon zum Dritten Reich: Wer War Was Vor und Nach 1945 by Ernst Klee. Weltbild, 2008.

'Das Spiel ist Aus – Arthur Nebe' by Bernd Wehner, *Der Spiegel*, 12 October 1949.

Dem Täter auf dem Spur by Bernd Wehner. Gustav Lübbe Verlag, 1983.

Der SS Staat: Das System der deutschen Konzentrationslager by Prof. Dr Eugon Kogon. Wilhelm Hehne Verlag, 1988.

Doctors From Hell: The Horrific Account of Nazi Experiments on Humans by Vivien Spitz. Sentient Publications, 2005.

Einwirkung der neueren Philosophie Sämtliche Werke nach Epochen seines Schaffens by Johann Wolfgang Goethe. Bd. 12, 97.

Encyclopedia of Camps and Ghettos 1933–1945, The United States Holocaust Memorial Museum, 2009.

False Gods: The Jerusalem Memoirs by Adolf Eichmann. Black Horse Publishing, 2015.

Goethe in German Jewish Culture, ed. Klaus L. Berghahn and Jost Hermand. Camden House, 2001.

Goethes Werke by Kunst und Literatur. Bd. 12.

Heinrich Himmler by Peter Longerich. Oxford University Press, 2012.

Hitler's Justice: The Courts of the Third Reich by Ingo Müller, translated by Deborah Lucas Schneider. Harvard University Press, 1991.

Hitler's Shadow: Nazi War Criminals, US Intelligence and the Cold War by Richard Breitman and Norman J. W. Goda. The National Archives, 2010.

'"I didn't know what Auschwitz was": The Frankfurt Auschwitz Trial and the German Press, 1963–1965' by Devin O. Pendas in *Yale Journal of Law & the Humanities*, vol. 12, no. 397, pp.387–446.

KL: A History of the Nazi Concentration Camps by Nikolaus Wachsmann. Little Brown, 2015.

KL Auschwitz Seen By The SS by Rudolf Höss. The Auschwitz-Birkenau State Museum, 1995.

Konrad Morgen: The Conscience of a Nazi Judge by Herlinde Pauer-Studer and J. David Velleman. Palgrave Macmillan, 2015.

'Law and Justice in the Nazi SS: The Case of Konrad Morgen', by James J. Weingartner in *Central European History*, vol. 16, no. 3, 1983, pp. 276–94.

Majdanek: The Concentration Camp in Lublin by Jósef Marsałek. Interpress Warsaw, 1986.

Mein Weg zur 31. SS-Freiwilligen Grenadier-Division by Fredo Gensicke. Nation & Wissen Verlag, 2016.

Men Against Fire by S. L. A. Marshall. William Morrow and Company, 1966.

Military Training in the British Army 1940–1944 by Timothy Harrison Place. Frank Cass, 2000.

On Killing by David Grossman. Little Brown, 1996.

RG 263 Detailed Report: Heinrich Mueller by Timothy Naftali, Norman J. W. Goda, Richard Breitman, Robert Wolfe. Interagency Working Group, https://www.archives.gov/iwg/declassified-records/rg-263-cia-records/rg-263-mueller.html

Sämmtliche Werke, Herder, volume 27.

Soldiers of Evil: The Commandants of the Nazi Concentration Camps by Tom Segev. McGraw-Hill, 1988.

SS Wiking: The History of the Fifth SS Division 1941–1945 by Rupert Butler. Casemate, 2002.

Strafvollzugslager der SS und Polizei: Himmler's Wartime Institutions for the Detention of Waffen SS and Polizei Criminals by Stuart B. T. Emmett. Fonthill, 2017.

'Texts Buried in Oblivion. Testimonies of Two Refugees from the Mass Grave at Poniatowa in Holocaust Studies and Materials' by Andrzej Żbikowski, in *Journal of the Polish Center for Holocaust Research*, 2008, pp.76–102.

The Buchenwald Report ed. David A. Hackett. Westview Press, 1995.

The Cruel Hunters: SS-Sonderkommando Dirlewanger, Hitler's most notorious anti-partisan unit by French L. MacLean. Schiffer Military History, 1998.

The Dual State by Ernst Fraenkel. Oxford University Press, 1941.

'The Ethics of a Truth-Seeking Judge: Konrad Morgen, SS Judge and Corruption Expert' by Raphael Gross, in *Years of Persecution, Years of Extermination: Saul Friedlander and the Future of Holocaust Studies*, ed. Christian Wiese and Paul Betts. Bloomsbury, 2010.

The German Trauma: Experiences and Reflections 1938–2001 by Gitta Sereny. Penguin, 2001.

The Last Days of Hitler by Anton Joachimstaler. Cassell, 2007.

The Last Days of Hitler by Hugh Trevor-Roper. Macmillan, 1947.

The Life of Ian Fleming by John Pearson. McGraw-Hill, 1966.

The Order of the Death's Head by Heinz Höhne. Ballantine Books, 1986.

The SS 1933–1945 by Christopher McNab. Amber Books, 2009.

The SS: Alibi of a Nation by Gerald Reitlinger. Viking, 1968.

The SS Dirlewanger Brigade: The History of the Black Hunters by Christian Ingrao. Skyhorse Publishing, 2013.

The SS-Division Wiking in the Caucasus 1942–1943 by Massimiliano Afiero. MMP Books, 2017.

The World at War by Richard Holmes. Random House, 2011. Also a boxed set DVD featuring Konrad Morgen.

Up Close and Personal: The Reality of Fighting at Close Quarters in World War II by David Lee. Greenhill Books, 2006.

Walter Krämer by Nico Wolzenburg, Thomas Wolf. Kreisarchiv Siegen-Wittgenstein, 2013.

We Wept Without Tears: Testimonies Of the Jewish Sonderkommando From Auschwitz by Gideon Greif. Yale University Press, 2005.

Weimar: From Enlightenment to the Present by Michael H. Kater. Yale University Press, 2014.

Who's Who in Nazi Germany by Robert S. Wistrich. Routledge, 1995.

'Why Adolf Hitler Spared the Judges: Judicial Opposition Against the Nazi State', Hans Petter Graver, *German Law Journal*, vol. 19, no. 4, 2018, pp.845–78.

ACKNOWLEDGEMENTS

WEDNESDAY 25 OCTOBER 2023

Fifty-two years to the day since Konrad Morgen, John Toland and Inge Gehrich were together in Frankfurt, I too am sitting in a room in Frankfurt, Germany. The room I'm sitting in has no windows and is full of shelves of boxes, books and files of paper.

It is the archive of the Fritz Bauer Institut at the Goethe University of Frankfurt. The building itself is large and imposing and I am on the fifth floor. On the way through the building I pass information panels, which tell me that the building was built before the war for the chemical company IG Farben as their headquarters. IG Farben used forced labour to build their factory at Auschwitz-Monowitz and an IG Farben subsidiary manufactured Zyklon B, the gas used to kill Jews in the gas chambers. One of the information panels has a picture showing a Nazi rally in the grounds I have just walked across.

On a trolley next to my desk, there are six large archive boxes containing the papers and letters of Konrad Morgen. The catalogue that describes these papers states that together these six boxes measure 1.05 metres. Inside these boxes are individual blue archive cardboard folders, each numbered and concerning a particular part of his life and work. There's another, smaller box, which contains photographs. One of the boxes reveals that at one stage, Morgen lived just around the corner from where I am sitting.

Alongside the paper documents, there are various identity cards. Although these are less useful in terms of information, as physical documents they do make an impact. One of these is bright red leather and shows the German eagle on the front in gold. This is Morgen's Nazi Party membership card for 1936, in which is inscribed his party number, 2,536,236. It is forty-eight pages long and starts with a personal exhortation to party members from Adolf Hitler. In the middle are stamps, which Morgen bought to support the party.

After Morgen died in 1982, his widow, Maria, left these documents and photographs to their neighbours at their holiday home in Niedernhausen, who then gave them to the Fritz Bauer Institut. The institute is named after the famous German prosecutor Fritz Bauer, whose work led to the 1963–5 Auschwitz trial in Frankfurt, at which Morgen was a prosecution witness.

There is another link as well. During the Second World War, Morgen tried to investigate Adolf Eichmann but he was blocked, a fact later confirmed by Eichmann at his trial in Jerusalem. Ultimately, it was Fritz Bauer who secretly gave the Israelis the information that led to his capture. He did this because his earlier attempts to get him extradited to Germany had been frustrated by former SS personnel within the German police.

The Fritz Bauer Institut exists, according to its mission statement, 'to pursue the study, research, and documentation of National Socialist mass crimes, especially the Holocaust'. Thanks to its work, authors like me have access to its archives and for this, I am very grateful.

Inside the archive room where I am working, there is lots of material about the 1963–5 Auschwitz trial and about Bauer, who was a tireless Nazi hunter. On the way to the airport to catch a flight home, I buy a biography of Bauer and learn that he was imprisoned in a concentration camp in Heuberg in 1933. In exchange for his freedom, he signed a document supporting the regime, something which Bauer never referred to for the rest of his life. It is a sober reminder about the reality of life in the Third Reich and it brings to mind something Bernie Gunther said in Philip Kerr's *March Violets*: 'Everyone in Germany was somebody different before 1933. And as I'm always saying, "Who isn't a National Socialist when there's a gun pointed at his head?"'

Although Bauer died in 1968, I was able to speak to Gerhard Wiese, one of the prosecutors who worked with him on the Auschwitz trials and later chief prosecutor in Frankfurt, and I am very grateful to him for his assistance in suggesting various avenues I should explore. I very much enjoyed our conversation and it's fair to say he probably asked me as many questions as I put to him!

Archivists at the institute have added to the Morgen papers over the years. There are copies of transcripts from the Auschwitz trial, as well as records of Morgen's interrogation by the Americans after they took him into custody at the end of the war and the transcripts of the Nuremberg trials. In addition, there are copies of papers from other German and US archives. These sections are extensive: transcripts in German of the interrogation sessions between Morgen and the Americans and summaries in English compiled for the Nuremberg trials run to hundreds of pages.

The current archivist, Johannes Beermann-Schön, re-catalogued Morgen's papers after he started at the institute and added to them. Thanks to the work he carried out, and his willingness to accommodate my visit at short notice, my research has been made much more straightforward.

The work of archivists in preserving, organising and cataloguing their holdings is crucial to people like me who are looking for specific information about historical events. Where I have looked for information for this book, I have been met with nothing but helpfulness and friendliness from archivists. Although most archive catalogues are online, sometimes an archivist's help is needed when search engines are not finding information that I know is in the archives somewhere.

Alongside Johannes Beermann-Schön at the Fritz Bauer Institut, I would also like to thank Matthew Hanson at the FDR Presidential Library and Museum, who tracked down and sent me the John Toland interview; Hartmut Obst at the Ludwigsburg State Archives, who helped with finding the Konrad Morgen de-Nazification papers; Heike Müller at the International Center on Nazi Persecution's Arolsen Archives and Doreen Wustig at the Staatsarchiv Leipzig for information about Eleonore Hodys; Dr Wojciech Płosa at the Auschwitz Museum Archives; and Jakub Chmielewski from the history department at the state museum at Majdanek. In addition, I would like to thank Horst Temmen at the publisher Edition Temmen for his help in tracking down the image of Oskar Dirlewanger and his staff and Kevin Quinn at the National Archives for his help with the picture of Konrad Morgen at the SS trial at Nuremberg.

Alongside archivists, academics have also been very helpful and approachable. Morgen is of enduring interest to historians, philosophers and legal academics who study and write about him and I am very grateful to Emeritus Professor of Law and Social Theory David Fraser at the University of Nottingham for sharing additional observations about Morgen with me and to Professor Joel Marks, Emeritus Professor of Philosophy at the University of New Haven.

Finally, I would like to say a huge thank you to the fantastic team at Biteback Publishing: to James Stephens for commissioning me to research and write this book, to Ella Boardman and Namkwan Cho for designing the book's cover and to Nell Whitaker and Suzanne Sangster for their work in marketing and publicising the book. Thanks also to Ian Allen for proofreading. I am a huge fan of the editorial process and a very special thank you goes to my editor Catriona Allon, whose suggestions, corrections and comments have resulted in a better book than would otherwise have been the case.

INDEX